the
REMIX

ALSO BY LINDSEY POLLAK

Getting from College to Career:
90 Things to Do Before You Join the Real World

Becoming the Boss:
New Rules for the Next Generation of Leaders

the REMIX

How to Lead and
Succeed in the
Multigenerational
Workplace

Lindsey Pollak

HARPER
BUSINESS

An Imprint of HarperCollins*Publishers*

HarperCollins books may be purchased for educational, business, or sales promotional use. For information, please e-mail the Special Markets Department at SPsales@harpercollins.com.

FIRST EDITION

Designed by Bonni Leon-Berman

Library of Congress Cataloging-in-Publication Data has been applied for.

ISBN 978-0-06-288021-5

19 20 21 22 23   LSC   10 9 8 7 6 5 4 3 2 1

To Evan and Chloe

CONTENTS

INTRODUCTION: From the Reorg to the Remix

Mention organizational change in any hallway, e-mail inbox, or Slack channel of any workplace in America, and you'll likely receive a collective groan and eye roll.

"We know the drill," seasoned employees will say as they prepare for announcements of revised and re-revised business priorities, shuffled leadership teams, and, of course, budget cuts and layoffs. As one longtime manager recently commented to me, "I've been re-orged so many times, at this point I could probably report to a dog."

Isn't it about time we find a less cynical, more optimistic approach to workplace change?

What if a new group of workers came along with more positive expectations of how change will affect their organizations and careers? What if organizations began to listen to and embrace this new group's mindset? What if even long-tenured, "jaded" employees felt that change was actually an opportunity to deploy their knowledge and experience in new and exciting ways? What if organizations found a way to integrate these two perspectives to create exponential success?

All these things are possible because all these things are already happening. I've been witnessing this more constructive, collaborative approach to change starting to take place over the past several years. The catalyst is the unprecedented generational overlap that is taking place in American business today.

Now that Millennials—comprising those born between approximately 1981 and 1996—have officially become the largest generation in the U.S. workforce, and Generation Z workers—those born in 1997 and later, the most racially and ethnically diverse generation in American history—are entering the labor force in large numbers, leaders and organizations have had little choice but to begin embracing new ways of working that appeal to younger, digital-first generations. At the same time, they must continue to appeal to members of the massive Baby Boomer generation, who are responsible for so many decades of success and are still going strong today.

While some companies are embracing the multigenerational mix, most organizations are struggling to appeal to all generations of employees at once. Today's employers say they want people with experience but complain that experienced workers are more expensive and stuck in their ways. Employers say they want people with bleeding-edge tech skills but lament that the young people with those skills don't always have the professional savvy they desire. As one painfully true job search Internet meme declared, "We're looking for someone aged 22 to 26, with 30 years of experience."

As a result, few feel entirely wanted and many are on the defensive. I encounter this all too often in organizations that invite me to consult or speak: Traditionalists and Baby Boomers feel like they're being elbowed out for younger workers. Millennials and Gen Zs feel like they're being held to an unfair standard. And Gen Xers—don't forget about Gen Xers—feel caught in the crossfire or ignored entirely.

All this tension, even if it stays below the surface, has an impact on how we show up as employees, managers, and leaders, and on the work we are capable of accomplishing together. Festering intergenerational resentment and insecurity is a threat to the success of our organizations and our individual careers.

Add to this generational tension the fact that we are currently living through an era of ever-greater disruptions—what the U.S. Army War College termed VUCA—volatility, uncertainty, complexity, and ambiguity. As leaders in a time of VUCA, we need to think about all the ways the tentacles of disruption affect every area of how we hire, manage, engage, and retain talent in our organizations.

The workplace can even serve as a microcosm for the larger issues facing our country. Kenneth Frazier, the CEO of Merck & Co. and the most prominent African American chief executive in the country, has said, "If you look around at what's happening in our society, there's more division than I think I can ever remember. . . . I actually think the workplace is the last place in our society where people can't choose necessarily who they work with."

This raises the stakes for leaders even more. The choices we make in our workplaces can impact the very feelings people have about our shared society. If we can get every generation feeling valued and pulling in the same direction at work, maybe we can do this on a larger scale. That's what gets me out of bed in the morning and what I want to share with you.

I have spent many years studying even the tiniest details of successful intergenerational teams and organizations to learn what makes them different. How do they thrive in times of change?

The secret sauce—the strategy I have observed again and again across a wide variety of industries and company sizes—involves a combination of keeping the best, "classic" workplace practices of the past while simultaneously embracing more modern and innovative approaches to work. It mixes the "old" and the "new" in positive ways.

The best way I've found to explain this approach is with an analogy from far outside the realm of business, in the world of music.

It is the remix.

In music, of course, a remix is a song, usually a well-known classic, that has been changed from its original state by a new artist who adds, takes away, or alters the original in some way to create something both recognizable and entirely new.

In business, the remix is a positive approach to organizational change that takes practices or habits embraced by a previous generation (Traditionalists, Baby Boomers, and/or Generation Xers) and adds to, removes from, or alters them in some way to better appeal to Millennials, Gen Zs, and future generations to come so we can all succeed together. The result is a workplace that mixes, matches, and blends the best of each generation's ideas and practices to design a smarter, better, more inclusive experience of work for everyone.

Producer and former DJ Briana Craig, a.k.a. Bri-Real, told me, "Some remixes take the original to the next level, and sometimes the remix becomes more popular than the original song."

This doesn't surprise me at all. I like music remixes because they celebrate the fact that I've been around for a while *and* they make me feel current. They offer a memory and a discovery. Music and culture writer Sharine Taylor commented to me that "a remix forces you to think outside what is comfortable. It can be both comfortable and uncomfortable." Nobody can exist in two eras at once, but remixes give us that liminal experience.

Importantly, a remix does not erase the past. Rather, in a workplace context, it involves examining the "classic" fundamentals—from management to workspaces to benefits to communication to compensation and beyond—and questioning:

- What are we doing because "it's always been done that way" that we need to stop because it no longer works?
- What are we doing because "it's always been done that way" that we should continue and add to it because it still works?
- What do we need to start doing in entirely new ways to succeed in the future?

Remixing opportunities are virtually endless and applicable to people and organizations across any industry and any current employee demographic mix. Remixes take place across organizations, inside teams, and within ourselves.

The remix is the Baby Boomer banking industry veteran who feared stagnation, so he gave up his corner office to "hot-desk" at a different spot every day to better interact with more colleagues and gain new perspectives.

The remix is the 24-year-old cosmetics industry employee who felt overlooked because of her youth, so she signed up for a reverse mentoring program that matched her with a company executive. Now she takes that senior leader on regular shopping outings to advise on what she and her Millennial peers want from a retail environment, and her opinions are impacting company strategy.

The remix is the Gen X entrepreneur who felt ignored in his corporate job, so as a side gig he created a new voice technology company based on the inspiration of two people: his two-year-old daughter, who loves interfacing with Google Home and Amazon's Alexa, and his aging immigrant mother, who equally loves these voice recognition devices.

The remix is the city pool in Galveston, Texas, that couldn't find enough teenagers interested in lifeguarding, so they started recruiting retirees instead. One, a 63-year-old former math teacher, was voted the city's best lifeguard.

Some of the remix examples you will read may feel uncomfortable (no more annual reviews?), some may feel surprising (apprenticeship is the oldest form of training people and still among the most effective!), and some may feel utterly revolutionary (transparent salaries?!). But all the strategies, tools, tactics, and recommendations presented in the coming pages are meant to position you and your organization for the realities of our increasingly multifaceted, multigenerational world.

To be a remixer is to see today's unprecedented generational change not as a challenge but as an opportunity. The individuals and organizations that don't adapt to the changing demographics of the workplace will not have a viable future, and the individuals and organizations that do successfully remix will win—and relish—our shared tomorrow.

My Perspective

I came to the topic of generational differences through a career remix of my own. After graduate school, I landed a job at a start-up website called WorkingWoman.com in New York City, and eighteen months later the company went bankrupt during the dot-com bust. I took the opportunity in 2002 to launch my own business as a writer and college campus speaker specializing in advising students and recent graduates on entry-level career success.

While generational experts Neil Howe and the late William Strauss coined the term "Millennial" in their book *Generations: The History of America's Future, 1584 to 2069* back in 1991, there were minimal Google searches on that term until around 2004. It was about that time that I began writing my first book, *Getting from College to Career: 90 Things to Do Before You Join the Real World*, which was published in 2007. In retrospect, I can hardly believe it, but the word "Millennial" does not appear a single time in my proposal for the book.

The year 2007 also marked my first request from a corporation to speak to them about college students and young professionals. It was a professional services firm, and they asked me to share my advice on, in their words, "what Millennials want." I didn't know it at the time, but this was the beginning of my career as one of the first "Millennial experts."

As a Gen Xer myself, I sensed quite a few differences in recent grads' work expectations compared to my own a decade earlier. And

I knew my preferences had seemed surprising to my early bosses, who were Baby Boomers and Traditionalists. And so, in order to explain Millennials to my new clients, I knew I had to understand earlier generations better, too. So I began exploring: What was work like for my parents and grandparents and great-grandparents? What had changed the most since those times and, just as important, what had stayed the same?

I have since spent the past decade researching, writing, and speaking about Millennials and generational differences to more than two hundred corporations, law firms, universities, business schools, high schools, professional associations, hospitals, nonprofits, summer camps, franchises, small businesses, veterans' organizations, and more. The generational mix of my audiences over the years has included virtually every age, from 8-year-old Girl Scouts to 90-year-old-plus World War II veterans.

I am not a social scientist or economist, and I don't profess to have all the answers. But I have been passionate about researching all things generational for my clients, my audience members, and myself as a business owner. The more I learn and teach, the more I want to know. Like you, I have personally experienced the incredible power of today's youngest generations to usher in a new, more positive, and adaptable model of work for all of us in the twenty-first century. And I have also been awed by the incredible wisdom, stamina, and reinvention of the older generations.

We'll begin with an overview of each generation in today's workforce and some key themes to embrace—what I call "rules for remixers." Then, chapter by chapter, we'll explore the different realms in which remixing can take place.

My goal in writing this book is to serve as a translator and tour guide—to inform you, to challenge you, to surprise you, and to help you and your organization navigate through today's multigenerational mix.

How do you, whatever your generation, job title, or organization size or industry, get things done—both big, long-term goals and small, daily tasks—when there are so many different people using so many different tools to do things in so many different ways?

The answer is to make yourself and your organization adaptable to change while remaining true to yourself and to the evergreen fundamentals of good business and leadership.

Yes, in the coming pages I will offer many suggestions specific to managing Millennials, since they are the largest cohort in the workplace today and will be for several decades to come. But rest assured this is not about doing a 180-degree flip and reinventing everything you do to appeal to what one particular generation wants.

My approach to organizational change is to embrace the fundamental fact that none of us, of any generation, will survive if we remain static and rigid. Members of every generation must build our adaptability muscles in order to achieve our personal and professional goals. We are incredibly fortunate to live in an era with more opportunities, choices, and diversity than ever before. This is often scary and confusing, but isn't it also exciting?

Welcome to the remix.

the
REMIX

1 FROG STEW

The Generational Remix

"Millennials Overtake Baby Boomers as America's Largest Generation."

IF YOU WANT to pinpoint an exact moment when remixing became essential, the proverbial tipping point, I'd go with April 25, 2016. That is the day the above headline appeared on the Pew Research Center's website. What was reported that day was that Millennials (the generation born from approximately 1981 to 1996, also known as Generation Y, who are in their 20s and 30s today) overtook three other cohorts: the Traditionalists (born from approximately 1922 to 1945, also known as the Silent Generation), the Baby Boomers (born from 1946 to 1964), and Generation X (born from approximately 1965 to 1980).

And while everyone focused on Millennials, another group, Generation Z (the cohort born in 1997 and later, with no exact endpoint yet) entered the workplace picture, too, thus bringing us to five distinct generations in the U.S. workplace for the very first time in history.

As a Gen Xer like some of you, I couldn't help but notice that

Millennials actually overtook our humble generation, not the Baby Boomers, as Pew announced in its headline (see chart below), but we'll get to other generations' brazen disregard for us Gen Xers in a moment . . .

MILLENNIALS BECOME THE LARGEST GENERATION IN THE LABOR FORCE IN 2016

U.S. LABOR FORCE, IN MILLIONS

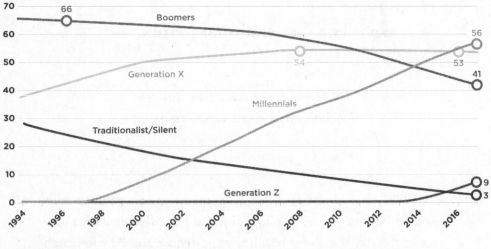

NOTE: LABOR FORCE INCLUDED THOSE AGES 16 AND OLDER WHO ARE WORKING OR LOOKING FOR WORK. ANNUAL AVERAGES SHOWN.

Source: Pew Research Center analysis of monthly 1994 - 2017 Current Population Survey (IPUMS).

If you work for a "hip" tech start-up, whose halls are filled with Millennials, the growing dominance of younger workers isn't surprising. If you employ or do business with people in India, home to the youngest workforce in the world, you've likely been engaging with younger and younger employees for the past several years.

But for the vast majority of organizations from Main Street to Wall Street to TheStreet.com and beyond, the movement from a Boomer-dominated workplace to a Millennial one has often felt sudden and confusing. It's kind of like the (apocryphal) story about a frog in boiling water. If a frog (Baby Boomer) is suddenly dropped into boiling water (a workplace full of Millennials), it will jump out. But if you put the frog in cool water that is then brought to a boil slowly, it will burn and die.

The goal of this book is to keep you and your organization from becoming frog stew.

It's Been a Boomer World

The reason today's generational change is so shocking for so many individuals and organizations is the length and power of the Baby Boomer generation's dominance in almost all of American culture (see rock music, Oprah Winfrey, the U.S. Congress, suburbia, jeans) and particularly in our workplaces. Often without consciously realizing it, many of us have accepted as "normal" the communication preferences, management styles, work ethic, office layouts, career path preferences, and other practices that were created and/or perpetuated by the Boomers. When your boss tells you, "That's just the way things are," the more accurate truth is probably that's just the way people born in the U.S. between 1946 and 1964 tend to do things.

That was certainly true for a Generation Xer like me. For the first decade of my career, there were only three generations in the workplace, and Boomers were overwhelmingly dominant in terms of their sheer numbers. My peers and I pretty much had no choice but to adapt to Boomer preferences if we wanted to get ahead. My bosses and clients were Boomers, and their bosses' bosses were almost entirely Boomers, too. No one gave workshops or wrote books on how to appeal to Gen X workers or changed the workplace for us. We simply weren't populous enough as a demographic group to challenge the Boomer dominance. (Approximately 76 million people were born in the U.S. between 1946 and 1964; only 55 million were born between the smaller number of years assigned to Gen X by the Pew Research Center, 1965 and 1980.)

Case in point: in that first job I had after graduate school at WorkingWoman.com, I was honored to be invited to a lunch meeting with my new boss, Rick, and a consultant named Betsy, who was working with our team. Before we talked business, Rick and Betsy proceeded to spend twenty minutes talking about their mutual obsession with the Watergate trial. Although I was trying to slink down underneath the white tablecloth, they eventually turned their attention to me, at which point they asked if I was even alive during Watergate.

As it happens, I was born in September 1974, about a month after the "Smoking Gun" tape was released, which I admitted very quietly. But if you want any proof of how dominant the Baby Boomer experience was and often still is, can we pause to note that this business lunch was taking place approximately twenty-five years after Watergate and it was *still* a topic of conversation?

Of course, time moves fast, and the white tablecloth flipped a decade later. At this point I had launched my own business and was about to deliver a speech at a college in upstate New York, when I noticed a student sitting in the front row wearing a New York Mets T-shirt. Trying to bond with him and act cooler than I am—always a mistake—I said, "Hey, you're a Mets fan? I actually went to the '86 World Series!" He smiled uncomfortably and said, "Oh. That's the year I was born."

I felt ridiculous. Why didn't I just say, "I love the Mets, too!"?

Just as wealthy executives might talk about an expensive sport like golf in front of employees who can't afford to play, generational myopia is another type of unconscious bias that can harm workplace relationships and interfere with our ability to achieve success together. Even as someone who lives and breathes generational differences and advocates for generational diversity, I myself sometimes forget that not everyone is the same age I am. If you've found yourself in a similar situation, I empathize.

Why Now?

Every year the workplace gets a new infusion of young people, so why is the current transition such a big deal? Here's the thing: right now, in this particular moment in time, generational change is happening more quickly, more broadly across industries, and in greater numbers than ever before. As I mentioned, over the course of my own career, the workplace has grown from three generations of workers to five, and this unprecedented age diversity is coinciding with rapid changes in technology, globalization, our environment, and more.

The generational change in the workplace over the past few years is also historically unique because it involves expansion on both ends of the age spectrum. Yes, Millennials are the largest group in the U.S. labor force today and will be for decades to come. At the same time, for the first time in history, there are now more Americans over the age of 50 than under the age of 18. While many of these Traditionalists and Baby Boomers (and the very earliest Gen Xers) are retiring or have retired from the workforce, many decidedly have not. Americans over the age of 65 today are employed at the highest rates in fifty-five years. And as of 2018, over 250,000 Americans aged 85 years old and over were working—the highest number ever on record.

This means that, within any team or at any client pitch meeting or conference you attend, you may find any combination of generations in the room with you, who might be up to *six decades* apart in age. And the age diversity is happening at all levels of the organizational hierarchy. In the words of Peter Cappelli, a management professor at the Wharton School, "Suddenly 20- and 30-year-olds are working with people their parents' and grandparents' ages who are subordinates or peers, not superiors as they used to be. And there aren't just a handful of seniors who are mostly in the C-suite and rarely seen. They're at all ranks." Another outcome of the extraordinary multigenerational mixing in the workplace is that 38 percent of Americans today report to a boss who is younger than they are. That is a totally new phenomenon.

Statistics show that a majority of us think all this mixing is a good thing. According to a 2018 Randstad Workmonitor study, 86 percent of global workers prefer working on a multigenerational team (defined as those who are at least ten to fifteen years different in age). Why the positive attitude? Because, according to survey respondents, age-diverse organizations allow them to come up with innovative ideas and creative solutions to challenges.

If you haven't already, take a few minutes and analyze your team or organization. Which generations are represented? Are any generations underrepresented compared to the general population or the makeup of your customer or client base? How does your generational mix compare to the U.S. labor force overall? The exact composition of your professional community will likely affect how acutely you are experiencing generational change and which elements of your organization or your own career to consider remixing first.

Why Generations?

Let's take a step back and review what generational theory is, what the generational definitions are, and why this is a valuable lens through which to view our organizations, our colleagues, and ourselves. And then I will summarize each generation working today.

At its simplest, a generation is defined as a group of people born and living at the same time. It can also refer to the span of time between the birth of parents and that of their children, which is one of the reasons I love generational study and find it an invaluable tool: we all have experience with generational differences, because we are all members of multigenerational families. I like to start with the mention of generations in families, because it's a reminder of the fact that our similarities as human beings outweigh our differences. While generational distinctions are real, we are all far more alike than we are different.

In fact, the longer I study generations in the workplace, the more similarities I find in what people want out of work. Those fundamentals—meaning, purpose, good leaders, professional growth—don't change. What changes is how each generation expresses these needs and what expectations we have about our employers' fulfillment of them. More specifically, Millennials want what all generations of workers have always wanted, but they now have the tools and the confidence to ask for these things earlier in their careers, and they no longer feel a stigma about leaving organizations that don't provide them.

As universal a topic as generations might be, some people dislike the concept, because it implies that millions of people who happened to have been born in the same window of time are all exactly alike. I certainly do not believe that everyone born into a particular generation is exactly the same. I appreciate Nilofer Merchant's concept of "onlyness," which she defines as each person standing in a spot that no one else occupies, with a unique point of view that is born of each person's accumulated experience, perspective, and vision. Gender, ethnicity, race, class, disability, age, and many other factors impact someone's experiences, and we must keep each of these potential differences in mind when we consider generational identity.

As just one example, Erica Cordova Zinkie, vice president and legal counsel at OneDigital, an employee health and benefits consulting company, is an African American Millennial woman in a leadership role. As she described her experience to me, "If I encounter a negative interaction, I have to assess whether that interaction is a standard, non-prejudiced interpersonal conflict or risk internalizing that as generationally oriented, race-related, gender-related, or position-related." Identity is complicated and personal, and, as in Erica's example, generational identity is only one component.

One of the ways I have found it helpful to approach generational differences is to consider them as similar to global cultural differences. I've heard it said that, depending on the era in which you were born, in many ways you perceive the United States as a different country from that of people born in a different era. While of course there are similarities among all Americans, it makes sense to consider that the U.S. of the 1930s, for example, was in many ways a different country from the U.S. of the 1980s, which was a different country from the U.S. of today.

(Note that while this book will primarily focus on generations in the United States, of course many of you reading this book were not born here or do not currently live in the U.S. While there are some commonalities among generations globally, each country has its own cohorts, generational monikers, and unique characteristics.)

Here are some notable changes in the American experience from just the past fifty years:

- 48 percent of Gen Z Americans identify as racial or ethnic minorities today, compared to 18 percent of Baby Boomers at the same age.
- 65 percent of Traditionalists were married by age 32, compared to 26 percent of Millennials.
- 9 percent of Traditionalist women had completed at least four years of college by age 36. By the same age, 36 percent of Millennial women have.
- Traditionalist men were ten times more likely to be military veterans than Millennial men are today.

- Between 1988 and 2018, the cost of a four-year U.S. college or university has jumped 129 percent for a private school and 213 percent for a public school (both adjusted for inflation).
- For the first time in more than 130 years, Americans ages 18 to 34 are more likely to live with their parents than in any other living situation.
- In 1978, 58 percent of American teenagers had paid summer jobs. By 2016, only 35 percent did.

When you look at facts like the ones above, you realize that comparing, for instance, a 25-year-old of the Baby Boomer era to a 25-year-old today is just not accurate or helpful.

Like Myers-Briggs personality type indicators, birth order iden-tification, or countless other ways we try to understand people, in no way are generational definitions meant to prescribe or guarantee how any single individual will or should behave. I like to think of generational characteristics as providing clues—never promises—as to how certain people or interactions might be better handled or understood. Generational experts Neil Howe and William Strauss explain it like this: "You may share many of these attributes [of your generation], some of them, or almost none of them. Every genera-tion includes all kinds of people. Yet . . . you and your peers share the same 'age location' in history, and your generation's collective mindset cannot help but influence you—whether you agree with it or spend a lifetime battling against it."

One more caveat. As you look through the descriptions below, the age ranges may differ from other generational year markers you've come across, or from your own personal experience. Since there is no official Ministry of Naming Generations, there are no rules and there is no day at the hospital where a doctor declares, "This baby is the last Millennial and the next one born will be the first official Gen Z!" I have chosen to put my trust in the Pew Research Center and its declaration of generational cohorts. Those are the numbers that you'll find throughout this book and in all my work.

The goal of these generational descriptors is to give us a shared language and context for the discussions ahead. Personally, you may find yourself identifying with the generation associated with your year of birth or you may not, and either feeling is legitimate. Some people with significantly older parents or siblings identify with an older cohort, and vice versa for those with much younger parents or siblings. You may define yourself as a "cusper," born on the cusp of two different generations, with a foot in each one. As you will see, two of these "cusper" cohorts have even earned names of their own as "micro-generations," thus further segmenting your identification options. Or, as some people tell me, you might just feel deep down inside like an "old soul" or "young at heart" and identify with a generation totally unrelated to your birth year. I leave it entirely up to you.

The Generational Sorting Hat: An Overview of Generations in the United States

GENERATION	BORN	U.S. BIRTHS	COMMONLY CITED CHARACTERISTICS
Traditionalists	1928–1945	47 million	Loyal, cautious, formal, proud
Baby Boomers	1946–1964	76 million	Self-focused, competitive, optimistic, "forever young" mentality
Generation Jones	1955–1965	45–50 million	Adaptable, balance of idealism and cynicism, openness to change
Generation X	1965–1980	55 million	Independent, cautious, skeptical, tech pioneers
Xennials	1977–1985	32 million	Adaptable, balance of optimism and pessimism
Millennials	1981–1996	62 million	Self-expressive, group oriented, purpose-driven, tech dependent
Generation Z	1997–to be determined	to be determined	Cautious, technologically advanced, diverse

TRADITIONALISTS

- Born approximately 1928 to 1945
- Born in the U.S.: 47 million
- Commonly cited characteristics: loyal, cautious, formal, proud

Most (but certainly not all) Traditionalists are now retired, but their influence can still be felt in workplace structures all around us. Think top-down hierarchy with clear reporting structures, the "uniform" of a suit and tie, and the expectation of loyally serving one company for life.

Children of the Great Depression, Traditionalists are also known for their frugality and caution. Hierarchy and rule following are also common to this generation, of which 50 percent of men shared the experience of serving in the military (compared to less than 1 percent of our population today). It was this group of adults to whom John F. Kennedy said in 1961, "Ask not what your country can do for you—ask what you can do for your country." Most women and people of color of this era did not have access to the same educational or professional opportunities as men, and women often did not work outside the home.

Many Traditionalists who did work retired in their early to mid-60s, thanks to pension plans and Social Security. Those with the means to retire were often happy to complete their careers and move on to the next stage of life beyond work. Traditionalists who have remained in or returned to the workplace want to be respected for their experience and knowledge and not discounted because of their age.

BABY BOOMERS

- Born approximately 1946 to 1964
- Born in the U.S.: 76 million

- Commonly cited characteristics: self-focused, competitive, optimistic, "forever young" mentality

Baby Boomers, children of older Traditionalists, were born in the post–World War II baby boom years of 1946 to 1964 (the only generational time frame to be officially designated by the U.S. Census Bureau), and thus became the largest generation in American history. Compared to Traditionalists, Boomers generally grew up with more siblings in their families, more children in their neighborhoods, and more students in their classrooms. This bred a strong sense of camaraderie but also of competition.

The Boomers are strongly associated with the dramatic social changes of the 1960s. The civil rights movement, gay rights movement, and women's rights movement opened up more educational and economic opportunities for previously excluded groups.

Boomers also came of age in an optimistic, powerful era of prosperity in and global dominance by the U.S. Technologically, Boomers are the first television generation and thus the first mass advertising generation, which led to more focus on mass culture, marketing, and conspicuous consumption. Recall the 1980s-era saying "He who dies with the most toys wins." This, of course, does not apply to every Baby Boomer, but the rise in U.S. consumer debt in their era was unprecedented.

Named and celebrated for their youth—"Baby" is still in their name, even now that every Boomer is over the age of 50, and "Don't trust anyone over 30" originated with this cohort—members of this generation often project a "forever young" mentality. One result, as we have discussed, is that many Boomers are staying in the workforce longer, not just because many have to for financial reasons (especially after the Great Recession), but also because many *want* to. File under "Sometimes Generational Stereotypes Are a Little Bit True": The design firm IDEO, founded by Baby Boomer

David Kelley, is currently working on several projects to "redesign death."

Boomers have enjoyed a lengthy period of generational domination based on their overall numbers and the era of economic expansion into which they were born. They also are the beneficiaries of many of the social programs begun by their Traditionalist parents' generation, such as Social Security and Medicare. Whether this generation will support laws and build programs that provide economic security to future generations remains an open question.

MICRO-GENERATION: GENERATION JONES

- Born approximately 1955 to 1965
- Born in the U.S.: 45 to 50 million
- Commonly cited characteristics: adaptable, balance of idealism and cynicism, openness to change

"Generation Jones" is a term coined by the writer and cultural historian Jonathan Pontell to describe those born sometime in the latter half of the Baby Boomer years to the beginning of Generation X, roughly from the mid-1950s to the mid-1960s. As writer Theresa Danna describes her Joneser peers, "You were more likely to have grown up watching *The Brady Bunch* rather than *Leave It to Beaver*. If you remember President Kennedy's funeral at all, you mostly remember your parents' reaction to the loss, rather than feeling a loss yourself. . . . You never really felt like a Boomer, even though your age slotted you in that category, and you never really felt like a Gen Xer, either." Jonesers were too young for Woodstock, too old for mosh pits.

"Jonesin'," as in having an intense craving, is another connotation for this generation's name, according to Pontell. Why? Because many members of this mini-generation came of age as younger siblings of Boomer brothers and sisters, who are perceived to have taken all the best resources for themselves. Older Boomers finished school and entered the workforce in a time of historic economic growth. This was over by the time Jonesers graduated just a few years later. From 1973 to 1982, the U.S. endured three recessions, two energy crises, inflation, and high unemployment.

What is notable about Generation Jones is that people born around this time don't identify with either the Boomers or the Gen Xers, which provides a reminder not to make assumptions about people based on their age or birth year. It also points to a questioning of how expansive generational cohort years really should be. Pontell himself explains that he originally came up with the idea of a separate generation in elementary school, when a teacher fifteen years his senior told the class that he and his students were all members of the Baby Boomer generation. Pontell says he laughed out loud at the thought.

GENERATION X

- Born approximately 1965 to 1980
- Born in the U.S.: 55 million
- Commonly cited characteristics: independent, cautious, skeptical, tech pioneers

Next we come to the generation I and many of you proudly belong to. We Gen Xers came along after the massive Baby Boomer cohort and thus were nicknamed the "baby bust" generation. (Not exactly a motivating concept, am I right?)

A generation almost as small in size as the Traditionalists, Gen Xers have often felt overshadowed by our Boomer predecessors. As mentioned about Jonesers, the economy began to turn south as we were born and grew up, which led to a very different childhood experience. While Boomer kids played stickball in the street with their many siblings and peers, Gen Xers were more likely to have fewer siblings or be only children, and to stay indoors due perhaps to fears of being kidnapped, like the children whose photos we saw on the sides of our milk cartons.

From 1960 to 1980, the divorce rate in the U.S. more than doubled, with 50 percent of marriages in 1970 ending in divorce. Approximately half the children born to married parents in the 1970s saw their parents split up, compared to only about 11 percent of Americans born in the 1950s. This left many Gen Xers in single-parent situations where, because that parent was out working, they returned from school to empty homes, leading to increased attention to the phenomenon of "latchkey kids."

All these factors combined to create a generation that grew up independent, self-reliant, and appreciative of technology that helped us take care of ourselves, such as microwave ovens, video games, and personal computers. When we entered the Baby Boomer–dominated workplace around the 1990s, we often felt alienated and unimportant. That helped fuel the independent instincts that led many Xers to move to Silicon Valley and start companies that bucked the norms of traditional corporate America. (It is notable how many Silicon Valley entrepreneurs are members of Generation X.)

If you closely review the generational chart on page 2, you will find that we Xers did actually become the largest generation in the U.S. workforce in the year 2013 for about fifteen minutes, and then we were overtaken by the Millennials. We never really had our generational moment—and believe me, I was looking for it. It is not uncommon in my workshops on generational differences for a Baby Boomer or Millennial to say, "Wow, I didn't know there was a generation between us!"

I don't think it's an accident that I am so interested in research-ing the multigenerational workplace, because Gen Xers are often positioned as outside observers, translators, or bridges. We had to adapt to the Boomers and now we're being asked to adapt to the Millennials. We have to be multilingual generationally, because no one else speaks our exact language. That can be a tough place for us to be, but it also gives us a unique positioning to succeed alongside the two very large generations that we're sandwiched between. We are natural remixers.

MICRO-GENERATION: XENNIALS

- Born approximately 1977 to 1985
- Born in the U.S.: approximately 32 million
- Commonly cited characteristics: adaptable, balance of optimism and pessimism

Like the Generation Jonesers, Xennials are another recently de-fined cohort who felt left out of the mainstream generational cat-egories. The term, invented by journalist Sarah Stankorb (born 1980), quickly went viral, likely because so many people technically in the Millennial demographic didn't want to be associated with all the negative stereotypes that accompanied that term. (We'll get to those.)

Nor did members of this cohort feel like "digital natives," a key characteristic of the Millennial description. "We use social me-dia," writes Stankorb, "but can remember living life without it. . . . We adapted easily to technological advances but weren't as be-holden to them as our juniors." This is where another name for this micro-generation—the "Oregon Trail generation"—comes in, recalling the bare-bones computer game released in 1985 that Xennials often played.

Similar to the Generation Jonesers, Xennials are also associated with a demographic perceived as growing up in boom economic times (in this case, the Millennials) without enjoying the fruits themselves. As one generational analyst described Xennials: "They are old enough to remember the end of a long period of growth (following a small recession) in the 1990s, but they came of age around the time that the 'dot-com bubble' burst and saw the decline and major recession of the 2000s. In other words, they were 'first given a sweet taste of the good life, and then kicked in the face.'"

MILLENNIALS, A.K.A. GENERATION Y

- Born approximately 1981 to 1996
- Born in the U.S.: 62 million
- Commonly cited characteristics: self-expressive, group oriented, purpose-driven, global, tech dependent

Millennials, the generation we will spend the most time in this book discussing, are also known as Generation Y, a term that tends to be more common outside the United States. Millennials are primarily children of the Baby Boomers (thus another nickname, "echo boomers"), and because of their large size Millennial preferences will dominate the workforce for the next several decades, just as the Boomers' preferences did before them.

Our two largest generations have more than a few similarities. Like Boomers, Millennials tend to be self-expressive, group oriented, and civic-minded. In fact, while I was writing this book, a lovely story appeared in the *New York Times* featuring Baby Boomer "freedom riders" from 1964, including 73-year-old Howard Kirschenbaum, working more than fifty years later alongside Millennials like twenty-five-year-old Arekia Bennett, executive director of Mississippi Votes, to register voters.

I am very deliberate in beginning a description of Millennials with a positive intergenerational story, because, unfortunately, too many stories about Millennials tend toward the negative. Articles, blog posts, and news stories often criticize Millennials for acting entitled, demanding constant feedback, changing jobs willy-nilly, wanting instant gratification, and believing they deserve "trophies for participation." As the cover of *Time* magazine declared in 2013, "Millennials Are Lazy Entitled Narcissists Who Still Live with Their Parents." Ouch.

As the *Time* headline suggested, many attribute these perceived negative characteristics—I call it Millennial shaming and I'll point it out many times in this book—to the way Millennials were parented. They grew up in an era in which children, particularly those in the middle to upper middle class, received a lot more personal attention and coaching from adults, and many parents "helicoptered" over their children to help them handle challenges and setbacks. Many Boomer parents positioned themselves more as buddies and mentors to their kids (hence the term "peer-enting"), and 55 percent of Millennials say that they consider a parent to be their best friend.

What I find irksome about criticisms related to these facts is that children cannot control how they are parented. If we find these behaviors problematic, shouldn't we be calling out Baby Boomers for how they raised children rather than bad-mouthing the generation they raised? Regardless of who we "blame," Millennials today are often forced to contend with negative perceptions of their desire for the personal fulfillment and self-expression that the adults who raised them encouraged them to pursue. As one Millennial commented in one of my multigenerational workshops, "We didn't give ourselves the participation trophies. The adults kept giving them to us."

Millennials also came of age alongside the rise of the Internet, thus the nickname "digital natives," which has had a massive impact on how they perceive the world and interact with others. It can't help but affect your perspective and expectations of your life and your career when all the information in the world is just one click away. And Millennials were the unwitting early guinea pigs in the grand experiment known as social media. Millennials were the college students who first experienced Facebook as a student-only environment and then were shocked when their parents, teachers, and ultimately potential employers were invited to the network, too. I can't help but feel sorry for Millennials, who did the same dumb teenage stuff we all did in previous generations but were unlucky enough to be the first people to be encouraged to photograph and post pictures of their exploits on a public platform.

Millennials are significantly more diverse than the generations that preceded them, with 44 percent identifying as part of a minority race or ethnic group (defined as a group other than non-Hispanic, single-race white). Millennials are more than three times as likely as Traditionalists to identify as LGBTQ, and 63 percent of Millennials, compared to 39 percent of Traditionalists, consider themselves to be allies of the LGBTQ community.

Financially, Millennials are the first generation to experience the more pronounced economic disparities that have arisen in our country. The average debt burden of Millennials is around $37,000 (primarily due to the rising cost of higher education), and, as *New York Times* columnist David Leonhardt has written, "For Americans under the age of 40, the twenty-first century has resembled one long recession," with people between the ages of 25 and 34 (read: Millennials) earning slightly less in 2017 than people in the same age group had been in 2000.

Millennials are also the generation to come of age amid increasing school shootings, terrorism, and hate crimes, from Columbine to 9/11 and beyond. While other generations also lived through these horrors, Millennials experienced them as children and young adults. This impacts their views on safety, community, and social trust. I was particularly struck by findings of the Pew Research Center, which asked Americans across generations the question "Generally speaking, would you say that most people can be trusted or that you can't be too careful in dealing with people?" Based on the most recent results available, about 40 percent of Baby Boomers and 37 percent of Traditionalists believe that, generally speaking, most people can be trusted. About 31 percent of Gen Xers agree. But only 19 percent of Millennials believe that most people can be trusted. That means that eight out of ten Millennials distrust their fellow citizens.

While this lack of social trust is not surprising given the times we live in, this characteristic of Millennials is essential for people of other generations to understand. Many leaders over the years have asked me why their young employees no longer seem to give them the benefit of the doubt or are quick to assume the worst intentions when company policy changes are announced. If you have felt this way about Millennials, it is not your imagination. (Note that we don't have statistics about Gen Z yet.) If you work with members of this cohort (and if you don't yet, you surely will soon) it is critically important to build and maintain authentic personal relationships to earn their trust.

Millennials, as we have established, are already the largest generation in the workforce and in the overall U.S. population; by 2020, experts predict this generation to make up 50 percent of our workforce, and by 2025 they are expected to comprise 75 percent of all workers in our country. There is simply no question that the Millennial mindset and style of work will have a tremendous impact for years and decades to come.

IN THE MIX: WHAT'S IN A NAME?

It is important to keep in mind that the very word "Millennial" itself is controversial. The vast majority of people I meet in this age range don't like it, mostly because of the overwhelmingly negative portrayal of their generation in the media.

At one company, I did a little market research and asked the 20- and 30-something audience to help me call them by the right name. I asked how many prefer the term "Millennial" and a few hands went up. The same for "Generation Y." A few were partial to "early-career professionals" or "20-somethings." One guy said, "Just call me Steve."

This unscientific result gels with the findings of a study by Pew of generational name preferences: while 79 percent of Baby Boomers consider themselves to be part of their designated generation, only 40 percent of Millennials feel the same way about their label. (For Xers, the percentage is 58.)

BuzzFeed, among the most youth-focused media companies of recent times, resisted the term for as long as possible, then in 2017 finally admitted the M-word into its official style guide. "Today we are waving the white flag, announcing our surrender to the term's unironic usage and acknowledging its journey from cheesy marketing buzzword we tried desperately to combat to just another everyday descriptive word in our vernacular."

I also have chosen to use the word "Millennial" in this book and in my work in general. I use it as a descriptor and do my best to strip it of the negative associations the word has unfortunately come to embody.

GENERATION Z

- Born: 1997; no end date yet determined
- Born in the U.S.: number not yet determined
- Commonly cited characteristics (so far): cautious, technologically advanced, diverse

You are probably hearing a lot about Gen Z lately, thus far mainly in their role as tween and teen consumers. While Gen Z is a larger generation than Millennials globally (roughly 32 percent of the global population in 2019), the American cohort is significantly smaller in size than the Millennials, just as Generation X is significantly smaller than the Baby Boomers. In fact, 2017 marked the lowest number of babies born in the U.S. in thirty years.

Gen Zs are notable for their diversity, which led to an early but since abandoned generational moniker, the "Plurals." I still like this concept as an entry point to understanding Zs. Consider that the youngest Gen Zs, beginning with those born in 2009, are the most diverse generation in American history, with 48 percent being part of a minority race or ethnic group. One in four are Hispanic, significantly higher than any other generation, including Millennials.

Many Gen Zs prefer to identify as "blended" or multiethnic, and question the need to "choose a box" on documents like school forms. Gen Zs are also the first generation to come of age with the legalization of gay marriage and greater acceptance of transgender and nonbinary identities.

Gen Zs are shaping up to be our most educated generation as well, with 59 percent of 18- to 20-year-olds enrolled in college, compared with 53 percent of Millennials at the same age. The high school dropout rate for Zs is also lower than that of similarly aged Millennials in 2002.

Akin to Gen Xers and Millennials, Gen Zs are coming of age

during a time of significant turmoil that can be particularly frightening for children. First is the Great Recession that began in 2008, which rocked many American families' sense of security. Next comes the significant rise in school shootings, including the massacre at Sandy Hook Elementary School in 2012. And finally, the opioid epidemic, which traces back to the late 1990s and has continued for the entire lifetime of Gen Zs. Colleges and universities have responded by increasing mental health services, sexual assault awareness, public safety, and various other policies to better provide security and safety for students' mental, emotional, and physical well-being. We are beginning to notice similar action in workplace environments.

Perhaps not surprisingly, statistics show that Gen Z teenagers are more risk-averse than previous generations. They are significantly less likely to have tried alcohol, gotten a driver's license, had sex, or gone out regularly without their parents than teens of the previous two or three generations. (Note that these declines appeared across racial, geographic, and socioeconomic lines and across rural, urban, and suburban areas.) This is likely related to the dangers present in society today, but also because teenagers can now have an active social life without leaving home. It almost goes without saying that Gen Zs were born into an era dominated by technology and social media. This cohort barely knows a world before personal computers, the Internet, and mobile devices. They can watch any TV show anytime, anywhere—there is no such thing as "Saturday morning cartoons" or "appointment TV" anymore—and when they don't know how to spell a word, they ask Alexa.

However, while they are deeply connected and effortlessly savvy technologically, I have also noticed awareness in this generation that constant connection has its downsides. There has been a pullback among young people from some social media and a desire among some to unplug. That said, there is zero doubt that Gen Zs are effortlessly fluid in their use of today's existing technologies and their willingness to adapt to new developments in virtual reality, artificial intelligence, and whatever else comes next.

GENERATION EVERYONE?

The term "Generation Alpha" has been used to describe the generation that will ultimately follow Gen Zs (since we need a new alphabet), but I have not come across any consensus yet on exactly when that next cohort will begin, except that they will be the children of Millennials. Believe it or not, I once received a phone call from a reporter from a well-known business media outlet who asked me for my opinions on the workplace preferences of Generation Alpha. I politely declined to provide any conjecture about the workplace preferences of a generation that is still being conceived(!).

Whether or not we eventually identify and define Alphas, I want to float the theory that we are likely nearing the end of the relevance of generational constructs. I am not the first one to posit this theory; the marketing agency sparks & honey titled its report on Generation Z *The Final Generation*.

It certainly makes a nice story to end the concept of generational theory with the end of the alphabet, but it makes sense for other reasons as well. As change happens faster and faster in our society, does it make sense that people born fifteen or twenty years apart will still share common experiences and expectations? And with the increased connection we all feel thanks to the Internet, mobile devices, and social media, perhaps in other ways we are moving closer together in our shared expectations and experiences.

Internet entrepreneur Gina Pell coined the term "Perennials" to describe people who transcend the entire concept of generations by remaining current and timeless. As Pell defines them, Perennials are "ever-blooming, relevant people of all ages who live in the present time, know what's happening in the world, stay current with technology, and have friends of all ages. We get involved, stay curious, mentor others, and are passionate, compassionate, creative, confident, collaborative, global-minded risk takers who continue to push up against our growing edge and know how to hustle. We comprise an inclusive, enduring mindset, not a divisive demographic." Her examples include Ellen DeGeneres, Lady Gaga, Emma González, Lorne Michaels, Lin-Manuel Miranda, Diane von Furstenberg, Ai Weiwei, and Serena Williams.

Consumer brand marketers are certainly embracing a perennial mindset. Whereas fifty years ago it would be almost unheard of for a parent and child to wear the same clothing styles (how often did your grandparents wear jeans?) or to like the same music, today this is commonplace. As marketing expert Gregg S. Lipman describes this:

> Fathers and sons comparing fantasy football rankings on matching iPhones or killing precious productivity hours on YouTube. . . . Teachers and students sipping from matching Starbucks latte cups or ordering the same items from Pinkberry. . . . Moms and daughters rooting feverishly for their favorite "American Idol" contestants. . . . Uncles and nephews cracking open cans of Red Bull. . . . Grandparents, parents, and their children conversing freely on Facebook or Skype.

These consumer experiences inevitably cross over into people's workplace expectations, which means that an organization's employer brand will need to appeal across generations just as consumer brands now need to do.

This is not just smart business; it is also the law. It is imperative to keep top of mind that when we talk about generations, we are also talking about age. Ageism is real and it is illegal. The national

Age Discrimination in Employment Act of 1967 (ADEA) forbids age discrimination against people who are age 40 or older. The law prohibits discrimination in any aspect of employment, including hiring, firing, pay, job assignments, promotions, layoffs, training, benefits, and any other term or condition of employment. The law does not protect workers under the age of 40, although some states have laws that do safeguard younger workers from age discrimination as well.

No matter what generation you personally identify with, if you identify with any at all, the most important point is to remember that generational understanding should be one tool among many in your professional toolkit to consider when you are facing a professional opportunity, a communication frustration, a management misunderstanding, or other personal or organizational inflection point. Always—always—keep in mind that some issues are generational and some are not. (I'm sure I don't need to convince you that there are irritating bosses and exasperating employees of every era.)

I have observed firsthand through my work how powerfully generational understanding has helped my clients to better manage their organizations and, quite frankly, to understand and enjoy their colleagues a whole lot more. That is why I personally believe so strongly in the importance of this tool and look forward to applying it to benefit you and your organization.

CHAPTER 1: KEY TAKEAWAYS

- Analyze your team or organization to understand which generations are represented or underrepresented and how your generational mix compares to the U.S. labor force overall. This will help you to determine which elements of your organization to consider remixing first.
- We as human beings are more alike than we are different. What changes from generation to generation is how we express our needs and preferences at work, and what expectations we have about our employers' fulfillment of them.
- Think of generational characteristics as providing clues— never promises—as to how certain people or interactions might be better handled or understood. Generational understanding should be one tool among many in your professional toolkit to consider when you are facing various challenges and opportunities.
- As change is happening faster and faster in our society, we may be coming to the end of the applicability of generational theory with Generation Z and moving toward a "perennial," timeless approach to life and work.

2 RULES FOR REMIXERS

Common Sense Is Not So Common

THE FIRST PLACE to apply the tool of generational understanding is within yourself. Organizations are ultimately a collection of human beings, and while it certainly takes two to tango, the way we each manage ourselves is critical to the way we interact with others. To begin to build your multigenerational muscle, here are eight essential rules that will recur throughout the coming chapters and are meant to steer you to consistent success whether you are remixing a small team, a large global organization, or only yourself.

Rule #1. Stop the Generational Shaming.

Take a look at this quotation:

"I see no hope for the future of our people if they are dependent on the frivolous youth of today."

In what era do you think this was written? This week's *Economist*? A political speech from the 1960s? The Roaring Twenties? The late eighteenth century of *Hamilton*?

In fact, these words are attributed to the poet Hesiod, a contemporary of Homer, all the way back in the eighth century B.C.

We have literally been shaming young people for all of human history.

This has never made any sense to me. Why does every generation criticize the next? Why do we do everything we can to discredit the people who will play a large role in creating our shared future?

The latest shamees, of course, are Millennials. I'm going to guess that, even if you identify as a Millennial yourself, most of what you have read about this generation is negative. As we discussed in the previous chapter, the popular buzz is that today's 20- and 30-somethings are any combination of entitled, narcissistic, lazy, living in their parents' basements, unable to make eye contact, and expecting those infamous trophies for participation.

Gen Xers were called "slackers" in our youth. And Baby Boomers were called "hippies" and the original narcissistic "me" generation. But the vitriol directed at Millennials from all directions has been off the charts. Even in the youth-dominated technology sector, one developer from a major tech company posted the hideous statement "We don't hire junior developers or interns . . . if you don't get a puppy, you don't have to clean up its messes."

We don't tolerate discrimination within the workplace, so we must condemn the constant, brazen shaming of Millennials.

I was struck in the many interviews I conducted for this book with young leaders by how many did not want to be identified as Millennials. Amy, who asked to be identified only by her first name, is a mid-level executive at a media company and former employee of a national senior citizen membership organization. She told me that she fears that being identified as a Millennial will bias leaders against her.

"I've been fortunate to take on some large responsibility and leadership in my career thus far," she shared. "I'm proud of that and certainly want to continue to grow, but to some extent I feel that as you move up to more senior and executive-level roles in an organization, there is often a perception or expectation that those roles will be filled with people with a similar profile as far as years of experience or age. I feel like having someone know my age could limit my immediate potential in terms of an executive thinking, 'She's not ready,' or 'She'll have plenty of time to get there—it doesn't need to be now.'"

Amy even admits that she has a small patch of gray hair that she used to pluck, but now she emphasizes it so senior leaders might think she is older.

This saddens me, not just for Amy's feeling that she needs to hide her age in order to succeed, but for any organization that might miss out on any Millennial's talents because members of this generation feel ashamed of their age. Ageism affects all generations (isn't it interesting that a Millennial wants to expose her gray hairs to feel more respected, and middle-aged workers often cover their grays to feel more relevant?), and for business leaders it is entirely against our own professional interest.

I am frequently asked why I am so supportive of Millennials, why I am so bullish on this generation. My answer is simple: we don't have much choice! We quite literally cannot achieve anything without them. We've discussed the fact that Millennials are already the majority—and soon to be the *vast* majority—of our country. And our workforce. And our clients and customers. And our vendors. And our investors. And our voters. No organization will succeed if it does not attract, engage, and embrace Millennials.

If you have ever been guilty of making fun of Millennials or any other generation, in a personal or professional context, you must commit to stopping right now. This includes shaming of yourself or your own generation. While a bit of light self-deprecation can be charming and build bridges between generations, be mindful of going too far. Stop clicking on articles about Millennials and Gen Z "killing" everything from paper napkins to shopping malls to home ownership to canned tuna. Stop calling yourself a Luddite if you are a Traditionalist or Baby Boomer who takes a bit longer to learn technology. And, Gen Xers, we need to stop complaining that everybody ignores us.

For some on the older end of the age spectrum, this also means letting go of nostalgia. I was once at a conference where an executive from a major beverage company told an audience of young professionals, "I feel sorry for you guys. Business was so much more fun in the '80s!"

That comment helped absolutely no one.

Patty McCord, former chief talent officer at Netflix, says that nostalgia for "the way things used to be" is one of the biggest potential pitfalls she advises business leaders to avoid. Her advice is to focus on your customers or clients instead of your memories, to be "constantly thinking about where you're going to be, who your customer's going to be, what you need to do differently, how you're going to scale, and how the world's going to look. Even if we wanted our companies to stay the same, our customers won't. The world's going to go on without us, whether we like it or not."

If you have any remaining nostalgia for the past, find a way to get it out of your system. Reminisce with a former colleague, write a memoir, pack a time capsule. To spark your thinking, here is a list of a few things I miss from the early days of my career:

- Knowing people's phone numbers from memory
- Putting fresh calendar pages into my Filofax each new year
- Spinning my Rolodex
- Bringing full-size toiletries on business trips

Of course, my beloved iPhone has replaced the most nostalgic items on this list, and I wouldn't give up my phone. But if anyone comes up with an app of a full-size shampoo bottle, I'm listening.

Rule #2. Empathize.

Next, replace your shaming with empathy. In order to successfully work with people of other generations, you have to be able to put yourself in their shoes and consider the world from their perspective.

It is critical to learn about the experiences of other generations in order to understand what values, preferences, and expectations they bring to the workplace. And most of us have a lot to learn in this regard. While many of us engage in intergenerational relationships in a family setting, we tend to be less generationally diverse in our other personal and professional relationships. According to Cornell University gerontologist Karl Pillemer, you are more likely to have a friend of a different race than one who is ten years older or younger than you are. (Consider as well that three-quarters of whites don't have *any* non-white friends, according to the nonprofit, nonpartisan Public Religion Research Institute.)

Think about it: Beyond members of your family, how often do you socialize with someone of a different generation? In the workplace context, beyond people you must interact with—colleagues, bosses, direct reports, clients, vendors—how often do you network with people outside of your general age range, or people in your age range who are a different race or gender? What opportunities are you missing because you are exposing yourself only to the limited perspective of people quite similar to you?

One of my observations about many Millennial professionals is their relative lack of knowledge about what the business environment was like before they entered it, with a particular lack of understanding of the technological realities. This is not a criticism. It is pretty difficult for anyone to imagine working without the tools you consider basic. Asking a Millennial to work without high-speed Wi-Fi is like asking a Boomer to work without electricity. In one of my all-time favorite studies, Cisco found that one of every three college students globally believes the Internet is as fundamental a resource to the human race as air, water, food, and shelter. Sometimes even a Gen Xer like me can't remember what we did before the Web. How did I track FedEx packages?

To better empathize with a Traditionalist or Baby Boomer, imagine what it would be like to be told for decades that one way of working is the "right" way—working for one company your whole career, rising up a prescribed ladder, sacrificing personal time for work, retiring at a certain age—and then suddenly, toward the later end of your career, the rules completely change. You have to learn an entirely new, tech-enabled way of communicating and working that aligns with the now-dominant Millennial cohort, and your leaders, wanting to appeal to those Millennials, tell you, "We're going to do things differently in the workplace now and change what kinds of experience and knowledge we value. And if you don't change, you will be considered an irrelevant dinosaur. Oh—and you no longer have an office."

To better empathize with a Generation Xer, imagine advancing through the early years of your career in the shadow of the largest generation in history. Your Boomer bosses preach the importance of "paying your dues," and so you keep your head down and do just that. Then, as you enter the middle years of your career, when you thought you might finally get the chance to take over leadership responsibilities, you notice that the long-tenured employees ahead of you are not planning to retire at the same age their predecessors did. And another enormous group of workers is coming in behind you, and they have a skill set of social media and technology understanding that appears to be more valued than your dues-paying hard work. You're perpetually caught in the middle and it feels like it will never ever be your turn in charge. On that note, I have heard Gen Xers referred to as the Prince Charles of the generations. (Pro tip: Do not repeat that joke in England. I did, and the audience was *not* amused.)

To empathize with a Millennial or Gen Z, think about the pressures of growing up and beginning a career in the age of the Internet and social media. Whereas earlier generations could make a lot of mistakes and professional blunders in private, you face the pressure to post your accomplishments and daily activities online for all to witness. While I was unemployed for a few months after grad school and searching for my first job, I didn't have the added burden of scrolling through Instagram photos of my friends' successes or watching their job titles advance on their LinkedIn profiles. FOMO (fear of missing out) is real and painful.

Empathizing with today's youngest workers also means giving thought to the financial realities of young adulthood. As we have addressed, the exponentially greater cost of higher education means that a large number of 20- and 30-somethings in today's workforce have student loan debt. Even worse, this investment in higher education has not significantly increased income for Millennial and Gen Z college graduates as it did for previous generations (who often had less debt to begin with).

College educations pay off only because it has become less viable in the twenty-first century for people to make a living with only a high school diploma, particularly during economic downturns, when jobs are scarce. For people of color, the challenges can be even greater: one recent study suggests that young Black men need two additional levels of education to achieve the same employment levels as young white men. Some trade school and reskilling programs, which used to serve as an alternative to college, are leading young people to take out loans, particularly those programs offered by for-profit colleges. The upshot is that many Millennials and Gen Zs are working hard and making payments on their debt—but they are still not able to buy homes or save for retirement at the same rates previous generations might have done at their age.

When you empathize, you can also take steps to correct what you perceive as inequalities and unfair practices. Daryl Dickson, vice president of talent development and human capital officer at Management Leadership for Tomorrow, a nonprofit whose mission is to empower a new generation of diverse leaders, deeply identifies with the Millennials and Gen Zs she coaches and mentors. "When I first started my corporate life several decades ago," she told me, "one of my biggest frustrations was that you were expected to do nothing but execute someone else's decisions unless you had spent years earning your stripes. I felt I was capable and worked very hard, and I wanted to be judged on that and not how long I had been in my chair. I see that same sentiment in young people today." This is why Daryl, and many other Baby Boomers I speak with, believe that organizations that are willing to advance and compensate talent without regard for age and time in their positions are the ones that will win the future.

Rule #3. Assume the Best Intentions.

Continuing on the theme of empathy, next time you experience a conflict—and especially if you suspect that conflict involves an intergenerational misunderstanding—I would ask you to pause before reacting.

For example, I hear a lot of complaints from longtime leaders who say, "It is so annoying that the Millennials and Gen Zs on my team always wear earbuds in their ears at work."

I often question back, "Do you think that they're doing it intentionally to irritate you?"

They always laugh and say, "Of course not."

So I ask, "Why do you think they're wearing them?"

At this point they either think about why this younger person might be wearing earbuds or they decide to ask the Millennial directly. Both of these are positive, constructive outcomes.

The answer from the younger employee usually turns out to be something along the lines of "I'm wearing earbuds because I'm trying to concentrate. Listening to music makes me more productive in our open office."

Some managers find this acceptable and live with the earbuds, especially those of us from other generations who also find it challenging to work in an open floorplan. Others might say, "Thank you for explaining. I understand that you feel more productive, but for our work it's more important that you be available. I'll let you know the projects when it's fine to plug in, but for now please take them off because we have clients in the office who may want to engage with you." Or you might allow employees to plug in at their desks but ask them to remove headphones when they walk around the office so they are available for engagement with other employees. Or this might result in a conversation about an employee's need for a special accommodation. Or, as we will discuss more in chapter 9 on the workspace remix, this conversation could lead to a decision to remix the team's workspace to include some quieter spaces where employees can better concentrate.

Assuming the best intentions allows you to better understand the "why" behind a behavior or decision you might question or disagree with. This then allows you to explain the "why" behind *your* reasoning. The end result is more understanding and effectiveness all around.

Rule #4. Think "And," Not "Or."

In the past, many of our experiences at work and at home were purportedly one-size-fits-all. There was the so-called nuclear family.

There were "standard" work hours of 9:00 to 5:00. There was Henry Ford saying, "Any customer can have a car painted any color that he wants so long as it is black."

And now we have Starbucks, Spotify, and Build-A-Bear Workshop. I call this Customization Nation, and we all live here. Rather than relying on a store or product designer to create an experience for us, today's consumers are cocreators in the process as we personalize and customize products and experiences to our exact liking.

Of course, it was never actually true that one size fit all—just look at how long it took for "nude" bandages to include more than one skin color—but in recent years, thanks in large part to technological advancements, our choices and opportunities for personalization have grown exponentially. As modern consumers, we live in a world of almost unlimited options. How could that not affect our workplace expectations? As we'll discuss in the following chapters, few organizations or industries offer a straight career ladder anymore. Work hours have become flexible. Job titles have become more personalized. Employee benefit offerings have multiplied.

What does all this variety and customization mean for you as a leader? When you are searching for ideas, solutions to challenges, innovations, and disruptions, you will satisfy more employees when you seek out solutions that include options and choice. As one example, if you want to reward your team for a successful quarter, consider that not everyone wants to go to a bar for drinks. Perhaps offer the choice to the team of a celebratory breakfast, lunch, escape room outing, or shared volunteer activity.

Here is another example: about 4 percent of employers are now offering their Millennial and Gen Z employees some relief for their student loan debts, which is a benefit I applaud. However, it was a concern that student loan repayment could take the place of retirement saving among young employees. Thinking "and," not "or," Abbott, the pharmaceutical and medical products company, announced in 2018 a new benefit to help its employees both pay off their student debt *and* begin to save for retirement. The Abbott program allows employees who contribute at least 2 percent of their pay toward their student loans to also be eligible for the company's 5 percent match in their 401(k) retirement savings plan.

If you find yourself torn between the "old" way of doing something and the "new" way, resist the pull to make that kind of choice. The better outcome will usually reflect a combination or confluence of both.

Rule #5. Remember That "Common Sense Is Not So Common."

Providing options does not mean providing unlimited options or a free-for-all. It might sound counterintuitive, but providing clear expectations, rules, and boundaries around people's choices actually allows members of all generations to feel more comfortable, creative, and empowered. Otherwise, you leave too much up for interpretation.

In the wise words of Voltaire, "Common sense is not so common."

For example, one of the trends that has received a lot of attention in recent years is the policy of unlimited vacation. While I support the concept of treating employees like adults who can be trusted to take the appropriate amount of time off at appropriate times, my definition of "appropriate" might be vastly different from yours. Many managers in unlimited vacation policy situations tell me their team members, especially those with less work experience, either take way too much vacation (in their opinion) or are too intimidated by the choice and take none at all. That is not an ideal outcome.

Similarly, in 2015 Netflix announced that it would offer employees up to one year of maternity or paternity leave and that employees would be trusted to take the amount they needed. By 2018 the company found that most people interpreted the rule as an automatic full year, which was not their intention. Now Netflix instructs managers to tell employees that it is most common to take four to eight months, and that has become the average.

Another example is the confusion that often surrounds social media sharing by employees. There have been many instances in the news—for example, a Millennial employee recording internal company discussions and then posting them publicly. Here is the argument that often ensues:

EXECUTIVE: But that was confidential!
MILLENNIAL: You never told us that!
EXECUTIVE: I didn't think I had to!

Most Traditionalists, Baby Boomers, and Generation Xers, who came of age and built a large portion of their careers before the existence of social media, tend to consider information private unless told otherwise. For Millennials and Gen Zs, the exact opposite assumption is made: everything can be shared unless you are distinctly told not to do so.

Neither side of this argument is right or wrong. And there is often no way to provide explicit instructions when you didn't even consider a situation could be interpreted in a way that was different from what you intended. This is why multigenerational teams are so important, especially for major decisions. You must consider a variety of perspectives and potential interpretations (generational and otherwise) if you want to survive and thrive in a diverse world.

Clarifying expectations and boundaries applies to the day-to-day completion of tasks as well. For instance, "Brainstorm some ideas for a new e-book product about blockchain" has no boundaries. Your team might come up with brilliant suggestions, but they might also come up with suggestions that are too specific when you wanted general, too U.S. focused when you wanted global, too theoretical when you wanted practical. People often give vague directions because they want to invite their team to "think outside the box," but that is difficult to do when you don't know what the box is.

It is also the case that many younger employees have not been taught the same "commonsense" skills that many members of previous generations often took for granted, such as typing, writing a professional communication, balancing a budget, and ironing a shirt. Millennials and Gen Zs themselves are more than aware of these perceived shortcomings compared to previous generations, hence their self-deprecating jokes about the challenges of "adulting."

Lots of people bemoan the fact that "kids today" don't know how to do things they consider to be "basic knowledge," but how many of us are taking it upon ourselves to teach those things to our children and employees? As a remixer, you might have to do so.

Rule #6. Don't Change What Works.

Another counterintuitive truth is that the best way to help people adapt to change is to focus on what will stay the same. Especially at a time when so many people are concerned that robots will take away their jobs, I would argue that the fundamentals—those things that should not change and will not change—are more important than ever.

This is particularly important in managing long-tenured employees, who often feel tremendous loyalty to their organizations and ways of working. They want to be assured that much of what they have built will remain, despite the VUCA all around us.

I was once delivering a workshop to a group of university professors on the topic of generational change. As I was describing Millennials' and Gen Zs' desire for shorter and more interactive learning opportunities, a chemistry professor raised his hand and asked—somewhat snarkily, I might add—if I was saying he should no longer teach the periodic table of the elements because his students might find it boring. Of course, that is not what I was saying at all. The periodic table of the elements is essential, fundamental knowledge. But isn't it possible that professors can find new and innovative ways of teaching it?

Fabrizio Freda, president and CEO of The Estée Lauder Companies, describes this beautifully as "separating your roots from your anchors." Your roots are the core identity of your organization or your brand (or your scientific discipline)—those elements that need to be preserved and should never change. Your anchors, however, are the practices or habits that are weighing you down and need to be released.

For The Estée Lauder Companies, roots include the quality of the company's products, a focus on prestige beauty, and the family values established and upheld by the Lauder family. An example of an anchor would be the belief that service from an in-person beauty adviser is the only way to learn how to put on makeup. As Freda has warned, "A root can become an anchor if you don't treat it in a new and modern way." And so some of the company's brands now offer virtual beauty advisers and social media chatbots.

As a personal "root," do not change what works in your leadership style and habits. Good people managers, for example, are good managers of any generation because they get the fundamentals right: they care about their employees, they give regular feedback, and they help their employees succeed. Sure, today they might sometimes coach an employee over Skype instead of in person, but the attention and commitment they are showing to that employee remain exactly the same.

Rule #7. Be More Transparent.

Were you ever given as an answer to a work-related question "That's above your pay grade" or "You don't need to think about that right now"?

Imagine saying that to an employee today. The likely reply in that person's mind might be "No problem. I'll just google it!" or "No problem. I'll just tweet my question to the chair of the board!" The Internet and social media have leveled the playing field tremendously when it comes to access to information and power. This means that, as a leader in the multigenerational workplace, you have no choice but to be more transparent and democratic with information and access.

It's okay if you find this off-putting or even somewhat terrifying. Many leaders in industries with a lot of regulation or confidential information—law, pharmaceuticals, defense—are the most concerned about transparency, which is understandable. The funny thing is, many leaders in such industries have told me that when they actually ask their employees what information they want to know, it's often not confidential or controversial at all. (Note that the recommended rule is not to be 100 percent transparent but to be *more* transparent.)

Most of all, these leaders report that junior employees in particular usually want more understanding around what happens at higher levels: how decisions are made, how the finances of the organization work, why a certain strategy has been set. One law firm told me they had a big win with Millennials by hosting open roundtable discussions with the firm's chief financial officer. Why? Because they found most junior associates at the firm didn't really understand the economics of the billable hour. Having more transparency into that essential topic helped them understand the fundamental role they had in their firm's financial outcomes and overall success.

Rule #8. It's Okay if Everybody Wins.

I know, I know. This sounds like I am pandering to the "Everyone gets a trophy" Millennial generation. But the thing is, they're right on this one. We should give more trophies for accomplishment.

Fortunately, we have a lot of guidance on this from the world of marketing. Marketers have been studying the Millennial generation ever since they came on the scene, and marketers want to sell to this generation. So marketers say, "Okay, we understand that Millennials like trophies. Great. How big, how shiny, how many trophies do they want? What's the hashtag?" And thus we have witnessed a huge growth in customer loyalty programs, website badges, reward coupons, and free gifts with purchase. It is another element of Customization Nation.

But in the workplace many of us recoil from the idea of trophies. We say things like "No one gave me trophies when I was just starting out! Those Millennials are so entitled!"

The problem is not giving trophies; the problem is giving trophies for participation and not genuine accomplishment. I worry that, in the backlash against trophies for participation, we stopped remembering why acknowledgment and rewards are so valuable and appreciated. Everybody wants to win. Everybody wants to be the hero of their own story. And if you've ever played a team sport, you know that winning with teammates is often the greatest trophy of all. (I have won exactly one sports trophy in my entire life, for coming in first at a girls' singles tennis tournament at Belvoir Terrace summer camp in the Berkshire mountains of Massachusetts when I attended nearby Camp Emerson at age 12. It is lavender and gold and I still have it and you will have to pry that little trophy out of my cold, dead hands because I absolutely earned it.)

I am often asked, "When there's an intergenerational conflict, which generation should win?" I don't think that's the right question, because this is not a zero-sum game where one generation's gain is equivalent to another generation's loss. The right question is "How do we flex and adapt to one another so each person can have the opportunity to be part of the winning team?" And then we find the best solution. We do that through listening to each other, we do that through communicating across employee levels and job functions, and we do that through shared values and a sense of common purpose and pride.

My favorite story of every employee feeling a sense of purpose as part of a winning team comes from 1961, when President John F. Kennedy was visiting NASA headquarters during the space race with the Soviet Union. While touring the facility, he noticed a janitor with a broom and went up to say hello.

"What do you do here at NASA?" Kennedy asked.

The janitor proudly replied, "Mr. President, I'm helping to put a man on the moon."

CHAPTER 2: KEY TAKEAWAYS

- Stop the generational shaming. If you have ever been guilty of making fun of Millennials or any other generation, in a personal or professional context, you must commit to stopping right now. This includes shaming of yourself or your own generation.
- Empathize. Learn about the experiences of other generations in order to understand what values and expectations they bring to the workplace.
- Assume the best intentions. Give members of other generations the benefit of the doubt when they make a decision or take an action you disagree with. This leads to more understanding and effectiveness all around.
- Think "and," not "or," because one size fits none. If you find yourself torn between the "old" way of doing something and the "new" way, resist the pull to make that kind of choice. When you are searching for new ideas and solutions to challenges, you will satisfy more employees when you offer options and choice.
- Remember that "common sense is not so common." Providing clear expectations, rules, and boundaries around people's choices allows members of all generations to feel more comfortable, creative, and empowered. People can't "think outside the box" if they don't have clarity on what the box is.
- Don't change what works. Determine your "roots"—the core identity of your organization and yourself as a leader— and separate them from your "anchors," the practices or habits that are weighing you down and might need to be released.
- Be more transparent. Since the Internet and social media have leveled the playing field when it comes to access

to information, leaders have no choice but to be more transparent and democratic with their knowledge.

- It's okay if everybody wins. One generation's gain is not equivalent to another generation's loss. Everyone wins when we acknowledge each other's contributions, communicate across employee levels and job functions, and share a sense of purpose.

3 THE TALENT REMIX

The Fall of Loyalty and Rise of the 80-Year-Old Lifeguard

IN THE PAST, the most common metaphor for long-term employment was the career ladder, provided by an employer, that an employee would climb up until reaching the top rung and retiring with the proverbial gold watch.

In recent years, careers have been described with very different imagery, ranging from lattices, to jungle gyms, to tours of duty, to chaos theory, to "every man for himself."

As a leader in the workplace today, you must accept that your employees and colleagues may view their career paths very differently from the way you have envisioned yours, especially if you are a Traditionalist, Baby Boomer, or Gen Xer who embraced the career-ladder climb. Some of this is because most younger Americans don't want to spend their lives advancing up the ranks of a single organization. More of this is because employers are no longer offering this possibility.

Back in the 1970s, over 70 percent of workers had health coverage through their employers and about 50 percent had defined benefit plans that guaranteed them a set amount of income for life.

This made it appealing for employees to stay at one organization for as long as possible. What many people don't realize is that this type of employment situation is actually a historical anomaly. As Rick Wartzman, author of *The End of Loyalty: The Rise and Fall of Good Jobs in America*, has discussed, the security and loyalty that corporations provided to employees in the two- to three-decade postwar era are far more the exception than the rule over 150 years of industrialization.

What is problematic for those of us on either side of the employer-employee relationship today is that the "exception" became an expectation for Baby Boomers. And, as we have established, if you held a job anytime in the past half century, you were undoubtedly influenced by Baby Boomer expectations. That includes the belief that a company will provide security for its employees, who should be loyal in return. Many Baby Boomers still have this model in their consciousness as the ideal, and subsequent generations have absorbed it. But in the current economy, it is considerably less common.

Most Millennials have never known a world of strong loyalty between employers and employees. In fact, many Millennials personally witnessed their Boomer parents suffer through the breakdown of the employer-employee loyalty relationship. The experience of watching a parent lose his or her livelihood, home, and retirement savings can make an unforgettable impression on a young person. Now add in shared experiences like the Great Recession beginning in 2008, including the overnight downfall of huge global corporations like Lehman Brothers. Millennials' skepticism about employment and loyalty, and their lack of social trust, as described in chapter 1, become difficult to refute.

The employment market for all generations today is characterized by shorter employee tenures, more temp and consulting positions, and higher rates of freelancing. Companies and entire industries are launching, closing, merging, and separating with head-spinning frequency. An astonishing 94 percent of the job growth since the Great Recession has come from "alternative work arrangements" such as temporary help agency workers, on-call workers, contract company workers, and independent contractors or freelancers. Thirty-six percent of U.S. workers participate in the gig economy through either their primary or secondary jobs.

I am not saying that you as an individual leader, or perhaps your entire organization, are not dedicated and loyal. I am saying that "employers"—as a concept—are rarely perceived as loyal today, especially by Millennials and Gen Zs. These younger generations' experience has been that if an employer's profits go down, if overseas talent becomes cheaper, if automation provides a robot alternative, employers will not hesitate to lay off their employees.

The very definition of "loyalty" has become subject to interpretation. According to one study, only 1 percent of HR professionals believe Millennials to be loyal to an employer, while 82 percent of Millennials self-identified as being loyal to their employers. How can there be such a disconnect? My interpretation is that HR professionals are defining "loyalty" as the notion of staying with an employer. Millennials are defining "loyalty" by how much they believe in their employer's mission and are currently contributing to it.

This is a massive mismatch of expectations, and the stakes couldn't be higher. It's like entering into a relationship where one person is expecting a commitment for life and the other thinks it is casual dating. When the fundamental, big-picture issues are so incompatible, how can you possibly build a sustainable team, not to mention get the budget forecast done by next Tuesday?

The talent remix requires leaders to rethink our expectations of whom we recruit, how we find those people, and what the relationship between employer and employee will be over time.

To begin, let's look at some key facts about the employment picture as it stands today:

YOUNG PEOPLE HAVE ALWAYS HAD SHORTER JOB TENURES. NOW EVERYONE ELSE DOES, TOO. It turns out the stereotype of Millennials as job hoppers has more to do with age and life stage than with the era in which they were born. According to the U.S. Department of Labor, the median length of time young people work for one employer has been pretty consistent over the last thirty-five years: about 3.2 years in the 1980s compared to 2.9 years for 25- to 34-year-olds now. Millennials in their 20s stay in jobs about as long as Boomers and Xers did in their 20s.

The biggest declines in average job tenure over the same thirty-five-year period actually relate to men aged 45 to 54, who stayed with one employer a median of 12.8 years in 1983 but only 8.4 years in 2017. According to economists, this is due to several factors, including the collapse of many semiskilled jobs and the decline of labor unions.

Overall as of 2018, the median number of years that wage and salary workers of all generations have been with their current employer is 4.2 years. That is only one year longer than the median rate for today's Millennials. In other words, Millennials are not the only job hoppers: we all are job hoppers now. Again, some of this is because we want to be; some of this is because we have no choice in today's labor market.

For employers, this raises a lot of questions around recruitment and retention. Should you sell candidates on a shorter-term commitment? Should you ask people how long they want to stay with your organization? Should some positions be short-term and others longer-term? Should we all adopt a Hollywood-like model where a large group of experts comes together to make a single product and then disbands?

There is no consensus yet on the answers to these critical questions, but one of the most innovative suggestions comes, perhaps not surprisingly, from one of the most successful entrepreneurs in

Silicon Valley. Reid Hoffman, a founder of PayPal and LinkedIn, along with coauthors Ben Casnocha and Chris Yeh, proposed a new approach in the book *The Alliance: Managing Talent in the Networked Age*. The concept is "tours of duty," defined as incremental employment alliances mutually agreed upon between employer and employee for set periods of time. When Hoffman founded LinkedIn, he set the initial employee relationship as a four-year tour of duty—almost the exact tenure of the average employee today (also the typical product development cycle in the software business).

As Hoffman, Casnocha, and Yeh describe the benefits of the tour-of-duty model, "The company gets an engaged employee who's striving to produce tangible achievements for the firm and who can be an important advocate and resource at the end of his tour or tours. The employee may not get lifetime *employment*, but he takes a significant step toward lifetime *employability*. A tour of duty also establishes a realistic zone of trust. Lifelong employment and loyalty are simply not part of today's world; pretending that they are decreases trust by forcing both sides to lie."

Will the tour-of-duty model replace the job-for-life model? We shall see, but I applaud Hoffman and his colleagues for experimenting with a remix.

GEOGRAPHY IS NO LONGER DESTINY. Another fact about employment today is that the increase in freelance, temp, remote, and gig work has decoupled the relationship between physical location and employment. One study found that one-third of freelancers said they were able to move as a result of the flexibility freelancing offered. This increases worker satisfaction by enabling people to live where they want—and, more importantly, where they can afford—while also increasing productivity by reducing commuting time and stress.

For employers, this can increase the potential pool of job candidates with the skills an organization needs. It can also reduce costs if your business is located in an expensive region. For a boutique organization like mine, hiring freelancers and consultants based outside my local area has been incredibly valuable. Over the years I have hired top-notch talent from North Carolina, Oregon, and Israel—and have met exactly none of them in person.

For those who want or need employees on site, I am frequently asked whether companies located away from major urban centers should move their location to attract top talent, and younger employees in particular. While it's great to locate your organization in a bustling neighborhood near lots of clean, reliable, and safe public transportation options and cool restaurants, that is not always possible or affordable. And, as I learned from my interviews for this book, it is less important than other factors.

When Millennial Tiffany Kuck graduated from the University of Kentucky, she took a dream job as a youth activities manager for Disney Cruise Line and lived onboard ships for three years. When her grandfather became sick, she wanted to travel less, so she looked for jobs on land and spent two years working for Radio Disney in her hometown of Indianapolis. When that office shut down, Tiffany received job offers in five different cities from five different organizations, including a position at a resort in Hawaii. Which offer did she decide to accept? The one from McGohan Brabender, a health insurance company in Dayton, Ohio, which is definitely not Hawaii.

Why did a talented, ambitious Millennial with multiple job offers choose to work at a 180-person company in a traditional industry in a small Midwestern city?

"The second I stepped into this office for my interview," Tiffany told me, "employees came up to say hello and welcome. The CEO of McGohan Brabender, Scott McGohan, toured me around the building and introduced me around. For my interview, I met with six different leaders who told me about themselves, the company, and what they believe in. I felt welcomed and like I belonged.

"I would have said yes to taking this job no matter the product or industry or location because of the leaders," Tiffany told me.

To attract Millennials—and top talent of any generation—what's happening inside your walls is far more important than where those walls are located. Just look at Silicon Valley, where some of the most innovative companies in the world are located in suburbs miles away from city centers.

That said, some geographic regions are not able to wait for individual employers to attract people—particularly Millennials and Gen Zs—to their regions. Several areas of the U.S. are so desperate for employees, particularly young people, to fulfill their workforce needs that they are offering cash to attract a more age-diverse workforce and tax base. The legislature in Vermont, currently the fastest-aging state in the U.S., passed a bill to pay people $10,000 to move there and work remotely. To market the program, the state hosts employment events for tourists visiting Vermont on vacation. Other areas offering cash and other incentives for young transplants, especially those with family ties to their region, include St. Clair County, Michigan; Grant County, Indiana; and North Platte, Nebraska—where they will pay you $30,000 to move if you are a diesel engineer. If you move to the state of Maine, the money you spend paying off your student loan debt each year is subtracted from your state income taxes. If you're a STEM major and your loan payment amount outweighs your taxes, Maine will even write you a check for the difference.

CAREER MOBILITY MATTERS. While the career ladder may no longer exist, employees of all generations do want to feel that they are on a growth trajectory. This is particularly important to younger employees.

James Frick is a former business school admissions director and currently an MBA prep coach with Management Leadership for Tomorrow. He told me that his biggest advice to organizations that want to attract a wide range of young leaders is to demonstrate that you want to partner with employees to create a "road map" for their careers. Even if you offer a job in one division or functional role, Millennials and Gen Zs want to know that multiple paths are possible—even paths that might lead away from your organization. Older generations appreciate this, too.

Pfizer offers a good example of this strategy. In 2014 the company launched an internal talent marketplace on the company's intranet where any employee of any employment tenure could post or apply for short-term development opportunities within the company, such as joining a small project or shadowing a leader in a different division. "It's rewarding to know that your employer supports your development and is open to you trying something different," said one Millennial employee who used the marketplace to take on a project in a division she hopes to transition into. "Also," she said, "the ability to transition cross-divisionally absolutely diminishes the likelihood that I'll have to look for a job outside of Pfizer when I ultimately decide I'm ready for a new role."

The talent marketplace concept feels to me like building a gig economy inside a large organization, similar to the "intrapreneurship" concept many companies pushed when dot-com start-ups were poaching their talent. Just look at the language the Pfizer employee uses about her career: "I'll have to look for a job," "I ultimately decide," "I'm ready for a new role." She appears in control of her career path. By providing a talent marketplace, Pfizer is acknowledging the power she feels over her career and offering a win-win platform for her to get what she wants while the company achieves its business goals and gets work done.

Challenging Recruiting Traditions

What can you do as an individual leader to adapt to the ongoing disruptions and varying generational perceptions around employment? You must become very clear on your non-negotiables and adopt some flexibility in other areas. In other words, now is the time to get creative about how you recruit and retain talent.

For inspiration, go take a dip in your local pool. You might be surprised at the person sitting in the lifeguard chair.

For decades, the majority of lifeguarding positions in this country, particularly seasonal summer positions, were held by teenagers. Municipalities, schools, beach clubs, community centers, summer camps, and other employers could rely on young people to apply. But, as we learned in chapter 1, significantly fewer teenagers now hold paying jobs, even during summer vacations.

"Back when *Baywatch* was on the air [in the 1990s], we had so many applicants that we had to turn people away," said B. J. Fisher, a spokesperson for the American Lifeguard Association.

This is no longer the case. Over the past few summers, pools have been struggling to hire enough lifeguards, and this forced a reckoning. When leaders in the industry took a look at what was fundamental to lifeguarding, it wasn't being young. It was being a strong swimmer and wanting to help people. And so they got creative.

"We're starting to think outside the box: Baby Boomers, seniors, retired lawyers, and accountants," said Fisher. "Employers are starting to look internally, too: maybe that custodian who swims laps after work can get certified." (The added bonus of older lifeguards? They can drive themselves to work.)

The city of Austin, Texas, found it so challenging to recruit lifeguards that officials began targeting high school students who may not even know how to swim. Over the past two years the city has recruited two hundred teens for a semester of free swim classes and lifeguard training, along with guaranteed jobs following the training. They also get school credit.

It has often occurred to me that many industries could vastly remix the age of people they have historically recruited for certain positions just as the lifeguarding industry has done. This has taken place with traditional notions of gender—consider the increase in male nurses and female fighter pilots—so why not with generation?

One organization provides an unexpected model. Encore.org is a nonprofit organization founded in 1998 by author and social entrepreneur Marc Freedman (still CEO and president), who felt that our growing aging population was being abandoned as a resource. Encore is an innovation hub tapping the talent of the 50-plus population as a force for good. According to Marci Alboher, Encore's vice president for communications, "We are trying to create a world that works for people of all ages and taps the talents of people of all ages."

Five years ago, Encore's management team realized they were not walking their own walk: they looked around at their staff and saw that almost every employee was over the age of 50. They themselves were not tapping the talents of people of all ages.

"Encore made a big transition in the last five years," Marci told me. "A quarter of our staff are now Millennials and Gen Xers, whereas the earlier team was primarily Baby Boomers. We intentionally age diversified because we realized: How could we be talking about the importance of age diversity when our own workplace did not feel very age diverse? And it is changing the way we operate in so many ways."

If an organization dedicated to aging Baby Boomers can further its success by hiring a group of Millennials, then I challenge every hip Millennial start-up to hire a group of workers over 65, too.

Recruiting habits and biases occur on an individual level as well, and offer a personal opportunity for remixing. Baby Boomer Donna Kalajian Lagani, chief revenue officer and publishing director of *Cosmopolitan* magazine, has been in the business of selling advertising for decades. "What never changes about who I look for," she told me, "is someone persistent, persistent, and more persistent. We're in sales, and in our business, persistence always wins out.

Smart, strategic, hardworking, and persistent—those are the things I have always looked for."

For Donna, hiring a salesperson with persistence is a root. It is fundamental and unchangeable whether that salesperson is selling a page of advertising in a magazine or a custom filter campaign on Snapchat.

But over the years Donna has had to let go of some anchors. When I asked her what has changed the most over the course of her career, she told me it is how she reviews résumés of job candidates.

"In the past," she said, "when I would look at a résumé, if somebody had jumped around a lot in their career, I would have worried. I was looking for long-term employees, someone who wanted to build a long career with us. Now it's almost the opposite. It's 'Why was that person at the same job for ten years?'

"It shifted when I realized young employees are not necessarily interested in long-term careers at the same place." Donna discovered that, if she wanted the best talent, she couldn't judge today's job applicants with exactly the same criteria she applied to previous generations.

Two major health care organizations recently changed their dress code policies to adapt to the reality of today's workers. Indiana University Health, a nonprofit health care system that includes sixteen hospitals, and the prestigious Mayo Clinic both announced that they would now allow nurses to have visible tattoos, which had previously been forbidden.

Why change the policy now? It comes down to demographics. An estimated 47 percent of Millennials in the United States have at least one tattoo, compared to 36 percent of Gen Xers and 13 percent of Baby Boomers. And this statistic doesn't only refer to potential job candidates. One nurse at IU Health commented that being able to show her tattoos had a positive impact on her relationship with patients, because so many of them had tattoos, too.

While tattoo statistics aren't available yet for Gen Z, I suspect the trend will continue. When I asked a summer camp director about why his camp had eliminated its policy requiring staff, mostly teenagers, to cover their tattoos, he said, "Because if I didn't change that policy, I wouldn't have any staff to hire."

(What if you consider it a "root" of your organization to dress in more formal business attire and you don't want to relax your policy? You can maintain a traditional dress code and still attract younger workers as long as you explain the reason behind your rules. You'll need to communicate that the policy exists, not because it is the default way people have always dressed in your office, but because, for example, professionalism is a core value of your company and team members reflect that in their dress. When people understand the "why" of a policy, they are more likely to accept it.)

Finally, some of the country's most prestigious employers, including Ernst & Young, Hilton, Nordstrom, Apple, and IBM have let go of a major anchor by eliminating the requirement for employees to have a college degree. Some other organizations that do still require a college degree for most positions, most notably Google, no longer include college grade point average in their criteria for hiring.

Are there any recruiting "musts" that you may need to reconsider?

Meaning over Money?

It's hard to talk about employment without talking about money. Over the years, I have asked people how they ended up in their chosen career field, and often a Baby Boomer would answer, "I took the job that paid the most money and that's how I ended up in this career."

I don't hear that answer as much anymore.

This does not mean money is unimportant to younger generations. We all need money to live, and, as discussed, many Millennials are in debt and the Great Recession wiped out a tremendous amount of wealth across generations.

But when I ask Millennials in particular about how important money is to their career decisions, the answer is often—but certainly not always—that money is important but other factors, like career opportunities, flexibility, and a sense of purpose, are more important.

It is often said in the media that Millennials will be the first American generation to be "less well off" than their parents' generation. When I discuss this with Millennials, they resist this characterization. "We may not make as much money or own a big house with two cars in the garage," they tell me, "but my definition of success is different. Success to me is doing work that I enjoy. I've already traveled more than my parents and I have great friends and time to spend on things I love to do."

It's hard to argue with that sentiment. And prioritizing meaning over money might be more common than we realize. Multiple cross-generational studies today show a marginal relationship between compensation level and job satisfaction. You've probably come across the 2010 Princeton University study that found well-being rises only with an income up to $75,000 ($86,000 in today's dollars). After that, money doesn't really make people any happier.

While I haven't studied the exact dollar amounts myself, I can certainly vouch for the fact that I have worked with professionals making tens of millions of dollars a year and they often complain about the same workplace challenges as those making much less: lack of communication from leadership, bad bosses, difficult colleagues, and unclear career paths. I have yet to see a retention bonus or salary increase keep an employee for all that long. As one very well-compensated banker said to me, "I care about my comp the day I get the number. The other 364 days of the year, everything else matters more."

What does this mean for you as a leader? It is important for the salaries you offer to align with industry norms—again, people do need to pay their bills and no one wants to feel undervalued—but it is not the most important factor to consider when attempting to recruit or retain top talent of any generation in today's market. If you are a leader who does not directly make compensation decisions, this is good news. One study found that 80 percent of American workers across generations would rather have a boss who cared about them finding meaning and success in work than receive a 20 percent pay increase. And employees who find their work highly meaningful are 69 percent less likely to quit within the next six months.

Keep in mind that different generations and different individuals may define "meaning" quite differently, of course, and leaders need to honor that. For example, a meaningful job to a midcareer Gen Xer might be one that allows him independence and more time to spend with his family. A meaningful job to an aging Boomer might be one that respects her desire to continue contributing to the labor force into her 70s. A Gen Z might find it meaningful to feel like she is saving the world.

Back in 1974, Studs Terkel wrote in his oral history *Working* that the "happy few" people who truly enjoyed their jobs had "a meaning to their work over and beyond the reward of the paycheck." I do see more leaders today incorporating discussions of meaning and purpose into their management toolkit; I would love to see more. In an environment obsessed with cost cutting and maximizing shareholder value, why wouldn't we put more effort into a management practice that has zero cost?

Industry Issues

How important is industry to attracting and retaining multigenerational talent? It is no secret that some industries are more popular than others, and that popularity can wax and wane over time. Let's look at the insurance industry, for example. The average age of an insurance agent in the United States is 59, and because of impending Baby Boomer retirements the industry overall is projected to have 400,000 to 500,000 open positions by 2020. But, according to the industry's own research, less than 5 percent of Millennials report being interested in working in the field.

As you can imagine, these numbers raised alarm bells across the insurance community, prompting several leaders in the field to come together to figure out how to better recruit a new generation to their workforce. Competitors including AIG, Lloyd's, Marsh & McLennan, and 850 other insurance industry organizations joined forces to create an industry-wide grassroots effort, the Insurance Careers Movement (insurancecareerstrifecta.org), to "inspire young people to choose insurance as a career." The program includes the offering of virtual career fairs, Twitter chats to discuss insurance career opportunities, discussions of the industry's diversity and inclusion efforts, and promotion of insurance as a great second-career option.

The effort by insurance companies provides a good model for other organizations or industries struggling to attract the next generation of workers. It also points to the shifting power dynamics between employers and Millennial talent, which can vary greatly by industry. I have observed countless examples of companies that refused to change in any way to appeal to Millennial workers—resisting having a social media presence, ignoring employee review sites like Glassdoor, and some even saying they simply won't hire Millennials if it means changing their ways(!).

But demographics are demographics, and this strategy simply is not viable. I empathize with the discomfort of feeling like you are bending over backward to win the interest of potential employees. But it is far less uncomfortable than the pain of having no future employees at all.

Several companies in the manufacturing industry—another realm of aging talent—came to a similar realization as those in the insurance industry. Although, as we have discussed, many older generations find it distasteful when parents "helicopter" over their Millennial children, manufacturing companies are so eager for young talent that they are willing to take advantage of the closeness between Millennials and their parents to attract young people.

According to the National Association of Manufacturers, there is an industry-wide push to market more to parents of potential employees after surveys showed that parents often held outdated views of their industry and its career prospects. Today's manufacturing jobs are often more technically complex and lucrative than some parents know.

Toyota Motor Corp.'s manufacturing plant in Indiana, for example, holds "Parents' Night Out" events to encourage parents to learn more about the benefits of a manufacturing career for their children. In Greenville, South Carolina, the local chamber of commerce held a manufacturing-themed parents' night where moms and dads were invited to network with local employers about job opportunities for their kids. In addition to hosting in-person events for parents of job candidates, individual leaders and entire companies across industries can and do reach out to parents in other ways. Some employers advertise in college campus newspapers during parents' visiting weekends to reinforce their brands. Others maintain Facebook groups or parent pages on their websites that describe the companies or departments and answers parents' frequently asked questions.

If you are a parent, please do not take this trend as an invitation to proactively contact your child's potential or current employer. It is uncomfortable for the employer and often works against the child rather than helping. Parents should only interact with a child's employer when explicitly invited. Believe it or not, I have personally witnessed a mother walking the floor of a job fair, handing out résumés on behalf of her young adult child, and multiple HR professionals have complained to me about receiving calls from parents about their children's performance at work. Those are definite don'ts.

IN THE MIX: TAKE YOUR PARENTS TO WORK

Have your parents ever visited you at work? If you work for LinkedIn, they probably have. Every November, the company hosts a "Bring In Your Parents Day," a concept embraced by many other companies with younger workforces as well. Like the long-running Take Our Daughters and Sons to Work Day, the parental version acknowledges that many professionals, especially Millennials and Gen Zs, want to share their professional lives with those who are important to them, and that includes their parents. Currently about 1 percent of companies invite employees' parents in to see their kids on the job.

It is not uncommon for audiences to laugh when I talk about this concept in my speeches. Inviting your parents to the office would have been absolutely unthinkable a few decades ago. But when you stop to think about it strategically, the concept is brilliant.

First of all, we have already established that today's young people are closer than ever with their parents. Many still live at home into their early 30s. So, if one of your goals is to retain Millennial and Gen Z employees, parents can be your allies on the home front. If they know and like your organization, they can be advocates on your behalf to their children and help them retain a positive perspective through the daily ups and downs of work.

Second, if your company markets to Baby Boomers and Gen Xers, your young employees' parents are potential customers, clients, referrers, or net promoters of your organization. LinkedIn is well aware that many of their employees' parents are LinkedIn users and potential advertisers or recruiters, too. The company reports that 3,700 parents have signed up for LinkedIn profiles after visiting their kids working at the company.

And finally, as the workforce becomes older and organizations look to source more Baby Boomer and Gen X talent, parents can be another opportunity for recruiting, as they themselves might be future prospects or referrers of talent.

Attracting Age-Diverse Talent: Remix Your Talent Toolkit

When you begin to remix the talent you aim to recruit, you necessarily need to remix the tools, methods, attitudes, and people you use to accomplish your recruiting goals. In other words, if you want to recruit different people, you will have to recruit differently.

Some new Gen Z–led organizations are modeling this behavior in their talent recruitment efforts. Ziad Ahmed, cofounder and CEO of the Gen Z firm JÜV Consulting and a current student at my alma mater, Yale University, says that diversity and inclusion are core to his company's mission to represent the voices of his generation. "We are constantly trying to think about which voices we are not bringing to the table. That is a fundamental part of building our business, because we are a better company when we represent and empower all of us, not just those of us who know to google that a Generation Z consulting firm even could or does exist."

Below are some specific examples from various industries to support you in recruiting a more diverse, age-inclusive workforce. Please know that I am absolutely aware of how overwhelming it is to find any talent at all now that people can apply for hundreds of jobs with one click of a button, and employers can be inundated. And I am equally aware of how overwhelming it is to find a job now that most employers use technologies like applicant tracking systems to sift through people without a human eye ever seeing your résumé. The human element of recruiting cannot be lost. I have split the below suggestions into two categories—technology-enabled and human—because every recruiting strategy needs a mix of both.

Technology-Enabled Recruiting Remixes

- Citi is one organization using data to rethink the talent they recruit for certain positions. Bill Fisse, managing director of human resources and global head of talent and diversity for Citi's Institutional Businesses, told me that the firm began to look more closely at the data they had about people they recruited from campus who stayed at the company and succeeded. Among the discoveries was a higher success rate among engineering majors, whereas in the past they had primarily recruited business and economics majors. This opened up an entirely new opportunity to recruit talent from campus. Many other companies are using data to assess and expand their recruiting efforts, and the trend is sure to grow.
- Construction materials maker USG Corporation now accepts applications by mobile phone to increase its appeal to younger workers and those without access to computers. In the first quarter of this recruiting change, applications jumped 26 percent. The company also added videos to job postings to

demystify various manufacturing positions, which increased by 50 percent the number of people who submitted an application after looking at a job listing.

- Employers continually look for new outlets to post open positions to a broader range of online job boards, ranging from a wider variety of campus career centers, to diversity job boards (e.g., Diversity.com, Out & Equal's LGBT CareerLink, SHRM-Veterans.jobs, SHRM-Disability.jobs) to senior job boards (e.g., AARP Job Board, SeniorJobBank.org, Workforce50.org), and more. Note that this does not mean ignoring "old media" outlets. Some of the municipalities looking to attract non-teenage lifeguards went back to placing ads in newspapers, employee retirement guides, and paper utility bills.

- In 2018, Synchrony relaunched its early-career recruiting website and marketing materials for the company's Business Leadership Program (BLP), a two-year rotational experience for high-potential recent college graduates. "We want students to get a feel for who they would be surrounded by working here and to see that this is a place that is inspired by having as many different points of view as possible," says Stephen Kennedy, vice president of leadership programs and employee experience. The updated website features videos and profiles of twenty-two Synchrony employees of different ethnicities, college majors, and work experiences, and the videos include zero stock photography.

  A few weeks into the new campaign, one of the BLPs featured on the website received a LinkedIn message from a student who saw her video, saying that it inspired her to apply for the program. The applicant did not attend one of the schools at which Synchrony usually recruits, but she was an excellent candidate. According to Stephen, this was the exact goal of featuring real employees. "Great talent should come from anywhere, not just target schools. We have to make it easy for students of any background to access the great opportunities we have." This is particularly important for organizations that want to recruit more diverse talent. Research has shown that Black and Hispanic job applicants are more likely to apply for a job when they see Black or Hispanic people in company recruitment materials.

- Location Labs, a technology company, actively responds to negative comments posted anonymously on Glassdoor as part of its recruiting strategy. The company says that job candidates have chosen to interview with the organization because they saw these transparent responses from leadership.

- Similarly, Intel implemented a "no comment left behind" policy several years ago on social media to ensure that every comment, post, complaint, and question about employment receives a personal response from a recruiter or other company representative. Many people tell me they look more closely at negative employer reviews than positive ones to see how the employer handles them. A few negative or unanswered comments could turn away potential talent of all generations.

Human-Enabled Recruiting Remixes

- Amy, the Millennial media company leader you met earlier, uses her own fast-moving career to challenge her team's notions of what level of experience is required when they are hiring for a particular role. "Because I have been successful early in my career," she told me, "I don't think experience alone should be the qualification for doing a job." For example, her team was recently seeking to hire someone for a position they deemed required seven-plus years of experience. However, they decided to interview and hire someone with two years of experience because that candidate demonstrated a lot of success and could get the job done.

- A consumer packaged-goods company reports that their recruiting "secret sauce" involves bringing its CEO and other VIPs to campus recruiting events and job fairs. "We used to bring branded water bottles, thumb drives, or other swag to make ourselves memorable to job candidates," the company's head of recruiting told me. "But we realized that *experience* is the new swag." I love this approach. Any company can put out a bowl of Hershey's Miniatures. What really stands out to job candidates of all generations is having a personal recruiting experience that makes them feel special. What could make job candidates feel more important than meeting the head of the company to which they are applying?

- Texas Capital Bank puts its Millennial employees in charge of recruiting students from their alma maters. "Most companies put the most senior person as head of a college recruiting team, but we put the most junior person," Tricia Linderman, the bank's former executive vice president of recruiting and onboarding, shared with me. Called "campus captains," Tricia explains, "they are the ones who decide what events to go back on campus for, they talk with the professors, they figure out the organizations we want to be part of. They do it all. It's great because they are more plugged in on campus and they have more time than senior executives." Each campus captain's job is to get as many résumés into the bank's system as possible. Some even participate in the interviewing process.

- On the other end of the career spectrum, Texas Capital Bank is one of many organizations embracing the concept of "employee boomeranging"—actively recruiting employees who had previously left the organization for another job,

entrepreneurship, personal needs, or any other reason. At
the bank, a senior vice president of treasury sales left to run
his own business and then returned, as did an employee who
left twice for personal reasons and came back to run all the
company's banking centers.

We began this chapter with a discussion of loyalty, and that is
where we return. Just because an employee has parted ways with
your organization in the past does not mean that person can't be an
asset in the future. For many organizations, this practice represents
a big shift in mindset. "I'm pretty sure when people left our organization in the past," one lateral recruiter in the financial services
industry told me, "we said, 'Don't let the door hit you on the way
out!' And then they were dead to us."

That attitude is no longer viable. As employees today, especially
Millennials, change jobs more frequently, and careers can last forty,
fifty, or sixty years, why discount talent that both knows your business from the inside and can offer an outside perspective? To find
"boomerang" employees and "unretirees," many organizations are
actively creating employee alumni networks on their own websites
or on LinkedIn to keep former employees of all ages connected and
aware of potential opportunities to come back. Perhaps, then, it
is not a ladder but a revolving door that will represent the future
career path model.

CHAPTER 3: KEY TAKEAWAYS

- The talent remix requires leaders to rethink our expectations of whom we recruit, how we find those people, and what the relationship between employer and employee will be over time.
- "Employers"—as a concept—are no longer perceived as loyal, and the very definition of "loyalty" has become subject to interpretation. Remember that your definition may not necessarily align with those of your employees or colleagues.
- Geography is not destiny. To attract talent of any generation, what's happening inside your walls is more important than where those walls are located.
- Challenge your recruiting "musts" by rethinking the characteristics and qualifications of talent you have historically recruited for certain positions.
- It is important for the salaries you offer to align with industry norms, but most employees would rather have a boss who cares about them finding meaning and success in work than receive a pay increase.
- Parents can be your allies in recruiting, engaging, and retaining Millennial and Gen Z talent. Consider hosting informational events for parents or inviting employees to bring their parents to see them on the job.
- Keep in mind that job candidates consider the vetting process to go two ways today, thanks to social media and employee review websites like Glassdoor. Deem it a recruiting strategy to respond to online comments, posts, complaints, and questions.
- Consider former employees and retirees as potential future talent for your organization and create alumni communities to keep in touch with them. Why discount talent that both knows your business from the inside and can offer an outside perspective?

4 THE LEADERSHIP REMIX

From Command-and-Control to Coaching

A FEW YEARS ago, there was a college football head coach who led his team all the way to the NCAA Championship game.

As is the case with many sports teams today, the players on this team were all at the younger end of the Millennial demographic, and the coach and his staff, who were primarily Boomers and Gen Xers, quickly determined that these players were raised in a different style than the previous generations they had played with and coached. In particular, the Millennials didn't respond to yelling or punishment. Getting yelled at didn't motivate them; in fact it did the exact opposite. Their play declined.

The coach realized that he had to change his leadership style in order to elicit the results he wanted from the talent he had. When asked by a reporter about his approach to leading Millennials, he explained that the fundamental requirements for his players did not change: the hard work, the stamina, the physical drills, the weight lifting, the healthy eating, the importance of being on time and of being an ethical player. Those things, he said, would never change.

But here are the things that did change. He assigned every player a mentor so they could discuss their challenges with someone they trusted. He shortened player meetings so that the players would pay better attention. The coach implemented a no-yelling rule with his staff.

Note that this wasn't because he and his fellow coaches didn't prefer longer meetings or didn't *want* to yell: "I used to like kids who you could get after and really coach hard," the team's former defensive coordinator admitted. "But society has changed."

The reason the coaches stopped yelling is that yelling stopped working.

Not surprisingly, some in the football community reacted very strongly to this team's changes and said things to the coach such as, "Are you kidding? You're coddling them. You're going to make them soft. This is football!"

But the coach had one simple response to any criticism, to explain why he and his coaching staff were willing to change their style.

"It works," he said. "We're winning."

This coach is not the first to take a positive approach to leadership in sports: the late Bill Walsh is said to have stopped drills as head football coach at Stanford University to remind his staff to "stop screaming, and start teaching." Nor is kindness the only success strategy: there are more than a few sports coaches you could name who yell and scream and rant and still win.

What this coach's story demonstrates is that generational change requires leaders to examine our existing practices and consider what actually works to achieve the results we want with the people we are leading today.

Why? Because it's what it takes to win.

The Power of Leadership Expectations

No matter your generation or current level of professional leadership, you undoubtedly have decades of experience as a follower: as a child with parents and caretakers, a student with teachers, a congregant with religious leaders, a citizen with government officials, an athlete with coaches, a musician with conductors, or in whatever realms you have participated. In every one of these relationships, you have been gathering data—consciously or unconsciously—about what it means to lead.

In writing my second book, *Becoming the Boss: New Rules for the Next Generation of Leaders,* one of my most striking takeaways was how many successful leaders across all levels and industries told me that they learned how to lead well by modeling themselves after existing leaders they had personally experienced. Even the "bad" leaders proved valuable, because they demonstrated what *not* to do.

But here's the thing: the leadership styles we have experienced can differ greatly based on the era in which we experienced them and other factors of our identity. To understand these differences, we can't start in the workplace itself; we need to look a bit earlier in our lives. Whenever any of us enters any new situation, environment, or relationship, we bring a set of expectations with us—some conscious and some unconscious—that are influenced by our previous experiences.

When we do enter the workplace and meet our bosses—and our bosses' bosses and their bosses' bosses—it's natural to expect that their leadership will be somewhat similar to our earlier experiences with authority figures. This means that members of different generations—and all different backgrounds, for that matter—can enter professional situations with radically different expectations. When you as a leader understand how your beliefs align with or differ from the people you lead, you can better anticipate what challenges might occur and how you can overcome them.

Here are the key factors that influence our beliefs and our employees' beliefs about leadership and authority before we even set foot into a professional workplace.

OUR FIRST LEADERS

Let's return to the issue of parenting. When I've asked Traditionalists and Baby Boomers to describe the way in which they were parented, memories range from "Do as you are told" to "Because I said so!" This makes sense when you consider that Baby Boomers were parented by Traditionalists, the generation in which half of the men served in the military. And in the military the recommended style of leadership was "command and control," which is defined by NATO as "the exercise of authority and direction by a properly designated individual over assigned resources in the accomplishment of a common goal."

This doesn't mean that every single parent for the first half of the twentieth century was dictatorial all the time or didn't love their children; it means that the parenting norms of the era were quite authoritarian. Parents usually determined food choices, bedtimes, curfews, and most everything else without consulting their children. As one Boomer client described his Traditionalist-parented childhood to me, "The parents were the bosses, and the kids were the employees."

Then, when it came time for the Boomers to parent their own children, the Millennials, many took a radically different approach to child-rearing. Yes, we must return to the Millennial stereotype of being helicopter parented. The term, as we have discussed, refers to the concept of hovering over one's children and swooping in when problems occur to shield them from harm. (I've also heard the even more aggressive parents described as "snowplow parents," who don't wait for the problems to occur to take action; instead, they proactively plow the problems out of the way.)

A lot of people laugh or scoff at helicopter parenting examples, which is understandable if you come from a different era, a lower socioeconomic status, another country of origin, or a family that did not espouse any of these parenting practices. But some of these parenting changes were reflected elsewhere in American culture as well, notably in the U.S. public education system. The average public school classroom in the 1950s (when Baby Boomers were kids) had forty students. By the 1980s (when Millennials were kids), the average classroom had just half that number.

For Millennials who went on to college, the attention and support of adults only increased. Perhaps because the cost of higher education has grown exponentially, many college professors have become more like cheerleaders than authoritarians.

One study found that an A is the most common grade on college campuses today, accounting for more than 42 percent of all grades. To put that into context, the practice of awarding As has leapt 5 to 6 percentage points per decade, making the top mark three times more common than in 1960. With positive feedback in the form of grades the norm across the colleges that feed the entry-level ranks of many companies, it's easy to see why many Millennials might crave positive attention and feedback at work more than other generations.

AN ARMY OF FEWER

Another realm in which many young Americans first experience leadership and authority is through military service, hence the comfort level of Traditionalists with a command-and-control style of leadership. Remember that among the Traditionalist generation (also, tellingly, known as the "G.I. Generation"), 47 percent of men served in the U.S. armed forces. That means that virtually every family of that era had a father, husband, brother, son, or neighbor serving. Almost everyone was familiar with military terminology, military structure, military language, and the life-and-death stakes of loyalty.

That shared experience transferred into the workplace of mid-century America: seriousness, strict reporting structures, dress codes, discipline, precision, and dependability. And, of course, a top-down pyramid management structure with a single general firmly leading from the top.

When the U.S. moved to an all-volunteer force in 1973, right around the time many Baby Boomers started becoming parents, the average American's connection to the military weakened dramatically. Although women are now able to enlist, only about 8 percent of Generation Xers have served and only 3 percent of Millennials. (For Baby Boomers, the percentage of veterans is 21.)

As recently as 1995, 40 percent of young adults had a direct connection to a service member or had a veteran as a family member. Today that number is around 15 percent. In terms of active military personnel, less than one-half of 1 percent of the U.S. population serves in the military today. This means that more Americans currently work for Walmart than serve in a branch of our armed forces.

This is just another reason that so many of the formal, hierarchical structures and practices of corporate America can feel unfamiliar to today's youngest workers.

SUMMER JOBS REPLACED

Another potential influence on what we expect from leaders is our prior experience with workplace bosses.

My first-ever paid workplace experience was clerking at a video store during my junior year of high school (yes, *VHS*). True to all stereotypes about the 1990s and people who worked in video stores, my boss at the store was a long-haired, pot-smoking guy whose password to unlock the cash register was "SSDD": Same Shit, Different Day.

While I would not call my video store job particularly formative, it did involve some level of professional learning and experience. I had to show up on time. I had to perform tasks I didn't really want to do (e.g., putting away the porn videos in the "Over 18" section). I had to take direction from a boss (e.g., "Try not to blush so much when people rent the porn videos").

Today, as I have noted, it is increasingly common for teenagers not to work, even in the summer. From the 1970s to the 1990s, more than 50 percent of teenagers ages 16 to 19 had summer jobs, but teen summer employment dropped precipitously after the 2001 recession and even more sharply during and after the Great Recession. Since then, the teen summer employment rate has gone up to about 35 percent, which is still well below pre-recession levels. And nonwhite teens are even less likely to be employed.

This is not because today's teenagers don't want to work. We know this because nearly 1.1 million teens were counted as unemployed in the summer of 2016, which means they were looking for work but couldn't find it. Another 432,000 wanted to work full-time but were working part-time because they could not find full-time positions.

Experts attribute teens' lower labor participation rates to many factors, including working gig jobs paid in cash and not tracked by federal data and an increase in older workers staying in the labor force longer because of a loss of wealth during the Great Recession.

Another reason some teenagers aren't working is that they are studying more. Compared to previous generations, education now takes up more of teenagers' time, with heavier academic loads, high school students taking classes for college credit, and more availability of summer enrichment programs. Martha Ross of the Brookings Institution has noted that teen enrollment in high school or college classes during the summer was 42 percent in 2016, compared with just 10 percent in 1985.

So a number of today's young Americans are more highly educated but have less work experience. This corresponds with my research and observations. In over a decade studying Millennials in the workplace across a wide variety of industries, I have frequently heard members of this generation criticized for many perceived characteristics—entitlement, narcissism, laziness, self-absorption—but it is rare that any employer ever calls them unintelligent.

What employers often perceive to be lacking in today's youngest workers includes such essential workplace "soft" skills as communication, time management, decision-making, and self-motivation—skills that members of previous generations often learned while working as teenagers.

If you are managing a Millennial or Gen Z employee today, you must consider the fact that you might be the first boss that young person has ever had.

ALL-ACCESS, ALL THE TIME

"The Internet" is cited so often as the answer to virtually every change in modern society. But it's true: the Internet has allowed unfettered access to extraordinary amounts of information and power. The teacher is no longer the only one with the answer key. The CEO is no longer the only one who knows how the company is perceived by shareholders.

Whereas leaders used to dole out information on a "need-to-know" basis, today everyone not only believes they *do* have a need to know but they know how to find the information out for themselves and potentially share it with others. And they do this by pressing a few buttons on a device conveniently located in their classroom, in their bedroom, in their office, or in their pocket or bag. It's harder to maintain a sense of authority when everyone has access to so much of the same information and devices. Or—let's be honest—when the oldest, most experienced person in the room sometimes has to ask the youngest for help in using those devices.

The Internet hasn't just fostered the ubiquitous availability of information; it has also spawned social media, which has created an insatiable expectation of constant, instant feedback and positive reinforcement in the form of likes and badges and points and coupons. (The bar on this is high: a Gen Z college student recently told me that if she doesn't get one like per minute on a particular post, she deletes it.)

While all this has become (relatively) normal to members of all generations, remember that most Millennials and Gen Zs have never known a world *without* this kind of nonstop instant recognition and availability of information. And that is contributing every day to their expectations for more ongoing, consistent communication and feedback. The ubiquity of information has also removed an enormous amount of power—the access to and control of information—from today's leaders.

Think about how access to the top leaders in government, business, and all other realms has changed in just the past few decades: before C-SPAN launched in 1979, the only way to watch our elected representatives at work was to go to Washington, DC, in person; now we can watch their every move from anywhere.

Prior to the launch of CNBC in 1989, very few people were conversant with the names of corporate CEOs; now we expect to see their faces and hear their strategies on a regular basis.

As of 2001, when the very first camera phone became available in the U.S., any comment or action that was previously private now has the potential to be recorded and shared with the entire world.

And, starting in 2004, Facebook and subsequent social networks made leaders even more approachable and accessible through their own profiles, Facebook Live town halls, Twitter chats, and more.

Leaders in the multigenerational mix must acknowledge the changed dynamics between employees and management that the Internet has brought, and continues to bring in new ways every day.

IN THE MIX: THE BOSSES OF DISNEY MOVIES

Movies—even beloved Disney children's movies—impact our expectations around leadership as well.

While mothers like me are generally horrified by how frequently we are killed off in Disney films, it seems bosses don't fare much better. According to a recent study out of the UK, the most common theme, which appears in thirty-five(!) Disney movies, is "manipulation and deception by managers."

Think of the puppeteer Stromboli telling Pinocchio, "You will make lots of money for me, and when you are too old you will make good firewood." Or, more recently, the arrogant emperor Kuzco in *The Emperor's New Groove*, who tells an aging female adviser, "You are being let go; your department is being downsized; you're part of an outplacement; we are going in a different direction; we're not picking up your option; take your pick."

As Professor Martyn Griffin has said of the examples in his research, these are films "about age discrimination in the workplace for 6-year-olds."

Things are looking up, however, with some new, notably female entrants in the Disney leadership canon. In *The Princess and the Frog*, Tiana ultimately opens her own restaurant and appears headed for a better management style than the boss from her waitressing days. And, of course, Queen Elsa and Princess

Anna from *Frozen* end the film in the role of benevolent leaders to the citizens of Arendelle.

Said Griffin's coauthor Mark Learmonth, Elsa and Anna "are aware of their weaknesses and vulnerabilities. I would quite like to work for them."

The Leadership and Management Remix: Coaching

Now that we've taken a tour through the many factors that impact the way employees of various generations think about leadership, the question becomes: Is it possible to synthesize all of this into one overarching approach that both appeals to and is effective with the five generations working today?

There is, and it is the reason I started this chapter with a story about a coach. My more than fifteen years of research, writing, and consulting with organizations about generational differences has led me to the conclusion that the style of leadership most effective in getting the best results from all generations is to consider yourself a coach.

I define a coaching style of leadership as guiding and supporting—as opposed to commanding or controlling—each person to his, her, or their greatest potential to result in a winning outcome. Coaches can be effective with employees raised in a hierarchical work structure and with those who expect more democratic organizations. And, above all, coaches maintain the belief that progress and improvement are always possible. Coaches are positive agents of change.

Leaders today must believe that all their employees, of every generation, are capable of adapting to and succeeding in our changing times. They must have what psychologist Carol Dweck defines as a growth mindset: the understanding that abilities and intelligence can be developed, that almost anyone can learn to do almost anything if they put in the effort.

This is in contrast to a fixed mindset, which assumes that people are either good at something or they're not—that potential is predetermined and people should stick to what they know.

A growth mindset is valuable in managing employees and also in thinking about one's self-leadership: when you have a growth mindset, you acknowledge that you as the leader don't have to have all the answers; you are always capable of growing, learning, and improving.

A simple habit to cultivate more of a growth mindset is to remember to use the word "yet" when describing a skills deficit in yourself or others. For example, a fixed mindset would be to say, "I am not good at managing Millennials." A growth mindset is to say, "I am not good at managing Millennials *yet*." It is a simple but powerful concept that I have been pleased to see spreading through the American education system, including at my daughter's New York City elementary school.

As a leader, you can practice a growth mindset through your willingness to try different management techniques yourself and your encouragement of employees to experiment as well. Leadership expert Daniel Goleman recommends the coaching style for when the leader wants to help teammates build lasting personal strengths that make them more successful overall. According to Goleman, if this style were summed up in one phrase, it would be "Try this." (You'll notice I have borrowed this phrase as I coach you through applying the concepts in this book.)

After reviewing the leadership expectations people bring to the workplace, it's time to file this away as research—like a coach watching film from previous games—and get out onto the field for action. The combination of knowledge about the past and a growth mindset adds up to an ideal starting point for change.

CHAPTER 4: KEY TAKEAWAYS

- We develop our attitudes about leadership, and how we want to be led, in many other realms before we set foot into a professional environment. When you as a leader understand how your expectations and experiences align with or differ from the people you lead, you can better anticipate what challenges might occur and how you can overcome them.

- As children, many Millennials received more attention from parents and teachers than previous generations. This impacts their expectations related to feedback, mentoring, support from leaders, and other workplace experiences.

- Significantly fewer young people today have experience or familiarity with the military, which helps to explain why formal, hierarchical workplace structures and practices might feel uncomfortable and unnecessary to them.

- Millennials and Gen Zs are, on average, more highly educated than previous generations but have less work experience. You might be the first boss a 20-something employee has ever had.

- While the Internet and social media have impacted all generations, Millennials and Gen Zs have never known a world without the nonstop, instant recognition and availability of information we now have access to. That is contributing to employees' expectations for more ongoing, consistent communication and knowledge.

- The style of leadership most effective in getting the best results from all generations is to be a coach. Coaches guide and support—as opposed to command or control—each person to his, her, or their greatest potential to result in a shared winning outcome. Coaches are agents of change who possess a growth mindset.

5 THE PEOPLE MANAGEMENT REMIX

"Thank You," "Because," and "Why"

MICHAEL ABRAMS IS a Millennial-aged former marine who served on active duty for eight years and is currently in the Marine Corps Reserves. He is executive director of Columbia University's Center for Veteran Transition and Integration and advises companies on their hiring and management of veterans. Recently, Michael was asked to consult with a large company because several veterans had left the organization after only a few months on the job, and the company was concerned it wasn't serving the needs of the veteran population.

"What really confused them," Michael said, "is that they had veterans on one team with high turnover, but others in the exact same role who were staying. What we found when we looked deeper is that non-veterans were leaving the same teams as veterans. The problem was the managers. The teams with high veteran turnover had nothing to do with the fact that the team members were veterans and everything to do with the generally poor people management skills of the leaders of those teams."

If you find yourself asking why your managers are struggling to manage Millennials or Gen Zs—or any specific generation or group, for that matter—it is worth asking if those managers are struggling to manage people in general. Other generations of employees might also be unhappy, but Millennials and Gen Zs just might be the only ones speaking up. (Thank you, "entitlement"!)

This is one of the most constructive changes younger generations have brought to the workplace: because they have the tools and confidence to expose bad bosses, they are doing so. When it comes to serious offenses like sexual harassment and abuse in the workplace, intergenerational movements like #MeToo are empowering employees to speak up even more.

As a Gen Xer, I had plenty of bad leaders and plenty of complaints; what I didn't have were RateMyProfessors.com, Glassdoor, Twitter, Facebook, Wall Street Oasis, Above the Law, and other outlets to vent my concerns. Add in the increase in 360-degree feedback and upward reviews at many companies today, and employees of all generations have even more of a voice in exposing poor managers.

The people management remix requires an acknowledgment that many people managers never learned the "classics" to begin with. In this chapter we will talk about some new tools available to managers, but much of what we'll discuss is about going back to basics.

Managers Matter More Than Ever

In 2008, Google's People Operations team (their term for human resources) launched Project Oxygen, in which the company studied 10,000 people to determine whether managers made a difference in team performance. Google defined manager quality based on two key measures: manager performance ratings and feedback on managers from Google's annual survey of employees.

The data definitively revealed that managers did matter: the highest-scoring managers saw less turnover on their teams, and retention correlated more strongly to manager quality than to seniority, performance, tenure, or promotions. The study also showed a connection between manager quality and worker happiness: employees with high-scoring bosses consistently reported greater satisfaction in areas such as innovation, work/life integration, and career development.

What exactly defined a high-scoring boss at Google? The number one quality their research determined in 2008 and again when they revisited the research in 2018 is that the manager is "a good coach." Google defined being a good coach as taking such actions as providing timely and specific feedback, holding regular one-on-one meetings, listening, meeting individual communication needs, and being aware of your own mindset and that of your employee.

All these actions and habits have existed for generations, and even some command-and-control leaders employed them. While Google used current data to prove that they make a manager effective, the findings are not innovative or high-tech at all. If the same, "classic" strategies have been available forever, why haven't all generations of managers been great?

Because they didn't have to be.

In the past—certainly in the 1990s, when I started working, and when there was more of a stigma for changing jobs—employees would continue working for poor managers even if it made us unhappy and less productive. Most of the time, we just accepted the managers we got.

Now, when employees—especially Millennials—are more comfortable jumping ship when they are unhappy, we can't help but notice the captains of the ships they are jumping from.

Several people with the role of staffer in their organizations—a common position in law firms, investment banks, and consulting firms—have told me there are certain leaders no junior person will agree to work for. These leaders rose up the ranks because of their superior work outcomes or skill with clients, so everyone looked the other way at their mistreatment of employees. That will no longer fly, and we have Millennials to thank.

Many of these leaders, in order to maintain their positions, are being required to take management training programs or executive coaching that, frankly, they should have had long ago.

As the workplace becomes more heavily dominated by the Millennial generation, there will be even more attention on managers. If manager training and effectiveness are weaknesses in your organization, now is the time to address them.

Where to Start: Lead Yourself First

As flight attendants say, put on your own oxygen mask before assisting others.

It's hard to pay attention to other people's needs when you yourself are stressed, feeling unappreciated, worried about losing your job to a robot, or carrying expectations, beliefs, and biases—conscious or unconscious—that might be interfering with your role as a manager in the multigenerational mix.

For starters, take a look at whether your own age bias may be getting in the way of effectively managing yourself and your team. Activist and author Ashton Applewhite advises,

> As a leader, you have to look at your own attitudes
> about age and aging, because everyone is biased. What
> language do you use about yourself and others? Do you

use "still" when it comes to ordinary activities, like "still
driving" or "still working," for example, or say things
like, "I don't feel old," when what you actually mean
is that you don't feel invisible or incompetent? Do you
make self-deprecating jokes, or blame things on age when
age actually has nothing to do with it? If so, try to break
the habit.

There is no need for blaming or guilt; just start to notice your habits. The goal of reflecting on your own beliefs and biases is to build
awareness and acknowledge what expectations you have that may be
different from those of your employees.

One media executive handled this in a simple and effective way.
When he examined his beliefs and biases, he found that his biggest
discomfort was around the fact that many of his Millennial employees worked from home. He knew it is common practice today,
and his company's policy is to allow remote work. However, since
he never, ever worked from home in the early years of his career, he
couldn't kick the feeling that his employees weren't working when
they weren't in the office.

What he did was share this with his team. "You are not doing
anything wrong by working from home," he told them. "But I want
to be transparent that, since I never did that when I was in your job,
I sometimes worry that you are not really working if I can't see you.
I want you to work flexibly and feel trusted, so I am doing my best
to overcome my bias. Please be patient with me."

He wanted to see his employees working; they wanted the flexibility to work from home. Everyone wanted to be part of a happy,
productive team. Applying Remixer Rule #8: It's okay if everybody
wins, this executive decided to request that employees check in with
him at least three times a day on their remote work days: first thing
in the morning when they logged on, for a video call around midday

so he could see them face-to-face, and then at the end of the day when they logged off.

Because his expectations and explanation were clear and reasonable, his employees said, "No problem." They worked from home like they wanted and he had his knowledge that they were working. Over time, the executive became more comfortable with the arrangement and no longer requested the check-ins. Everybody won.

A similar self-awareness and clarity of expectations can be applied to a manager's expectations around work product. One law firm partner told me that he was unhappy with the writing quality of the firm's Millennial-aged junior associates. He blamed it on the casualness of texting culture, but he learned pretty quickly that blame and judgment were not going to solve the problem.

So he and his colleagues took the time to create a binder of what they considered to be well-crafted writing samples—client e-mail messages, briefs, memos, and more—that associates could refer to for guidance. "*This* is what I think good writing looks like," he told them. And so they learned how to meet his expectations.

Where can you take the time to create a document or folder of strong work examples that everyone can access—you only have to do this once—or make it a practice to copy your team on correspondence that meets your standards? For me, this meant drafting a few template client e-mails that my assistant can use for reference when handling specific types of correspondence, such as a speaking request or invoice follow-up.

The more clearly you communicate your style and expectations, the more your employees can meet them. I always found it a bit unfair that, during job interviews, employers ask all sorts of questions and learn all sorts of details about a candidate's style, experience, beliefs, strengths, and weaknesses, but candidates rarely learn these things about their new bosses. I can't help but imagine that, in the not-too-distant future, choosing to work for a particular boss will involve a process not unlike shopping on Amazon. What if, before interviewing with a particular manager, a candidate could read reviews and advice written by other people who have worked for that manager about how to meet that person's expectations? What would happen if managers provided this information themselves?

What a gift it is to communicate, especially to new employees, any information you can about how best to work with you. A simple statement such as "I'm very laid-back except when it comes to deadlines," or "I come from the product side of the business, so I'm a stickler for details" can go a very long way with employees of all generations, but especially those who are different from your cohort.

How to Manage Someone Older Than You

How does people management change if you are one of the many leaders today who is managing one or more employees who are older—sometimes significantly older—than you?

The answer is that my recommended management strategies don't change much at all, but their implementation becomes even more imperative.

This begins with leading yourself first. The primary piece of advice I find myself giving to younger managers of older employees is not to assume that the older person minds the age difference. There is no need to apologize for being young or even to point out the issue if you don't sense any concern or discomfort. Some older workers actually like reporting to someone with a different generational perspective. Trust that you are in your leadership role for a reason, and don't be afraid to be the boss.

On the other hand, if an employee you oversee does comment about your younger age or appears uncomfortable or even resentful, there are some steps you can take. The first is to spend some time getting to know the older employee. Ask questions about the person's experience, opinions, expertise, and interests. Listen. A lot. When you give others time and respect, they are more likely to reciprocate.

Next, try to focus on end results and be flexible about how people accomplish their work. You might find that older employees (or any employees, for that matter) have ways of working that are different from yours, and that is okay.

Finally, be willing to have a direct conversation about your age difference if necessary. While you may never be beloved by this employee, you can ask explicitly for the person's respect.

Be open, flexible, and communicative, and you just might find that the younger boss–older employee dynamic is a refreshing and positive remix.

Goodbye, Annual Review; Hello, Daily Feedback

Back in the day, managers and employees across a wide variety of industries and employer sizes lived and died by the annual review. Many companies, perhaps most famously GE, would rank employees and jettison the bottom 10 percent in a system derisively referred to as "rank and yank."

But not only are annual reviews a lot of work for everyone involved; it turns out they aren't even particularly effective. One study found the traditional performance-review process can hurt more than it helps; in fact, nearly 30 percent of the workers surveyed said they have looked for a new job after a performance review. No one likes to be blindsided by negative feedback, and even positive reviews feel a bit stale if they are months old. The entire process of annual reviews tends to feel backward looking at best, pointless at worst. It is also the case that many organizations provide little or no guidance to managers on how to conduct a performance review, so individual experiences can vary tremendously.

What's a modern, multigenerational organization to do? Many have decided to supplement or fully replace annual reviews with more frequent, ongoing feedback, believing—and I strongly agree with this belief—that it is more valuable to employees, managers, customers, and organizations to offer instant feedback right when it matters and can lead to better outcomes.

(It reminds me of the Waze navigation app, which is constantly receiving information on traffic patterns, weather slowdowns, and other factors that will affect a driver's route and travel time. Every time the app receives new data, it immediately applies the information to recalculate the route and ensure an improved outcome. That is what regular feedback does for employees.)

Desire for more feedback in general is a cross-generational issue. According to a PwC study, 72 percent of employees under 30 said they want feedback on a daily or weekly basis. That sounds like a high number, perhaps indicative of "entitlement," until you look at the corresponding statistic for other generations. The same study found that 60 percent of employees over the age of 30 also want daily or weekly feedback. And, I can't help but note, about 30 to 40 percent of employees of all ages do not want such regular feedback, again proving all individuals are not the same in their preferences. Many Gen X employees in particular tell me that they don't feel as eager for feedback as their older and younger colleagues. As we discussed in chapter 1, many Xers prefer to be more independent.

People often express surprise that older generations can want more feedback, but this doesn't surprise me. Some of us who came of age in earlier decades may have become accustomed to having bosses who tended not to provide a lot of guidance. That doesn't mean we didn't want it; we just learned not to expect it. So when you answer a need attributed to Millennial employees, you are often serving other generations' needs as well.

Just be sure that, when you do offer feedback, your performance criteria are calibrated to employees of different ages. For example, Paul Irving, chairman of the Milken Institute Center for the Future of Aging, points out that most companies' performance evaluations focus on individual achievement as opposed to team success. "This may inadvertently punish older employees who offer other types of value," he writes, "like mentorship, forging deep relationships with clients and colleagues, and conflict resolution, that are not as easily captured using traditional assessment tools."

If you are ready to remix the feedback you and your fellow managers offer to your multigenerational employees, here are some strategies to consider.

ONE-MINUTE MANAGEMENT. When I was writing *Becoming the Boss*, I surveyed a wide variety of successful leaders and asked, "What is the most indispensable management book you have read and would recommend to new managers?" Far and away the number one answer was *The One Minute Manager* by Kenneth Blanchard and Spencer Johnson, which was originally published in 1982.

I don't think it is a coincidence that the first-ever revised edition of this book, now called *The New One Minute Manager*, was published in 2015, just as Millennials were becoming the largest generation in the U.S. workforce. The authors knew back when Millennials were in diapers that the best way to manage people is to provide regular, specific feedback in exactly the way the book title describes: short bursts of one-minute praising and one-minute correction. It really can be that simple, as long as managers are consistent.

If you lead too large a team for ongoing individual feedback to be realistic, then consider offering regular "office hours" during which anyone can schedule an appointment or just pop in to talk—in person or via phone, Skype, text, instant messenger, or any other medium.

One of my clients, a Millennial IT leader, offers office hours to his intergenerational team from 8:00 a.m. to 9:00 a.m. every weekday morning. If no one shows up, he uses the time to catch up on his own work. And if any of his direct reports want to talk about a non-urgent business issue at any other time in the day, he feels no guilt reminding them exactly when he is available for feedback and career-related conversations.

EXPLICIT INSTRUCTIONS. If I had to pinpoint the advice I offer most often to older generations managing younger employees, it is to be more specific not just in feedback but in initial instructions. Remember Remixer Rule #5: Common sense is not so common.

A law firm partner once complained to me that he had tried to support a young associate's career by bringing her with him to a client meeting, but she blew it. When I asked what happened, he said with disdain, "She *talked*."

According to this partner, a junior associate absolutely should not speak in a meeting with clients. When I asked him if he had told her that in advance, he said, "She should have known not to talk."

That is absolutely a failure on the part of the partner. "You should have known better" is not exactly helpful feedback.

After sharing this story at a workshop with day camp leaders, one camp director told me that this gave him an aha moment about his "bagel problem." Trying to treat their counselors well and solve the problem of counselors not eating breakfast and having low energy with the kids, the camp decided to provide a small spread of bagels and coffee in the mornings in the staff lounge. The problem was that they would sit eating the bagels and not go out and engage with the kids.

What was the aha moment? "I realized I never told them the idea was for them to grab a bagel on the go and not sit down and take a break."

The need for more explicit directions may be related to the fact that Millennials had more oversight from parents, teachers, and coaches, or it just may be the simple issue that we don't know what we don't know. Specific, explicit instructions are important no matter what generations you manage.

ONE-ON-ONE CHECK-INS. Adobe is one company that has abolished annual performance reviews and decided to replace them with "check-ins," frequent meetings between employees and managers. One-on-ones are by no means a new concept, but if more managers actually held them, imagine how much more productive and engaged employees of all generations could be.

Quite simply, one-on-one check-ins signify to employees that they matter. Human resources expert Jaime Klein, founder and CEO of Inspire Human Resources, likes to remind people managers, "Everyone wears this invisible necklace that says, 'I am important. Pay attention to me.' In our busy high-tech world, so many leaders have gotten away from the basic nurturing of relationships. I advise managers to go back to basics and just get to know people. Break bread." A little personal attention can go a long way toward building trust and engagement between boss and employee.

STAY CONVERSATIONS. A more formalized variation on one-on-one check-ins is known at some organizations as a "stay conversation." This is a deliberate conversation between manager and employee about the employee's future at the organization. While not a promise, a stay conversation is an opportunity for a manager to explicitly tell key talent how much they are valued. In today's uncertain times, stay conversations can be critical to alleviate stress and support retention.

Sometimes, we are least transparent with people about their own careers, and this can be particularly frustrating for early-career professionals. From their recent experiences as students, Millennials and Gen Zs are generally accustomed not only to frequent feedback in the form of grades, but also to constant, transparent discussion of their next steps.

I was once sitting on an airplane next to a young professional who worked in sales for a major beverage company. (We started chatting because I noticed him flipping over his napkin, snack menu, and other items on his tray table. When I inquired, he told me the items had the logo of his company's biggest rival brand and he couldn't risk someone snapping a photo of him with the enemy logo. Brilliant.)

When I told him about my work, he identified himself as an ambitious and frustrated Millennial. He asked for advice on talking to his manager about how he could advance more quickly.

"I keep asking my boss what else I need to do to get ahead," he told me, "and my boss keeps saying, 'Be patient. Your career is a marathon, not a sprint.'

"And I understand that," my brand-loyal seatmate said. "But can't he at least tell me what mile of the marathon I'm on?"

That sentiment makes sense to me, and this is why stay conversations can be so valuable. When was the last time you talked to your top talent about the future? You don't have to make any guarantees, but you can talk generally and take an employee's temperature. If you don't have these conversations, your best people may leave while you are making other plans for them. So many people are told in their exit interviews, "Why are you leaving? We had big plans for you!" And they reply, "Why didn't you tell *me* that?"

FEEDBACK APPS. Some organizations, such as IBM and Warby Parker, have replaced their annual performance reviews with apps that provide employees with ongoing feedback. PwC even has an on-demand system by which employees can request fine-tuning whenever they want it: the app overlays a visual that compares past results with current ones.

Law firm Reed Smith recently developed a feedback app based on suggestions from the firm's own associates. According to Casey Ryan, the firm's global head of legal personnel, "We decided to provide the app as an addition, not a replacement, to our annual review process so associates can essentially have the best of both worlds. An annual review is valuable, but it could be about a piece of work from twelve months ago. The goal of the app is to offer an opportunity for partners and associates to talk more regularly and in real time about case and work developments. Particularly in a highly demanding and stressful job, the app is a way to both raise the performance culture and make a big firm feel smaller."

At other organizations, app-based feedback doesn't only come from one's manager. Companies like Goldman Sachs and J.P. Morgan have developed tools that allow any colleague to ping someone with feedback at any time.

In a twist on the assumption that young leaders always prefer technology, Amanda Ward, a Millennial-age director of Camp Chinqueka—an all-girls sleepaway camp my mother, my aunts, and I all attended—told me that she was struggling to provide enough feedback to the Gen Z–aged counselors she managed. She came up with the idea of giving each counselor an index card every week: she wrote each counselor's name on a card and then passed the cards around to the whole staff to write feedback (usually positive) for their peers. She then wrote a few pieces of feedback (both positive and constructive) on the other side of each card. The process was simple, fast, inclusive, inexpensive, and effective.

MBWA. Another simple, effective, and economical people management strategy and feedback opportunity is the decades-old Management by Wandering Around, which is as easy as it sounds: walking around and chitchatting with your team. This simple, classic practice has tremendous benefits among employees of all generations. One Harvard Business School study found that managers with the lowest levels of respect are those known for shutting themselves in their offices.

Donna Kalajian Lagani of *Cosmopolitan* magazine, whom you met in a previous chapter, is a practitioner. "If I have a question for someone on my team, I never e-mail," she told me. "I jump up and see them. I want them to see my face, I want it to feel more personal. And on the way to them I'll see three other people. It's important to be very visible."

If you choose to implement MBWA, remember to be inclusive in your wandering. Be careful not to visit only the areas where Gen X employees sit, or chat only with outgoing personality types, or longer-tenured staff of a certain level. And let people know explicitly that your goal is chatting and listening, not checking on them. One non-profit executive director told me that he tried this strategy when he first took on the job and employees "almost passed out" when he came into their cubicles and said he wanted to talk. They thought they were about to be reprimanded or fired. "I realized I had to be a little more casual and careful with my approach," he told me with a humble smile.

The Return of Apprenticeship

In college I had an unpaid summer internship with a nonprofit women's small business development center. The downside was that I had to answer the phone with the longest greeting in history—"Hello, American Woman's Economic Development Corporation, this is Lindsey speaking, how may I help you?" (my friends used to call up just to make me say it)—but there were many upsides. First and foremost was a simple act by the executive director that provided more value than I knew at the time. One day she said, "Come sit in my office and listen to me make fund-raising calls."

It was the kind of sales and communication training money can't buy. I was able to hear firsthand how my boss started each call, created rapport, refuted objections politely, and closed on a positive note, no matter what the outcome had been. When I set off with my own round of calls, I felt much more confident than I would have otherwise.

These days, you can watch a YouTube tutorial on pretty much any topic imaginable, but no training is as powerful as observing someone in your own organization doing the exact work you will be asked to do. In most professions, even if you learned the educational aspects in school—say, how markets work if you're in finance or how to source a brief if you're an attorney—class can only offer so much. There are so many daily nuances that cannot be taught.

Apprenticeship is a low- to no-cost people management technique that is particularly valuable in generationally diverse teams. The remix is that apprenticeship now goes in multiple directions depending on the skills that need to be learned. Apprenticing can take place in a variety of combinations, from manager/employee to mentor/mentee to employee/employee to intern/employee and more. This is valuable to the employee who is learning, and also honors the knowledge and experience of the employee in the modeling role.

Here are some apprenticeship strategies to consider:

CARVE OUT OPPORTUNITIES. Scott McGohan, CEO of McGohan Brabender, the Dayton-based independent health insurance broker you read about in chapter 3, gives a lot of presentations to clients, potential clients, and industry and community organizations. For each speech, he invites a member of his organization to practice their public speaking by introducing Scott and the company, and then staying to listen to his presentation. Since public speaking is one of the areas in which members of all generations tell me they want more experience, this is a simple and effective apprenticeship habit that is inclusive and, according to McGohan Brabender employees, highly valued and appreciated.

COPY EMPLOYEES ON HIGHER-LEVEL MATTERS. A hedge fund manager recently told me he wanted to foster apprenticeship among his junior employees, but he was just too busy to do so. His solution was to cc or bcc his junior employees on more of his e-mail corre-spondence, so they could understand how he works, how he phrases conversations, and how he handles various situations. (Of course, he gave the junior employees clear instructions not to jump into those conversations but just to observe.) In this way, he was able to model a skill without spending a huge chunk of his time. Where there's a will, there's a way for most things, and apprenticeship is no exception.

BE A ROLE MODEL. If you're a leader, ask yourself if you are truly modeling the behavior that you want your employees to demon-strate. For example, if it seems your employees always have their noses in their phones, take note of your own phone-checking hab-its. If you want your employees to be more available, to talk more in person, to have more attention to detail, are you practicing these behaviors yourself? As former UCLA basketball coach John Wooden said, "The most powerful tool you have as a leader is your own personal example."

(This tip applies to those of us who are parents as well. Although it's commonplace to bemoan today's screen-addicted children, we might need to look at our own contribution to this phenomenon. A study by the nonprofit Common Sense Media found that 33 percent of teens wish their parents would spend less time on their devices.)

Acknowledge and Praise

Acknowledgment and praise are vastly underutilized management tools across all generations. And that's a shame, considering that thank-yous are free, fast, and require no particular training. The in-dividuals and companies that are good at gratitude reap the rewards.

Seattle-based law firm Perkins Coie, one of the few "biglaw" firms on *Fortune*'s 100 Best Companies to Work For list, gives out thank-you cards to attorneys and staff members in recognition of their work. When I praised this practice during a workshop for another firm, one partner scoffed. "That's like giving people trophies for participation," he said.

Before I could respond—and you know my position on this topic already—another partner jumped in to reply to his colleague: "No it's not. You *choose* what work you acknowledge. You *choose* which people you thank, but nothing is more valuable to people than gratitude."

Before I could agree, yet another partner jumped in to further comment on this topic. She shared that she worked as an employment attorney, and one of her responsibilities was to listen to her clients' employee complaint hotlines. She said, "I can't tell you how many employee complaint phone calls start with the person saying, 'My boss never thanks me. My boss never acknowledges me.' And the conflict grows from there into expensive litigation." Needless to say, gratitude is cheaper than a lawsuit.

Thank-you notes and grateful comments are practically high-tech compared to an even easier—and just as important—level of acknowledgment for employees of all ages and skill levels. I have conducted more than a few focus groups at investment banks where junior employees' biggest complaint was not that they didn't receive enough praise. "We'd be thrilled," they told me, "if a single senior executive just knew our names."

If you're ready to up your organization's acknowledgment and gratitude game, try this:

KNOW PEOPLE'S NAMES. Learn and use people's names, particularly those working on any projects you oversee. This is equally important to the brand-new intern as it is to the long-tenured, back office employee who has been with your company for years and rarely engages with you in person. If you are not good at remembering names, then your remix involves getting better. There is no shame in jotting down names until you memorize them or asking people a few times before you get it right.

SHARE SUCCESSFUL OUTCOMES. Another way to acknowledge people is to form the habit of sharing the glow of any successful project, program, pitch, or other task to which they contributed. That assistant who typed up a letter: Did you send him a quick e-mail or text to let him know that the outreach had a positive result? The junior person who did the math behind the sales pitch: Did you stop by her desk to let her know you won the business? People want to know not just that you're grateful but that their work had meaning.

PROMOTE MORE FREQUENTLY. Promotions are a major incentive for all generations. Competitive-minded Baby Boomers enjoy the bump in prestige. Oft-ignored Gen Xers appreciate the acknowledgment of their hard work. Fast-paced, success-minded Millennials and Gen Zs like to have visible evidence of their forward momentum. And all of us in Customization Nation enjoy the feeling of a personalized career path. While all promotions need to be earned, it's time to be less stingy with title bumps.

This is the strategy undertaken by Texas Capital Bank. "We have tiered everything now, creating more levels in almost every area of the bank to give people a sense of movement," Tricia Linderman told me. "We were getting feedback that people wanted to understand the expectations and be rewarded for excelling at a faster pace than we were used to. It also helps managers separate stronger talent."

Note that acknowledging employees isn't just a "nice" thing to do; it's a business improvement strategy. Gallup research has found that 80 percent of employees across generations said recognition is a strong motivator of work performance, and 70 percent said they would work harder with continuous recognition.

Explain the Why

Another common knock you may hear against Millennials is that they don't want to "pay their dues." Always eager to bust a shaming stereotype, I frequently ask younger professionals in focus groups if it is true that they don't want to do "grunt work." (Which, by the way, is how I learned that the term "grunt work" does not translate globally. Oops.)

While no one says they *love* menial tasks—because, you know, they are human—Millennials tell me they are willing to do almost any type of work asked of them, with one major caveat: they want to know *why* they're being asked to do it. And "Because it's always been done that way" or "Because I said so" are not what we're talking about.

Explanations and context resonate with Millennials; they grew up with information at their fingertips and expect to know what's going on and how their work impacts an organization's larger purpose. And again, this is not true only for Millennials, but they are often more vocal about this desire than members of other generations may be. Who doesn't appreciate having their manager take the time to explain why a task needs to be completed or why leadership is implementing a strategy? Transparency breeds trust.

So if your employees are coming in late or leaving early, discuss *why* your required work hours exist. For example, you might explain that clients start calling at a certain time; or, if time zones play havoc with your hours, explain that you need to be in early on the West Coast to work with East Coast customers.

Stephen Kennedy runs Synchrony's high-potential leadership program for recent college graduates called the Business Leadership Program (BLP), whose recruiting practices you read about in chapter 3. The two-year program concludes with a cross-functional capstone project during which teams of ten participants (referred to as

"BLPs") from across the country each work on one of five different strategic projects for the business and then present their solutions to the company's leadership. The capstone experience challenges BLPs to support business priorities and teams outside their functional area of focus, leading them to develop new skills and work with employees of all experience levels within the business.

"We do a survey at the end of the program," Stephen told me, "and one common piece of feedback was that the program participants said it would be easier to be in the same physical location as their teammates for the capstone project." Stephen told the employees that he agreed, and that is exactly why the program was designed *not* to be that way.

"That is not how today's workplace works," he told them. "And that is exactly why we developed the capstone project the way we did. When you leave this program, you will need to be good at working across our locations and resources all across the country."

Rather than dismissing the participants' feedback, he acknowledged it and helped them understand why overcoming the challenges of the project would be beneficial to their careers.

I'm aware that not everyone, including your superiors, will necessarily agree with the strategy of providing a "because." Sometimes you might not know why your team is being asked to do something. But that doesn't mean you can't give your own team an explanation even if your leaders don't give one to you. It can be as simple as conveying "The regional manager likes to give each client a report by 5:00 p.m. Friday so we need to pull together this data and get it done." Even if you doubt the effectiveness of said reports, you've accomplished what you needed to for your own position and you've helped your team understand why they are being asked to hustle.

As a grad student in Australia, I took on a part-time job at a film festival and did a lot of mind-numbing data entry. It was a lot more palatable because I had a supervisor who used to say things like "On a boringness scale of 1 to 10, I'm going to estimate this one's a 13. I recommend a large latte." Humor always helps.

It is also okay—when asked "Why?"—to admit when you don't know the answer. Acknowledging "We don't know yet" or "I will get back to you when I know more" can be as powerful as having a complete explanation. Employees of all generations appreciate authenticity and candor.

And, finally, it's also important to listen carefully when your employees ask why, and you don't have a very good answer. When Volvo wanted to turn around its brand and business, one of the initiatives implemented by then CEO Stefan Jacoby was to create a "catalyst group," mostly of younger employees. One of the questions the group asked was, "Why does each design change in a car require a dozen signatures?" Jacoby and his leadership team couldn't come up with a response, so the company took action to cut that number in half.

That is a great example of the importance of two-way communications in today's workplace—the act of both talking and listening across levels of an organization and, of course, across generations. In the next chapter, we'll explore the next important element of leadership success in the remix: how we communicate with one another.

CHAPTER 5: KEY TAKEAWAYS

- The people management remix requires an acknowledgment that many people managers never learned the "classics" to begin with.
- Because employees have more power today to "review" bosses online and there is less stigma against frequent job changes, managers are under more pressure to be effective people leaders.
- Take a look at whether you possess any ageist views or expectations that are getting in the way of effectively managing yourself and your team. Stop any self-deprecating jokes about age or experience and help employees understand why you hold certain expectations.
- Consider supplementing or fully replacing annual reviews with more frequent, timely, ongoing feedback in the form of one-minute management, one-on-one check-ins, or feedback apps. All generations appreciate having more regular insight into their performance.
- Apprenticeship is a low- to no-cost people management technique that is particularly valuable in generationally diverse teams. Look for small opportunities, such as copying team members on more e-mail communications, to offer guidance and model behavior.
- Acknowledgment and praise are vastly underutilized management tools across all generations. Share successful outcomes with your team, write thank-you notes/e-mails/texts, and consider giving more promotions. Remember that thank-yous are free.
- Always explain the "why." Employees of all generations appreciate transparency and honesty, and knowing the reasons behind decisions makes employees at all levels feel like they are part of the team.

6 THE COMMUNICATION REMIX

COPE Like a
Transparent Chameleon

WHEN I ENVISION the "before" way of communicating in the Traditionalist- and Baby Boomer–dominated workplace, I picture a black-and-white television image of Walter Cronkite delivering his signature sign-off: "And that's the way it is."

The "after" image of today is 7 billion people of all ages tapping their version of "the way it is" into their phones, back and forth to each other and all over social media.

According to research, generational differences are most acutely experienced around communication issues. Eighty-one percent of today's workers say the primary difference between generations in the workplace is communication styles, and 38 percent find it difficult to communicate with coworkers who are not in their own age group. This means that companies that enable intergenerational communication among employees—by teaching colleagues how to communicate with one another—will have a tremendous advantage.

Almost all conversations have become two-way, including those between leaders and employees, not to mention between companies and customers. When world leaders, celebrities, and CEOs launch Twitter accounts and participate in Ask Me Anything (AMA) sessions on Reddit, you as a leader or an individual employee have little choice but to accept this reality.

The communication remix involves acknowledging that communication in organizations has moved from primarily top-down to more transparent and two-way. In this chapter we'll talk about "macro" best practices for leaders to communicate organization-wide and "micro" best practices for employees of all positions to better communicate at the one-on-one level.

Let's begin with how today's most effective CEOs and senior leaders have adapted the way they communicate for changing employees and changing times.

The Importance of CEO Visibility

In the past, it was common for senior leaders to lead from behind closed doors in hidden offices on faraway executive floors. This model is not gone, but it becomes less common every day. Millennials and Gen Zs have grown up in the era of the celebrity CEO, and most of the rest of us have embraced this newfound access to our leaders, too. This means that if you are a CEO—or owner, president, executive director, etc.—your employees will have certain expectations of your visibility and transparency. It's just not optional anymore.

Speaking as a New Yorker, Michael Bloomberg always comes to my mind as an example of a leader who embraced this reality. When he was mayor of New York City from 2002 to 2013, Bloomberg—who generationally is on the younger end of the Traditionalists, based on his birth year of 1942—re-created the workspace of City Hall to be an entirely open space, a rarity in government. Mimicking the trading floor model of his Wall Street days, he sat at a desk the same size as every other employee's and held standing meetings in plain view of his team.

As you can imagine, not every longtime government employee was comfortable with this arrangement. But most eventually came to embrace the idea of transparency in their role as public servants. As one city employee commented, "As a work space, it is something that you do not think that you can ever get used to. But when you see the mayor hosting high-level meetings in clear sight of everyone else, you start to understand that this open-communication model is not bullshit. And that it works."

(Note that Bloomberg was quite private about his personal life during his mayoralty, so being visible does not mean that you must post daily selfies or photos of your kids. I'm talking about accessibility of leadership in a professional context—although we'll get to social media expectations and appropriate boundaries in a moment.)

In addition to increasing a leader's everyday visibility, there are key moments when such transparency can make a particular impact. One of those moments is during employee onboarding and training.

Glenn Van Ekeren, president of Vetter Health Services, an operator of thirty senior living facilities with employees ranging in age from 16 to 85, personally participates in every new leader training. His role, he says, is to inspire and instill the importance of the company's mission, vision, and values in leaders. "Sometimes my team probably thinks I am too intricately involved," says Glenn, "but I can't think of a better way for me to devote my time than to invest in new leaders."

Another opportunity for CEO visibility is during recruiting events. This can be an especially effective strategy for recruiting Millennials and Gen Zs to "old-fashioned" or less popular industries or organizations. Who better than the CEO to sell young people on a career choice they may not have previously considered?

This was a key practice of former Land O'Lakes Inc. CEO Chris Policinski, who was well aware of Millennial students' relative lack of interest in food and agriculture careers. He took it upon himself to help sell MBAs in particular on his company and his industry. Policinski visited campuses once or twice a month, working directly with students on business school case studies and giving "fireside chats" with small groups. He even personally spoke on the phone with students mulling multiple job offers.

Policinski has said, "When I started, it was a very hierarchical world. I saw the CEO once a year when he gave the state of the union speech for the company." Now young talent expects personal interactions with leaders. This is a fantastic development and goes a long way toward building engagement and trust across levels of an organization, especially a large one.

Some additional ways leaders can increase their visibility include: writing blog posts on your company's website, intranet, or LinkedIn (and engaging with commenters); holding regular town halls, all-hands meetings, or Ask Me Anything sessions (in person and/or virtually); participating in social media on internal networks or externally; making appearances at employee events or volunteer activities; or simply walking around the lobby or halls to say hello and chat with employees. To build visibility with remote employees, CEOs can host virtual town halls that include live online chats, Skype, or Zoom-based Q&A sessions.

Leadership visibility is especially important if your organization is launching a new initiative or establishing a new way of working. For example, when the accounting firm BDO wanted to encourage adoption of a more robust flexible work policy, the company shared stories of its employees' flexible work arrangements on the firm's internal social media site, and encouraged leaders to share their own remote work practices. The firm's CEO at the time even declared publicly at meetings, "My name is Jack Weisbaum and I am a flexible worker."

Another leader who comes to mind when I think about visibility is Massimo Bottura, the chef who runs the number one restaurant on the annual World's 50 Best Restaurants list, Osteria Francescana, in Modena, Italy. "Every morning people pass by to say hello, from the mayor to the postman," he has said. "They often find me sweeping the street in front of the restaurant or my wife fixing the flowers because we are the first ones to care about where we live and work." Bottura is also known to help his team unload delivery trucks and prepare staff meals.

Imagine how it feels for a brand-new dishwasher or a long-serving, loyal line cook to see your boss, the top chef in the world, sweeping the street in front of your workplace as you walk through the door.

Next-Level Transparency: Show Them the Money

Chief financial officers are getting in on the visibility and transparency, too. We addressed earlier in the book how some law firm CFOs are offering junior attorneys and staff more insight into how their firms make money. Some companies debrief their employees after quarterly earnings calls to help the rank and file understand the financial big picture of their employers.

At Netflix, a company known for its radically transparent culture, virtually every employee can access sensitive information, like the number of subscribers in each country or the contractual terms of Netflix's production deals. While not all employees thrive in a culture this transparent—and the company has received some criticism for its encouragement of blunt feedback and open discussions of whether people should be fired—the commitment to internal information transparency is admirable.

Patty McCord, former chief talent officer of Netflix, emphasizes the importance of this practice, particularly to start-up companies. As she shared on a *Wharton@Work* podcast, "I call it the constant setting of context. I [often tell] start-up companies, 'One of the most important people on your team to communicate to the rest of the organization is your CFO.' If you can teach everybody in the company how to read a profit-and-loss statement, then you have a capability in your company that serves you and them for the rest of their careers. They understand how it works and where they sit in the organization."

Have you trained your team on how your organization makes and spends money, and how their job plays into that financial picture? If you are an individual contributor, have you taken advantage of opportunities to receive such training?

Some organizations are taking financial transparency even further. I'm talking about salary transparency, a practice that feels blasphemous to many people who came up the ranks in more traditional, secretive, hierarchical organizations.

Although the National Labor Relations Act of 1935 made it unlawful (with some exceptions) for private-sector employers to forbid employees from discussing wages and compensation, a recent survey by the Institute for Women's Policy Research found that nearly half of all U.S. workers reported being "strongly discouraged" from discussing pay with their colleagues. Few topics have been as hidden in our society as our salaries.

Salary secrecy is changing thanks in large part to the Internet and to Millennials, who came of age relying on the Web for all kinds of information. (I have personally witnessed many instances of young employees creating and sharing spreadsheets of each other's compensation for comparison, with no apparent discomfort about doing so.)

I know this concept is scary to many longtime leaders, but it is worthwhile to look at the positives of this practice. A 2010 experimental study by economists found that sharing information about workers' pay relative to others significantly boosted work effort, even after controlling for the effect of individual pay. Each one-unit change in salary rank (out of five) led to a jump in employee effort that was equivalent to giving them a 33 percent pay increase. Buffer, a software company well known for its transparent salary policy, even found that job applications increased when it posted its employees' salaries publicly online.

On the flip side, another study of employees at the University of California found that—not surprisingly—salary disclosure led to lower job satisfaction among workers who felt underpaid. One potential benefit of salary transparency is that it will help address pay inequity based on race and gender. Angela Cornell, director of the Labor Law Clinic at Cornell Law School, has said that open discussion of salaries among peers and coworkers can be a powerful tool to fight pay inequity.

Now is the time for all leaders to take a good, hard look at their pay structure. What would happen if suddenly the salaries of everyone on your team became public? Would you be comfortable with that information being available? There is no doubt in my mind that salary transparency is inevitable as Millennials take over more leadership roles. Millennials have come of age at a time of significantly more visibility of previously invisible information. When your high school friend drops a few pounds, he posts his daily weigh-ins on Facebook. When your neighbors sell their home, you can check the exact sale price on Zillow. We list our work history on our LinkedIn profiles. Why will salary be any different?

Social Media Communication: It's Complicated

Since your blood pressure may already be rising, I might as well go all in and talk next about your employees wanting to engage with you on social media. And I'm not just talking about the professional environment of LinkedIn. This means Instagram, Facebook, and Twitter, too.

If you're a Millennial or Gen Z, this may feel like no big deal. A recent survey reported that 75 percent of workers aged 18 to 24 are connected with colleagues on social media, compared to 54 percent of workers overall. I actually thought these numbers were a bit low, given the fact that so many of us make friends with our coworkers and want to connect (online and off-line) outside of work. Many people even befriend their bosses: 33 percent of workers connect with their direct managers on social media.

The desire to post about work on social media is surprising to some people. But it is critical to understand why it matters to young workers. As Joan Snyder Kuhl and Jennifer Zephirin, authors of *Misunderstood Millennial Talent: The Other Ninety-One Percent*, have pointed out, the perception is that Millennials want to post on social media to build their brand outside of work. The reality, they say, is that Millennials want their loved ones to understand and approve of their careers. Remember, again, how close many young people are with their parents.

This is exactly what I have observed among many Millennials and Gen Zs who post about their work on social media. It's frequently positive and often even promotional for their employers. And the trend seems to be catching on with other generations as well. I follow all my clients on social media, and my feed is full of posts—usually photographs—of employees of all generations and levels sharing their attendance at conferences and events, selfies with senior leaders, selfies with customers, any recognition or awards they receive, participation in community service projects with colleagues, sharing company news like new product launches, and much more.

Following your employees or colleagues on social media—if they are open to it—is also another way to acknowledge them as individuals. This is especially important to your employees from marginalized communities. Anisa Flowers is a Gen Z, and chief of staff for Pipeline Angels, an organization that is changing the face of angel investing and creating capital for women and nonbinary femme social entrepreneurs. Anisa, who is Deaf, told me, "The beautiful thing about my generation is that we literally wear our hearts on our sleeves. Our sleeves just happen to be on our social media accounts. If you want to recruit and retain us, it is crucial for leaders to take serious steps to learn what different individuals of this generation value and how your business stacks up against these values."

I know that some people prefer not to engage on social media at all, but there is no question that social media is a fact of daily life and decision-making for millions of people today. If you choose not to engage, be aware that your employees' and colleagues' social media shares are often being viewed by your current and future job applicants, investors, shareholders, and vendors across generations. Sometimes being a remixer requires stepping out of your comfort zone.

How to COPE

I can't tell you how many focus groups I have conducted where, as soon as the door is shut, the participants start to pump me for information: "Do you know anything about the new comp plan?" "Did they tell you when the new location is opening?" "Is it true that we won't be able to order lunch anymore?"

In one instance, I was conducting a focus group with a team of mid-level employees at a particularly hierarchical nonprofit, and one participant had recently been promoted to a new level but still came to the group. She had answers to all her former peers' questions about what was going on at the higher levels of the organization, and her view was remarkably positive, not just because she had been promoted. "I can't believe how much I'm being told now," she said. "They are doing so much more than I knew."

This is not about secrets or proprietary information. It's about people wanting to know what is happening in the organization where they spend the majority of their daily lives. Office gossip and complaints are as old as time, but so much of it is completely unnecessary. Another common outcome of focus groups is that I report back on what employees say they want (for example, more information about volunteer opportunities, more information about other divisions of the company, more training programs), and the leaders reply, "But we offer those things! Don't they know about them?"

They don't.

Leaders often worry about the dangers of being transparent about potential "bad" stuff, but often I find they could do a much better job of being transparent about the good stuff, too.

It is undoubtedly part of employees' jobs to read messages sent by their bosses and leadership ("But we sent them an e-mail!" is a common reply when I share with leaders what their employees don't know), but that doesn't mean the way we provide this information isn't due for a remix.

Leaders today need to communicate early and often. And then communicate some more. In different ways. I know this puts additional burden on leaders, but that is what it takes to be effective in a multigenerational work environment.

As an author, I know this all too well. Just think of all the ways you might be reading this book. This paragraph might be an excerpt you are reading in an e-newsletter or magazine attempting to entice you to read more. You might be listening to the audiobook, reading on your mobile device, or skimming a summary on an app like Blinkist. Maybe you're hearing it aloud at a book signing or watching a live stream or recorded video of my reading. (If so, hi!) My goal is to provide you with beneficial and applicable information in as many formats as possible to reach you; how and when you consume it is your choice. This is how leaders need to think about communicating with employees.

In other words, you have to provide options and be agnostic about how your employees choose to consume your information. (See Remixer Rule #4: Think "and," not "or.") The challenge is to do so without significant additional effort or cost. Fortunately, there is a solution, and it goes by the acronym COPE: create once, publish everywhere, a philosophy credited to Daniel Jacobson when he was director of application development for NPR Digital Media.

COPE-ing does not mean offering unlimited options. It means putting thought into what employees need to know, empathizing with the time they have to consume information, and then finding creative ways to provide that information so that people of different generations, schedules, job functions, family situations, and learning preferences can access and digest it.

This often leads to the realization that most communications can and should be a lot shorter, especially now that we have all become accustomed to the brevity of texting, instant messaging, and social media. A sales executive once told me he tries to write all e-mail messages to be short enough to fit on the screen of an early version iPhone, since he knows most people will read his messages on the go.

Amanda Ward of Camp Chinqueka, who employs a large number of Generation Z teenagers, told me that she was dismayed at how few counselors were reading the camp's forty-five-page staff manual. She knew some staff members read it diligently, so she didn't eliminate the book, but she decided to add a box at the bottom of each page called "TL;DR" (too long; didn't read) to highlight the most important one or two tweet-length takeaways from each page. She likened it to providing SparkNotes or CliffsNotes versions of novels. Of course, she would prefer that everyone read every page of the manual, but what was most important was expressing the manual's most critical information.

Warby Parker has always conducted all-hands meetings with its employees, but as the company expanded and launched multiple retail locations and labs, it became more challenging for all employees to attend in person or by video. So the company founders remixed the all-hands meetings to create what they called "the Weekly Briefing," a three- to five-minute highlight reel to provide all employees with the key messages they need to know on a weekly basis. Cofounder and co-CEO Dave Gilboa has advised other leaders to "think through your employees' schedules. Who might be missing out on key communication touch points and why? Are they constantly traveling? Do they not have a lot of time? Are they working remotely? Create new communications products that fit their particular habits and needs. Get them the information they need how they need it."

IN THE MIX: AN EXERCISE IN COPE-ING

Let's walk through an example of COPE-ing. Let's say your organization is launching a new volunteer program and you want to announce it to your entire employee base. Your communication team decides to announce the program with a video from you, the CEO. Here are all the ways you could potentially remix that content to reach your employees most effectively, depending on your particular mix of people. Note that I have attempted to make this list as inclusive as possible. As you read through the exercise, ask yourself a few questions:

- Which of these communication methods do we currently use and should *continue* to use because it still works?
- Which of these communication methods do we currently use and should *stop* using because it is no longer effective with our employees?
- Which of these communication methods should we *add* to our mix to see if it may help us achieve the results we desire?

Goal: Announce and educate employees about new volunteer program

"Create once" action: Record CEO video

Potential "publish everywhere" actions:

- Caption the video with text overlay. This will ensure that every word is clearly understood and that you are reaching employees with disabilities, those for whom English is not their first language, and those who simply prefer to digest videos with the sound off.
- Post the video link to Slack or any other internal communication tool.
- Turn the text into a full-length transcript for those who prefer to read the announcement.
- Provide the audio recording of the video as a downloadable MP3 for employees who prefer to listen to the announcement on their commute or while exercising at lunchtime.
- Remix excerpts of the MP3 into a shorter podcast episode.
- Edit the transcript into key bullet points to share in a blog post on your organization's intranet, in employee newsletters, or on social media if the program is public.
- Use the key bullet points to create a simple poster to display on break room bulletin boards, factory floor announcement boards, bathroom stalls, or other physical employee

announcement locations. (Some organizations continue to place paper memos on each employee's desk. Used sparingly, this can still be a very effective tactic.)

- Provide the bullet points to all team leaders and recommend they share them at their next team meeting or all-hands gathering to "cascade" the announcement to all levels and put the announcement in their own words. Keep in mind that in a multigenerational environment some employees will view formal language from management as appropriately professional, while others view phrases like "It has come to our attention" and "As per our recent communication" as glaringly inauthentic. Know your audience, know your company culture, and allow for some variety in each manager's style.

- Collect any questions that arise from the program announcement, write up answers, and provide them as an FAQ accompanying the video and blog post.

- Provide all leaders with a "toolkit" of the above resources to share with their team members, to again help cascade the information to all levels, and to gather feedback or additional questions to share with senior leaders.

All of the above options will not be appropriate for all organizations, but my goal is to challenge you to expand your thinking about additional ways in which your particular employee mix may like to receive information from leadership. Also think about how you can eliminate any methods that have stopped working for generational reasons, technological reasons, or otherwise. Early in my career, for instance, I worked for a company where the favorite communication tool of the CEO was to record long voicemail messages that would suddenly show up as a blinking red light on the phone extensions of all employees. I'm thinking that method would not be super-popular today.

The final step is to track the success of your communications. Do you know the open rate on your employee communication e-mails? Do you track the number of replies to questions you receive? Do you conduct surveys—formal or informal—on what programs employees are aware of?

If, even after COPE-ing, you find people are still not digesting your communications, you might need to pay more attention to segmentation. Remember that one size fits none in Customization Nation, and some communications may simply be too general to feel relevant to all employees. Think about how you might customize a larger message to smaller audiences, such as employees in a certain region, workers in a certain function, remote workers, long-tenured employees, or members of specific employee resource groups. Sometimes just a simple customized opening sentence makes all the difference.

Leaders Are Listeners

Now let's address the other side of the two-way communication remix: listening. My grandfather used to say, "There's a reason you have two ears and one mouth; use them accordingly," and I find that's a pretty good guideline for leadership.

Listening to employees doesn't have to be complicated. It can be done through formal or informal employee surveys, focus groups, and question-and-answer sessions with leaders during a town hall or all-hands meeting. You can solicit questions anonymously to answer in public if you're concerned people won't be candid in a large group. (Old-fashioned employee suggestion boxes are due for a comeback.) Or you can even channel your inner Ed Koch and just walk around asking everyone, "How'm I doin'?"

As someone who frequently conducts focus groups and listening sessions on behalf of my clients, I am endlessly astonished at how candid employees across all generations will be when asked for their opinions—even when the sessions are being videotaped. And the most common feedback at the end of a focus group always conveys this sentiment: "I know everything we discussed won't necessarily be addressed, but I'm really glad to have an opportunity to share my opinions."

When you don't listen as a leader, resentments fester, especially among younger employees who are used to the constant communication of social media and frequent requests from stores, restaurants, airlines, and apps to "rate your experience!" or "tell us what you think!"

"When we talk to companies having intergenerational conflict, we often learn there is no avenue for younger employees to feel their voice is being heard," says MaryLeigh Bliss, vice president of content at Ypulse, a youth marketing and millennial research firm. This is not true just for Millennials and Gen Zs. If you make an effort to listen to one cohort of employees, you have to listen to all employees. Traditionalists, Boomers, and Gen Xers may not have the same expectations of being surveyed, but they will certainly notice if they are excluded.

Ready to remix your leadership to include more and better listening? Try this:

BE INCLUSIVE. When you send out employee surveys, host Q&As, or engage in any other form of listening, invite *all* employees to participate rather than just a sample. Depending on your situation, this should include remote employees, call center staff, factory workers, distribution center team members, and potentially contractors and consultants. You will not only receive a more diverse and representative set of data, but you will also make sure everyone feels important enough to be heard. Sometimes you might only need information from a segment of employees, but whenever you are in doubt, err on the side of inclusivity.

Inclusivity also means expanding the number of tools you use to collect information from multiple generations. Amanda Ward of Camp Chinqueka told me that when she sent out a SurveyMonkey e-mail survey to her team, only a few people responded, because many Gen Zs consider e-mail to be "too much work" to check. When she edited the same survey into a fun visual image and posted it to Instagram, her counselors responded in droves.

ENGAGE AT ANY LEVEL. If you work for an organization that does not embrace listening, then do your best to have two-way dialogue with the employees you do oversee. While you may not change your entire organization, you can improve your neck of the woods.

REPORT BACK ON RESULTS. You are under no obligation to implement all, or even any, of the feedback you receive, but you do need to acknowledge that you have listened. No matter what your ultimate decisions, thank people for contributing their ideas and feedback and explain how their recommendations contributed to any subsequent outcomes or decisions, even if you choose to go in a different direction or to take no action at all.

You will even learn a lot about employees who choose not to respond to a survey or feedback opportunity. Author and psychologist Adam Grant, who studied employee survey results at Facebook, found that people who chose *not* to fill out the company's annual surveys were 2.6 times more likely to leave in the next six months. When people don't reply, it often means they are disengaged from their work or don't believe their opinion is valued. High response rates are usually a positive sign even if people's feedback about certain topics is negative or critical.

Communicating One-on-One: Be a Communication Chameleon

So far we have addressed primarily communication at the organization or team level. Now let's revisit one-on-one interactions, which make up the majority of our workdays. In the last chapter we discussed more formal, feedback- and coaching-related one-on-ones. Now let's expand the topic to include all conversations.

If you've ever felt like you are communicating in a totally different language from your colleagues, especially those of other generations, you are not alone. Too many people believe that effective communication is about communicating the way *you* find easiest or best. Sometimes that works, but what is more important is communicating in the way that will best be *understood* by the person you want to influence.

No matter what your role or job title, if you want to communicate across generations—and all differences—you have to become an expert on how to best communicate with the people you want to communicate with. How do you do that? It's quite simple. You ask.

That's it.

In the wise words of Swedish blogger Henrik Edberg: "Ask instead of guessing. . . . This will help you to minimize unnecessary conflicts, misunderstandings, negativity, and wastes of time and energy."

I recommend beginning with your boss(es), or, if you are the CEO or a business owner, this could be your board of directors or investors. An excellent recommendation for how to approach the ask comes from Harvard Business School professor Michael Watkins and his book *The First 90 Days: Critical Success Strategies for New Leaders at All Levels*. One of his recommended strategies for succeeding in any new role is to have a "style conversation" with your new manager about how you can best communicate with that person.

Instead of wondering and worrying, *Should I e-mail this person? Does this person mind if I stop by to ask questions or should I schedule a meeting? What kind of feedback does this person give?* discuss these preferences in advance. And if for whatever reason that feels untenable, then instead you may ask people who have worked with this person in the past, or you can take time to carefully observe this person's communications to learn the answers.

When I teach workshops to employees on "managing up," I recommend treating your boss as your client. Even if that person's style is not your own, you have to be the one to adapt when you are reporting to someone else. And if you report to multiple people, as is so common in many of today's matrixed organizations, you have to adapt your communication style to each person you report to. My friend Lisa Brill, a law firm partner, advises her associates to be a "communication chameleon."

I apply this myself. For example, e-mail is far and away my favorite communication method, because I best express myself in writing. But if I have a client who prefers to talk on the phone, then I must adapt to their preferences and dial their number.

When you are in the manager or client position, one of the most generous and timesaving actions you can take is to clearly tell the people who work for you exactly how to best communicate with you. It is the employee's responsibility to adapt to the leader's style, but you can make that job a lot easier. For example, does each of your direct reports know the answer to questions like the ones below?

- What is the best way to receive an answer from you quickly? By phone? By e-mail? By instant message? By dropping by your desk?
- How do you give feedback? Should they schedule a one-on-one? Should they come up with their own feedback and present it to you, or do you like to start the conversation? Do you like to give feedback on a regular basis or in a more ad hoc way?
- What are your e-mail preferences and pet peeves? In general,

do you prefer shorter or longer e-mails? Full sentences or
bullet points? Are emojis okay?

- How formal are you? Do u mind quck txts w typos?
- How do you like your documents formatted? What is your
  preferred font? (Believe it or not, I once had a boss who insisted
  on 11-point italic Arial font.)
- Are you open to FaceTiming, Skyping, or videoconferencing
  when they are not in the office?
- What are your general work habits? Are you a morning person
  or should they leave you alone until you've had coffee? Do you
  like to work from home or do you prefer to be in the office? Do
  you leave early on Wednesdays to attend your kid's tae kwon do
  class? Do you catch up and send a flurry of e-mails on Sunday
  nights? (Some leaders add directives to the subject lines of
  their e-mails such as "Not urgent" or "When you are back in the
  office" to advise people on their expectations in terms of timing
  a reply.)

Sometimes people's communication habits are stereotypically
generational—such as a Gen Xer preferring e-mail (guilty!), or a Baby
Boomer preferring the phone—but you absolutely cannot make assumptions about someone's communication preferences based on
their age. I have come across plenty of Boomers who text constantly
as well as plenty of Millennials who love to meet face-to-face. As we
have discussed many times, all members of a given generation—or
gender or ethnic group or level of the organization or job function
or marital status or physical ability—do not communicate the same
way or want to communicate the same way.

To be an effective leader in the multigenerational workplace, the
bottom line is that you must always be mindful, thoughtful, and deliberate about every aspect of your communications. It is no longer
effective to wing it.

IN THE MIX: LET'S TALK ABOUT SLACK

If you work at a company that uses Slack, you likely think of nothing else. If you work at a company without Slack, you may never have heard of it. (As a member of the generation stereotyped as "slackers," I have to admit it gives me enormous pleasure that one of the hottest topics in workplace communication today carries this name.)

For those not familiar, Slack is an app—viewable on desktop or mobile—that describes itself as a shared "hub" where members communicate and collaborate. The platform appears a lot like a very large text message chain with people posting written messages, visual images (including plenty of GIFs and emojis), and shared documents. The name is an acronym for "Searchable Log of All Conversation and Knowledge." As of 2018, Slack reported over 8 million active daily users worldwide.

I myself have personally struggled to adopt Slack, mostly because it has felt like yet another communication tool added to many others. Knowing that I need to embrace it, I reached out to two heavy Slack users, one Millennial and one Gen Xer, one from a small consultancy and one from a large corporation, for their take on Slack and its role as a tool for remixers.

First up is Millennial Jillian Kramer, vice president of research for Ypulse. Jillian describes Slack's main value as "an archive of every idea we've ever had as a company. For example, we have a Slack thread for each client project. There might be fifty-seven messages back and forth, approving documents and timelines. Everything is organized together in one place, which is not possible with e-mail. On Slack, everything for one client can be funneled in one spot."

Jillian also points to the casual aspect of Slack, which can boost the workday online in the same way that office banter or water cooler interactions can improve morale in real life. "The emojis are a nice way to lighten your day," she says. "You can also use Slack to publicly say thanks or give your colleagues points of encouragement."

For my Gen X peer Stefanie Spurlin, vice president of workplace solutions for Capital One, Slack did not come as naturally, but she became an avid user thanks to her Millennial team.

"I have some team members very ingrained in the agile practice of doing work, and they started using Slack as a tool to facilitate how they were communicating and sharing information," Stefanie told me. "For me, e-mail was my main form of communication. One of my team members who reports to me challenged me to use Slack and gave me a tutorial. Now I only communicate with them on Slack. I've even introduced the tool to an organization I'm involved in outside of work as a communication vehicle."

I admitted to Stefanie, Gen Xer to Gen Xer, that I still didn't get it. What's wrong with my beloved e-mail?

"Think of it this way," she said patiently. "Imagine you are having a conversation at the dinner table. You step away from the table to take a phone call and then come back and rejoin the conversation. Other people have been communicating while you have been away. On Slack you have that entire history. It's super-searchable and includes conversations and documents. You don't miss or lose anything. There is still a need for e-mail, especially to communicate with people outside of your team or organization, but there is less e-mail, which is a definite benefit."

I was starting to feel convinced, and then, unprompted, Stefanie called out the same value of Slack that Jillian did: "It's also great as a recognition channel," she said. "I love how people use it to give shout-outs and props and recognition throughout the day."

Remixer Rule #8 is that everybody wins. Everybody deserves recognition and praise. And, as we know, acknowledgment is one of the most effective, time-tested management tools for all generations. If Slack is providing a better way to acknowledge employees, then I am all for it.

The Daily Communication Remix

There are infinite opportunities every day to communicate more transparently and effectively across generations. Knowing that all individuals and organizations are different, here are a few more strategies to try.

SHARE MORE DOCUMENTS. More organizations are switching to collaborative platforms like Google Docs and SharePoint to make information more available. Whereas in the past one person "owned" a document, today it's possible for multiple people to collaborate in real time on shared work products. If this is a new practice for you, just try collaborating on a single shared document and see if it improves the final result or shortens the time it takes to complete the work. If you're not yet ready to collaborate in real time, think about documents you are willing to post to shared employee drives for colleagues who might want to access them, such as an industry analysis or client history overview. Consider how much work is probably being duplicated when everyone works separately.

KEEP IT SHORT AND SIMPLE. Sometimes I find when leaders attempt to appeal to multiple generations with their communications, they default to simply writing or saying more words—as if the more they talk, the more likely someone will find something to connect with. This is not only ineffective but also, frankly, lazy. As Mark Twain said—apparently apocryphally, but I love it anyway—"I would have written a shorter letter but I didn't have the time." The best approach to reach the most people is to simplify your communications as much as possible.

REMIX YOUR MEETINGS. A simple meeting remix is to ask participants in a regular meeting to sit in different seats from usual. This can help less-tenured employees or those in back-office functions to achieve more visibility if they usually sit in the back of a room or otherwise away from the action.

Another idea is to host a meeting in a different location from usual, such as in the company cafeteria or in an area of your organization's premises that your team rarely visits.

When working with employees across time zones, it is a best practice to rotate the time of the meetings so no one region is always staying late or speaking in the middle of the night. Some teams even rotate the leader of regular meetings so employees of all generations and levels have the opportunity to take the helm.

BE MORE VISUAL. There is nothing as classic as the saying "A picture is worth a thousand words" and few trends as popular right now as visual social networks such as Instagram and YouTube. Where can you remix any of your communications with the addition of more visuals? Can you record a quick video message to thank an employee rather than sending an e-mail? Can you revise an upcoming presentation to include more photos or an infographic? If you haven't yet added a photo to your LinkedIn profile or internal social network, now would be a great time to step out of your comfort zone.

As you think about remixing your communications and begin to implement some of the strategies we've discussed in this chapter, you might find there are areas where you or your colleagues need additional skill building. The next chapter, on the training and development remix, has you covered.

CHAPTER 6: KEY TAKEAWAYS

- The communication remix involves acknowledging that communication in organizations has moved from primarily top-down to more transparent and two-way.

- Generational differences are most acutely experienced around communication issues. Companies that teach diverse colleagues how to communicate more effectively with one another will have a tremendous advantage.

- In today's world of social media, people expect their leaders to be accessible and almost all conversations to be two-way. This means if you are a senior leader, your employees will expect you to be more visible and transparent. This is not optional.

- With salary transparency a growing trend, now is the time for leadership to thoroughly review your organization's pay structure. What would happen if suddenly all salaries became public? Would the organization be comfortable with that information being available?

- To most efficiently communicate across an organization today, the recommended remix is to COPE: create once, publish everywhere. This means offering information in multiple formats and styles—short, long, formal, informal, audio, video, written, etc.—to reach people of different generations, schedules, locations, job functions, family situations, and learning preferences.

- Good multigenerational communicators are good listeners, and listening doesn't have to be complicated. Consider implementing formal or informal employee surveys, focus groups, question-and-answer sessions, and town halls to listen to employees more frequently.

- The best way to communicate one-on-one and ensure
  your messages are heard and understood is to become a
  communication chameleon. Ask your key stakeholders how
  they prefer to communicate and share your preferences with
  the people you lead.

7 THE TRAINING AND DEVELOPMENT REMIX

Everyone Is a Valedictorian

WHEN TRADITIONALISTS, BOOMERS, and Gen Xers started a job, typically we were given an outdated training manual and a throwaway offer to "ask questions if you need to." Then maybe once a year we would attend a training class on a new software program. We learned on the job and we often did just fine.

Times have seriously changed.

Today, business operations often evolve too quickly to keep a manual current. Updated software programs are introduced every day or week, not once a year. New roles with new skill requirements are arising with unprecedented frequency.

What is the remix between a training desert and a training fire hose?

In this instance, I do not recommend a compromise. In our VUCA world, in which entire industries can collapse overnight and automation may soon make many jobs and careers obsolete, this is a clear case of needing to add to "classic" practices. In other words, I'm team fire hose.

The training and development remix involves expanding our thinking about how much training and development to provide employees of all levels. It's certainly not radical to believe that employees need training. What is radical is how much more training is necessary today and the currency that training carries with employees.

This is especially true for Millennials. According to one study, a whopping 65 percent of Millennials said the opportunity for personal development is the *number one* element they desire in a job. And, yes, that means they often want training even more than money, which only 21 percent of Millennials in the same study identified as the top reason for accepting a position.

Let's pause for a moment and make sure this point is perfectly, absolutely clear: today's Millennial employees—the majority of the American workforce now and for the next several decades—would often prefer learning opportunities to cold, hard cash.

Writing in the *Atlantic* about why Millennials aren't buying homes at the same rate as previous American generations, journalists Derek Thompson and Jordan Weissmann put it like this: "In an ideas economy, up-to-date knowledge could be a more nimble and valuable asset than a house."

Millennials are not the only ones valuing knowledge so highly. Given declining net worths since the Great Recession, the elimination of pension plans, and fears that Social Security will run out of money before many Americans are able to collect it, many people's greatest asset is their employability. This means that employers who provide ongoing training and development in the years to come will have a distinct advantage in attracting and retaining talent of all generations.

Begin on Day One

You begin to retain or lose employees from the very first moment they accept your offer. This means that training must begin that same day for employees at all levels.

This reality should empower you. Every moment, including the first, is a new opportunity to build each person's contribution and commitment, starting with some simple early strategies that appeal to all generations. And yet, one study recently found that 50 percent of new employees receive no onboarding training whatsoever. Onboarding training should involve the "hard skills" of learning to do the job for which the employee has been hired, but also training in your organization's culture, people, and processes.

Tricia Linderman admits that Texas Capital Bank used to welcome new employees the old-fashioned way: by not doing much at all. "We spent so much time recruiting people and then, when they started the job, we said, 'Good luck!' We thought if we hired smart people, they would know what to do. Now I am passionate about onboarding because I have seen the positive result on our culture."

Today, every new hire in every position at every level at Texas Capital Bank attends the same full-day orientation at the bank's Dallas headquarters. A receptionist, a bank teller, and the company's new chief risk officer might all be sitting next to each other during training.

"We integrate people into our culture very quickly by bringing everyone to orientation," says Tricia. "No matter what position or location you are hired into, you spend a whole day in Dallas and meet leaders from across the company. Our CEO and chief lending officer spend time with all new hires and tell our story. When people leave orientation, they know what this place is about."

Liz Wiseman, author of *Rookie Smarts: Why Learning Beats Knowing in the New Game of Work*, advises employers to think even bigger and remix their expectations of new employees. She suggests that employers ask their "rookies," whom she defines as employees of any age or career stage who are new to an organization, to make a difference to the company right away.

According to Wiseman, eBay revamped its onboarding process to both teach new employees about the company and explicitly invite them to make an immediate contribution. The directive to rookies was to jump in and share their ideas without holding back. One group of newbies a few years ago submitted an average of 25 percent more ideas for patents in their first few months of work—and more that ultimately led to formal submissions—than the entire rest of the company.

If your onboarding efforts could use a remix, try this:

REACH OUT IN ADVANCE. Have all the people who interviewed the new hire send a welcome message in advance and plan to come up and say hello on their first day. A quick note or video from team members can ease a new person's transition and, with video especially, put names with faces and help to forge earlier collaboration opportunities. Encourage teammates to reach out to connect in advance on LinkedIn as well.

ASSIGN AN ONBOARDING BUDDY. Some organizations match each new hire with a buddy to help them feel welcome and have a person to ask questions who isn't their direct boss. You might choose a person with a particular affinity—perhaps alumni of the same university or a fellow veteran.

CONNECT THEM IMMEDIATELY. Make sure a new employee's e-mail address and phone are set up if they work in an office or remotely, or their uniform and locker are prepared if they work in a retail or factory environment, or prepare in advance whatever else will make someone ready to communicate with their team from day one. Having the right tools will make the employee feel that their team wants to connect with them immediately, both literally and figuratively.

OUTFIT THEM FOR YOUR TEAM. I always love that moment during a sports draft when the chosen player is given a premade jersey of the team they have joined with their name stitched on the back. The athlete holds the jersey in triumph, the audience cheers, and the cameras flash. Wouldn't it be cool if a new employee were that excited to join your team? While calling the paparazzi might be a bit much, you can still provide new people with some branding. To serve all generations and preferences, provide a combination of "old-school" and "new-school" (Remixer Rule #4: Think "and," not "or"), such as a branded notebook and pen as well as a preinstalled desktop screensaver and company PopSocket for the back of their mobile phone.

When Tiffany Kuck, the Millennial insurance professional you met in chapter 3, accepted her offer to join McGohan Brabender in Dayton, she received a delivery to her home of a bouquet of flowers and a laptop bag. I love that combination of one welcome gift to keep at home and one item to bring to the office. I also consider such welcome gifts to be a sign of gratitude. It is common practice to thank an employer after a job interview; in today's world where employees have more choice, why shouldn't the employer thank the job candidate for accepting their offer?

What Makes a Modern Skill Set?

As I have mentioned, I have truly never, in over a decade of studying Millennials, heard people complain that this generation is not as smart as previous cohorts. What I do hear people say is that today's younger professionals are lacking in certain soft skills that more experienced workers consider to be "common sense." Likewise, younger workers are often shocked at the lack of technological understanding and aptitude of some longer-tenured workers. The reality is likely that people have always entered the workplace with vastly different skill sets, but the differences are starker today because of the speed of technological change we've been experiencing and the wider spread of ages in the labor force.

What this means is that managing the multigenerational mix requires leaders to get clear on the exact skills that employees need to have at every level. And you might have to train and develop people in ways that might be surprising. Remember Remixer Rule #5: Common sense is not so common.

I have led training sessions for high-potential junior talent at top-tier corporations that have included the following topics, which might have been considered common sense to earlier generations of professionals:

- How to answer a phone professionally
- How to write professional e-mails
- How to have a face-to-face meeting
- How to appropriately decline a job offer (Yes, some employers are volunteering to teach college recruits how to decline their own job offers because the lack of knowledge and etiquette—including "ghosting" after a formal job offer or even after starting a job—has become a pain point for employers of Millennial and Gen Z talent)

When you haven't grown up learning how to do these types of things on a regular basis, you might not know how to do them.

For example, just think about the phone. When I was growing up in the 1980s and 1990s, everyone had a house phone, and for most of my childhood there was no such thing as caller ID. I had to answer calls from my parents' friends and work associates. I had to speak politely to my friends' parents when I called their houses. I had to call to order pizza. I had to call to request college applications. I had to call my boss at the video store if I was sick. There were no options other than the phone.

Young people today generally didn't grow up with house phones, almost always had caller ID, and could often use e-mail or texting to avoid potentially prickly interactions. This has made many of them not just uncomfortable but actually fearful of using the phone. A young insurance company employee said to me recently, "I don't like answering the phone at work because I don't know what the other person is going to say."

I have enormous empathy for this feeling. If you've spent most of your life texting and e-mailing, this discomfort makes total sense. You don't know what you don't know, especially when starting out in the workplace for the first time. I'll never forget the first time I negotiated a contract at WorkingWoman.com. I made edits directly to the text of the contract and was yelled at for not using Track Changes. I had never heard of Track Changes.

There is some value in learning things the hard way—you better believe I learned how to use Track Changes after that experience— but organizations and individual leaders can and should anticipate many of the common mistakes entry-level employees make. I'm simply referring to keeping a list of the skills or knowledge you notice are lacking with each new hire and making sure the next person receives training on those things more deliberately.

If talking on the phone is important to success in your organization and you notice a lack of this skill in recent grads, then you need to offer training in how to do it well.

(Now you do want to put your marketing hat on. I don't advise offering a training class called "How to Answer the Phone." You probably want to call it something appealing like "Executive Leadership Communication Skills.")

If you are a Millennial, you might be surprised by some of the knowledge or skills your Traditionalist, Boomer, or Gen Xer colleagues don't possess. This might relate to cultural references (insert name of celebrity I have never heard of), work methods (the "new math," anyone?), or tech etiquette (free tip: when you are on a FaceTime or video call, look up at the camera, not down at the screen!). For example, I had a Millennial colleague invite me to "slide into her DMs." "I'd love to," I replied, "if you can explain to me what that means."

If you are adamant that you want your employees to be thrown in the deep end of the pool and learn by making some mistakes, then I would advise that you say so. Instead of making someone feel fear or shame about what they don't know, a coach-style leader might say something like "I'm not going to give you a lot of direction on this project, because I want to see what you can do on your own. You're going to make a lot of mistakes, but that's how I want you to learn."

A powerful case study in thorough employee training comes from an unexpected industry: fast food. It is Pal's Sudden Service, a burger and hot dog joint that provides extensive employee training at all levels. CEO Thomas Crosby has said, "We realized that we are in the education business, just like any school or university."

Crosby takes employee education to a new level. "Schools are usually satisfied with having a valedictorian in each class, a range of people they graduate, and those that don't make the grade," says Crosby. "We want everybody that we hire to be the equivalent of a valedictorian if we are going to beat the competition."

At Pal's, this means teaching employees every single aspect of the business, ranging from how to iron the employee uniform to statistical quality control to how to get french fries to stand up straight in a bag. The goal of all training is mastery and excellence, and employees who demonstrate that are eligible to become coaches of other employees.

It is also a reminder of the importance of making no assumptions about what people know and don't know when they join your organization at any level. Recall Vince Lombardi's famous speech to the

Green Bay Packers on their first day of training camp after ending the previous season with a heartbreaking loss in the championship. "Gentlemen," he said, holding a pigskin in his right hand, "this is a football." The more complex our world becomes, the more we need to revisit the basics.

Reskilling for the Age of Automation and Augmentation

All the training we have talked about thus far relates to the skills needed in the workplace of today. But what about tomorrow? And the next ten years? Huge changes are barreling toward us in the form of automation, virtual and augmented reality, artificial intelligence, and who knows what else. As just one data point, the World Economic Forum predicts that machines will do 42 percent of our labor by 2022, causing 75 million workers to lose their jobs in that time period. Many are referring to this as the Fourth Industrial Revolution, and it is coming at us quickly.

The usual reaction to such statistics is shock and fear—and rightly so. But there is a big "if" in many of the automation predictions: *if* workers are reskilled for the newly automated workplace, the World Economic Forum says, employers *could* create 133 million new jobs in that same time period, more than compensating for the jobs lost. That is a remix of epic proportions.

I am not an expert on this topic, so I have turned to more knowledgeable sources to help me understand how to discuss this issue with my clients and with you.

According to futurist Tom Cheesewright, it is important to understand the difference between automation—robots replacing the work of people—and augmentation, which expands and enhances human capabilities rather than replacing them, and might even help make people better at their jobs.

Researchers from Deloitte argue that the best way for leaders to prepare for the future of automation and augmentation is to focus on defining the difference between essential human *skills*, such as creative and ethical thinking, and nonessential *tasks*, which can be managed by machines. An example of augmentation that you may have already experienced as a customer is when an airline uses a chatbot to uncover useful information, such as your itinerary, and then a human customer service rep steps in to handle more complicated problems that require negotiation and empathy.

To demonstrate how augmentation can add more jobs than it replaces, consider that bank ATMs, for example, have actually increased the overall number of bank tellers, who are now freed up to advise and sell to customers rather than conducting basic transactions. Automation and augmentation can also be used to help companies employ older workers as our population continues to age. BMW and Nissan have designed "cobots"—collaborative robots—that help employees lift heavier objects.

What does this mean for you as a leader of yourself and others? In short, be prepared and learn the landscape. You don't necessarily have to be an early adopter, but you can't ignore the coming changes, either. Pay attention to the most talked-about technologies related to the work of your job function, your organization, and your industry. Approach the most tech-savvy people in your field about what developments they are following. Sit in on the most future-focused sessions at any conference you attend. And then share everything you learn with the people you work with.

Freelancers, it appears, are leading the way. In a recent study, this group of workers reported being nearly twice as prepared to succeed in a world where artificial intelligence or automated technology augments or replaces the work of humans—and 30 percent of nonfreelancers agreed with that assessment. Perhaps the preparedness of freelancers is because they are taking it upon themselves to reskill: the same study found that more than half of freelancers participated in a reskilling sometime in the last six months, compared to less than a third of non-freelancers who did so.

AT&T, which employs 250,000 people, determined that nearly half of its workers lacked the skills they would need to keep the company competitive in the future. The company faced a choice, said its vice president of human resources, Bill Blase: "We could go out and try to hire all these software and engineering people and probably pay through the nose to get them, but even that wouldn't have been adequate, or we could try to reskill our existing workforce so they could be competent in the technology and the skills required to run the business going forward."

They chose the latter, and embarked on one of the largest mass reskilling efforts in history. Known as Future Ready, the initiative is a $1 billion effort that includes online courses, collaborations with online and traditional universities, and an internal career center that allows employees to identify and train for new jobs at the company. In 2017 the company provided an average of more than 78 hours of training per employee (compared to the average of 42.2 hours for employers with 10,000 employees or more). Other large companies like Boeing, Disney, and Accenture have launched similarly expansive education programs for employees.

Salesforce is not only reskilling its own workforce but also making its training programs available outside the company. The 10,000-employee tech company has adapted its customer training program to train its own contractors—and anyone else—with new, job-specific skills for the future. The program, called Trailhead, is free, available online to the public, and plans to reach 10 million users—called "Trailblazers"—by the end of 2019. A survey found that one in four Trailhead users found a new job because of the program.

While these large corporate programs have received a lot of press, they are far from common. Only 3 percent of organizations overall report planning to dedicate significantly more resources to upskilling their workers in the next three years.

In 2018, MIT took the ambitious step of raising $1 billion to create an entirely new college for artificial intelligence. The goal of the college, MIT's president L. Rafael Reif announced, is to "educate the bilinguals of the future," whom he defines as people in fields such as biology, chemistry, and the humanities who are also skilled in modern computing. Rather than positioning automation or technology as replacing more traditional academic disciplines, the goal of the college is to create a remix. As MIT's dean of humanities, Melissa Nobles, said, "That's how the humanities are going to survive—not by running from the future but by embracing it."

If you don't have access to the above programs, how can you as an individual leader prepare for the future of automation when so much is still uncertain? I asked Alexandra Levit, author of *Humanity Works: Merging Technologies and People for the Workforce of the Future* and an expert on the future of work, for her advice. What she recommends first and foremost is a change in perception.

In addition to paying attention to trends in your industry, she advises individual leaders to see the coming changes as an opportunity. "Consider where automation can add value to *your* career or business," Alexandra says. "There is already software helping with everything from CRM [customer relationship management] and marketing to financial management and time tracking. Spend some time reassessing how you can save time and money by streamlining administrative tasks with the available technology."

When you think of all the ways you likely already use augmentation personally, such as asking directions from Siri or using Gmail's auto-complete to process e-mails more quickly, it can make reskilling for the future feel less intimidating.

The Perils of Training and Reskilling

You may be thinking at this point, perhaps because you have been burned before, "But what if I provide my employees all this training and reskilling and then they leave?"

At Pal's Sudden Service, leaders have made a conscious effort to be okay with that potential outcome. Thomas Crosby has said, "We want the experience here to be that, for your entire life, when you're a doctor or a chemical engineer, you'll look back and say, 'The things I learned at Pal's I still apply today.'"

Yes, people may leave after you train them. Keep in mind, however, that training itself is a remarkably effective retention tool, which is another reason I advocate for more of it.

This is true even in an industry known for high turnover. At Pal's, turnover at the assistant manager level is a remarkably low 1.4 percent. At the front lines, turnover is 32 percent, roughly a third of the fast-food industry standard.

Training is undoubtedly a big investment of time and money. But what if we don't train people and they stay? Isn't it worth the risk? In an ideal world, all employers would take responsibility for training people, and we could be satisfied knowing that somewhere another leader is paying for training for an employee who might someday leave that company and come to ours, bringing that expertise with them. This is not an ideal world, though, so some risk is necessary.

Recently, Laszlo Bock, formerly of Google and currently CEO and founder of the Silicon Valley start-up Humu, was among the first leaders I've come across to challenge "the way things have always been done" when it comes to concerns about other companies poaching the talent you've worked hard to train. Bock announced that Humu would stop including a non-solicit clause in employee contracts.

"Since most startups (including Humu) get our templates from the same handful of law firms," Bock explained in an article he wrote, "these clauses go in by default, barring employees who leave a company and join a new one from inviting former colleagues to join their new cause, usually for at least a year."

Among the reasons Bock cited for eliminating these clauses from Humu's employee contracts is that it forces his organization to be better.

As he says, "If I know that when employees leave they are prohibited from recruiting my people, I work that much less hard on creating a strong culture. On the other hand, if I know that everyone who leaves for something better can turn around and recruit my best people, I'm left with no option but to create an amazing work environment. I'm forced to compete for talent not only when I recruit, but on each day that someone is with me."

According to Bock about his time at Google, "For 11 years I encouraged my staff to go out and interview for other jobs at least once a year. This forced me to invest in their growth, and to prioritize culture. I didn't lose a single person."

Today's leaders need to think of training your team members as a lifelong investment in your relationships with those people. At a time when companies rise and fall and merge with more frequency than ever before, this makes good sense. As HR expert Jaime Klein describes the ideal relationship, "I am going to invest in you while you are here and teach you as much as I can, and we are colleagues for life. You might be the one recruiting me in twenty years!"

Serving Multigenerational Training Needs

Once you agree that employees need robust, ongoing training, the next issue to address is how to deliver that training to employees with a wide variety of developmental needs and learning preferences. This is a good time to incorporate Remixer Rule #4: Think "and," not "or."

Here are a wide variety of strategies—macro, micro, and mixable—for training and developing your multigenerational employees with a "hybrid learning" approach that combines live and virtual components. Try this:

REMIX YOUR TRAINING MIX. As someone who delivers a lot of workshops, I can report that many organizations are remarkably rigid about their training offerings. I'm surprised by how often I hear statements like "We never offer trainings longer than an hour—our people get antsy" or "We only do all-day trainings—our people like a thorough program" or "We don't do online training." It is simply not the case that all employees want the exact same format or that the same format is the best for vastly different training topics. The answer is usually—you guessed it—a remix.

For many years, individual contributors at Citi had participated in a two-day in-person leadership course. Recently the company's learning leaders reassessed this program and converted it into a multi-modality virtual program where employees convene virtually once a week over five weeks, do self-paced video assessments, and work together in cohorts. When the participants convene virtually, they work as these cohorts in virtual "breakout rooms" and interact as a larger group by using online polls and whiteboards collaboratively.

According to Laine Joelson Cohen, director and North America regional lead of Citi Learning, this approach has a number of benefits. It sustains learning over a longer period of time, provides employees with the opportunity to build their internal networks, enables people to work at their own pace and with their own learning styles, and limits people's time away from the office.

That doesn't mean all training at Citi will follow the same model.

The company is currently redesigning its new manager onboarding training, and Laine wants to cocreate the program with employees. To do this, her team is hosting a hackathon, bringing together current new managers to help design the new offering.

MAKE TRAINING (AND RETRAINING) ACCESSIBLE TO ALL. Do your longer-tenured employees receive as much training as people new to their positions? Is it clear to employees at every level exactly which skills are required to do their jobs today? If so, when was the last time you updated this list for long-tenured employees in particular? During every shift at Pal's, a computer randomly chooses the names of two to four employees at each location to be recertified on a skill. "It's our belief that human beings, just like machines, need to be recalibrated," says Thomas Crosby, the CEO.

In 2018, The Estée Lauder Companies partnered with LinkedIn Learning to offer online education and training to all of its full-time office employees across generations, job functions, and various regions around the world. Employees can choose what they want to learn, including both hard skills and soft skills, and the company also has experts curating what topics would be best for employees in different roles.

According to Phebe Farrow Port, chief of staff to the president and CEO and senior vice president of global management strategies, The Estée Lauder Companies chose to offer this training benefit because, after much research, the company felt that LinkedIn Learning offered the most comprehensive subject matter and compelling ways to view content. After selecting LinkedIn Learning, they discovered that over nine hundred employees had already signed up for the service on their own. From executive assistants to executive leaders, employees wanted to upskill and reskill on such topics as leadership, social media, and data analytics—the exact areas in which the company had been focusing its training efforts.

The Estée Lauder Companies is wise to acknowledge that its

employees are interested in seeking out learning and development opportunities and to fully support and supplement that desire. Providing meaningful training across generations and levels of your team promotes engagement, career advancement, and the innovation required to succeed in today's tech-driven business environment. If you don't offer it, it is possible your employees will take it upon themselves to reskill—and then take those skills elsewhere.

EMBRACE MICRO-LEARNING. Today's employees are busier than ever, so smart organizations create training that fits into their schedules. To borrow from the consumer world, think of the popularity of YouTube beauty tutorials as a model. You could watch a thirty-minute video on creating an entire nighttime look or a thirty-second video on the single topic of how to apply liquid eyeliner. Micro-learning modules—in the form of short videos, blog posts, audio recordings, e-mail updates, infographics, quizzes, or even text messages—can provide employees with learning and development when they are at their desks, at home, traveling, or anywhere else they need a quick information boost. I know I have gotten little helpful tidbits of training simply by scrolling through my Twitter feed. That counts as learning just as much as paying for an expensive conference. It's just shorter. Where can you offer more micro-training modules by splitting larger topics into smaller chunks of education?

OUTSOURCE. Employers have been hiring subject matter experts to train their employees for decades, but a variety of new services have popped up to assist in employee training, especially on higher-tech topics. For example, employer-financed programs account for about half of the business of General Assembly, a company that offers classes for coding and other skills. GA can customize its curriculum for companies' most immediate needs. According to Charlie Schilling, a general manager at General Assembly, "Someone can take an assessment on a Friday, sit through a part-time data science class in a week or two weeks depending on their flexibility, and immediately return to their job and do things in new ways."

OFFER STAFF-LED TRAINING AND DEVELOPMENT. In addition to working with external trainers, consider tapping your own internal talent as well. At Synchrony, many training programs are facilitated from within, after leveraging an external lens to explore industry best practices. Stephen Kennedy says this is especially important for the training programs delivered to entry-level talent in the rotational Business Leadership Program. "We invite staff, from BLPs' peers to senior executives, to present on their areas of expertise. This helps build a bridge at the company between generations. For example, if a Boomer is presenting, she is also connecting with and hearing from the Millennials she is training and learning what questions they are asking." This type of internal cross-pollinating through training can take place at any level, from members of any generation to another, depending on the subject matter.

ADVOCATE EXPERIENTIAL AND ROTATIONAL LEARNING OPPORTUNITIES. In rethinking your mix of training opportunities for employees, also consider how people of different skill sets, generations, and tenures at your organization can learn from experiential opportunities, such as rotational programs, special assignments, department or client secondments (a.k.a. temporary assignments), and more. At one insurance company I've worked with, managers get together and offer employees the opportunity for informal micro-rotations, in which an employee from one team might work on a short-term project with another team. Or an employee from one team might sit in on a few meetings of another group to learn more about that group's function.

Rotational programs can take a lot of work to create if they are not already ingrained in your culture, but they yield impressive results. According to the National Association of Colleges and Employers (NACE), about 43 percent of large employers have a rotational program for new hires, but—not surprisingly—they are far less common in smaller employers with under five hundred employees, only about 7 percent of which offer rotational experiences.

As a tool for retaining Millennial employees, the programs do pay off. A 2016 study by the NACE found that organizations with a rotational program had a one-year retention rate of 91.1 percent, compared to 72.3 percent at companies without them, and a five-year retention rate of 70.9 percent versus 59.8 percent for those without a program.

Reed Smith began offering an internal secondment program based on the suggestions of the law firm's own associates. According to Casey Ryan of Reed Smith, "Internal secondments started because we had an associate in London who made a compelling argument about why the client needed her to be in Paris. We approved a two-week secondment and that turned into two months. Clients told us they appreciated meeting the associate in person, and as a result more work has followed. It also had the added benefit of allowing the London associate to get to know the Paris lawyers much better, and overall created a stronger bond between our Paris and London lawyers. Because a lot of our work is done in teams, the secondment created a double benefit.

"That led to the broader program, and it's clear why: interoffice secondments require a pretty modest investment, they are not hard to implement, and they lead to better working relationships and better client results."

TRAIN PEOPLE TO LEAD. A worrisome study by CareerBuilder found that 58 percent of managers report having received no people management training at all. As we discussed in chapter 5, people management has been due for a remix for a long time, but it is more important now than ever, given the fact that a new generation of leaders is taking the reins at so many organizations. We should all be concerned by the findings of a Deloitte study that 64 percent of Millennial leaders felt unprepared when entering their first leadership role. As you know, it is the goal of my work and this book to help change this.

One realm where leadership training is not lacking is in the military. Michael Abrams of Columbia University's Center for Veteran Transition and Integration told me that not only does the military provide all its soldiers with leadership training, they provide leadership training *before* skills training. What would happen in your organization if every single employee had training in leadership from day one?

What About Actual Schools?

The CEO of Pal's Sudden Service believes that employers today must be like schools, but where does that leave *actual* schools in the remix conversation? What is the role of our education system—particularly colleges and universities—in training the workforce of today and tomorrow?

It is a fraught topic, to say the least. According to Gallup, while 96 percent of chief academic officers at higher education institutions say they are effectively preparing students for work, only 11 percent of business leaders strongly agree.

Yikes.

To better understand this gap—and what we might need to do about it—I reached out to Farouk Dey, vice provost for integrative learning and life design at Johns Hopkins University. Farouk, who has also held leadership positions in career services at Stanford University, Carnegie Mellon University, and the University of Florida (and started as an RA like me!), spoke candidly about this issue.

"There is absolutely a gap between higher education and the world of work," he told me. "Some say higher education is not preparing students for the jobs of tomorrow—but I worry about not preparing them for the jobs of today!

"Most schools are mainly focused on providing an academic experience and may be missing the integration of all the learning that happens outside the classroom. While I agree that the goal of higher education is to shape global citizens and expand their minds, we need to do more to prepare talent for the future workforce.

"Right now, industry still hires from higher education and sees value in it," he continued. "They haven't walked away yet. But companies are investing in education like boot camps to train their own employees, and that is the beginning of the disruption."

Farouk's goal is to remix higher education and career services using yet another example of Remixer Rule #4: Think "and," not "or." His vision is for higher education to provide students with a holistic, or "integrative," learning experience.

As such, he had to remix his own job first. At Johns Hopkins, he is the first career services professional to have a seat at the university senior leadership table and to have influence over curriculum educational structures. He led the university in reconstructing a whole set of departments to create a fully holistic learning experience that helps bridge the gap between higher education and industry. There is now collaboration among previously disparate areas of the university, including undergraduate research, study abroad, on-campus employment, alumni relations, and the university's technology ventures incubator.

I am inclined to agree with Farouk, especially given the exorbitant cost of higher education. If schools don't adapt to the next generation of students, they will go elsewhere for educational resources and career readiness.

Lifelong Learning

Farouk's former colleagues at the Hasso Plattner Institute of Design at Stanford, commonly known as the d.school, have put forth a remixed, hybrid vision of higher education. In 2014 the school sponsored a project called Stanford 2025, which asked students to envision a university of the future. One of the concepts that emerged is that of Open Loop University, in which students would "loop in" and "loop out" for six years of total study with no graduation year. Under this system, students could "loop out" after two years to go work and then "loop in" a few years later to use more of their time, and then come back to retrain for a new career in their 30s, 50s, 70s, or whenever.

Forward-thinking professionals have adopted this model on their own. Emma Lee Hartle, a Baby Boomer community college employee who recently changed jobs late in her career, credits her career longevity to her growth mindset and willingness to reskill.

"In my former job," she told me, "I was 54 and the youngest of the four people in my role, but I was the only one who went on to get more training. I got a new certification for résumé writing in 2011 and a coaching certification in 2013. I know we've all been teaching this stuff since the '70s, but things change. We are not using typewriters or requiring skirt suits anymore, and LinkedIn is essential for our students now. You have to have a willingness to keep learning."

Northeastern University has already started referring to "learners" rather than "students" to reflect the expansion of higher education beyond traditional college-age students.

"Through Northeastern's regional and online programs, we are available to all learners, all levels, and all locations beyond our main campus in Boston," says Manny Contomanolis, the university's senior associate vice president for employer engagement and career design.

"'Learners' is deliberately meant to be multigenerational. When you refer to somebody as a learner as opposed to a student, it suggests a different set of responsibilities. 'Student' sometimes implies a passive receptacle. A learner is a more active participant, and the term is more inclusive. It doesn't matter if you are online, on campus, working and taking classes part-time, older, younger. Learners are learners. I'd like to think we'll see more language like this," he told me.

Manny is absolutely right, and many universities are already catering to multigenerational learners. One of the pioneers of this practice is Dr. Philip Pizzo, founding director of the Stanford Distinguished Careers Institute, a one-year fellowship for successful professionals, mostly Baby Boomers, seeking their "next act."

Pizzo has said, "Since the eleventh century, universities have focused on young people. Now, with longevity being what it is, we need to expand the role to lifelong learning and intergenerational learning and teaching."

Lynda Gratton and Andrew Scott, authors of *The 100-Year Life: Living and Working in an Age of Longevity*, agree: "It is impossible that a single shot of education, administered in childhood and early adulthood, will be able to support a sustained, sixty-year career."

The Stanford program has launched many similar versions, including one at the University of Minnesota, which mixes the fellows in some classes with traditional age (Gen Z) college students. Not surprisingly, one 20-year-old student taking a multigenerational class called The Future of Work and Life in the 21st Century commented, "The first time I walked into the class I was like, 'Why are there a bunch of old people in here with us?' I was afraid it was going to feel like taking a class with my mom." But as the semester advanced, she began to see the incredible value of a multigenerational perspective. "My peers aren't in the workforce. [The Baby Boomer fellows] were able to share the problems they have actually seen."

It makes sense to me that one of the best ways to ensure we are preparing young students for the workplace is to bring the workplace to them. In the next chapter we will explore multigenerational relationships in more detail, through the experience of a variety of forms of mentoring and networking.

CHAPTER 7: KEY TAKEAWAYS

- The training and development remix involves expanding our thinking about how much training and development to provide employees of all levels, roles, ages, and tenures.
- Today's Millennial employees—the majority of the American workforce—would often prefer learning and development opportunities to money. They understand that in today's world of ever-changing disruptions, keeping one's skill set sharp is the most valuable commodity.
- Many companies fail to appreciate the importance of onboarding, but this is a critical moment to begin retaining employees of all generations. Help people feel welcome, informed, connected, and valuable from their first day on the job.
- Get clear on the exact skills that your employees need to have at every level, and make no assumptions about what people know and don't know, from how to answer a phone professionally, to how to update software, to how to manage a client. Emphasize the importance of mastering the fundamentals at every level.
- The best way for you as an individual leader to prepare for the future of automation and augmentation is to educate yourself and your team early and often. Pay attention to any up-and-coming technologies related to the work of your job function, your organization, and your industry.
- It can be painful to train employees who might eventually take their skills elsewhere, but you need to train everyone anyway. Think of educating your team members as both a way to serve your organization today and as a lifelong investment in your relationships with these individuals.
- To provide the most effective training to a multigenerational workforce, experiment with multifaceted, hybrid options.

Consider online and off-line courses, various lengths of
training offerings, individual coaching, educational games and
quizzes, bite-sized videos, rotational assignments, and more.
Be creative and track results to see what is most effective with
your mix of employees.

- Consider yourself a lifelong learner whose education does
not stop with graduation from school. We will likely see more
colleges and universities embrace a lifelong learning model,
perhaps inviting them to "loop in" and "loop out" of educational
programs their entire adult lives.

8 THE MENTORING AND NETWORKING REMIX

"What Don't I Know?"

WHEN I FIRST started out in the workplace in the late '90s, I had zero functional skills. I am not being modest. It was simply the case around the turn of the millennium, and for roughly the entire course of history before that moment, that an entry-level employee almost never brought a skill set to an organization that a more senior employee did not already possess.

Sure, we often arrived with some of the "soft" skills we discussed in the previous chapter, such as good communication, a work ethic, and lots of enthusiasm and potential, but we rarely offered knowledge or experience directly related to our employers' businesses.

Little did I know that, right about the time I sat down in my first rolling chair and plugged in my brand-new PalmPilot, this was about to change.

The tipping point, of course, was technology (and I don't mean the PalmPilot). As the Internet grew in importance to the core business of almost every organization in the late 1990s and early 2000s (albeit at different points, as some industries move faster than others), and then social media roared onto the scene, the balance of knowledge and power in organizations began to shift. For the first time, an entry-level employee could arrive with a skill set—namely, comfort and experience navigating the Web—that her boss, or even her organization's most senior leaders, did not have.

Some leaders chose to ignore this. Perhaps, as I did, you had a boss or colleague at some point who refused to read e-mail and insisted that all messages be printed out. Or an employer who opted out of high-speed broadband because dial-up was "just fine." Or a board member who said, "Who would ever provide their credit card information to a website?"

Other leaders embraced the change. In 1999, Jack Welch, CEO of General Electric at the time, required five hundred(!) of his top executives to pair up with junior employees for the purpose of learning how to use the Internet. He called it reverse mentoring.

A 2000 *Wall Street Journal* article about the program led with a comment from Lloyd G. Trotter, at the time aged 54 and head of GE's industrial systems operation. Asked about his knowledge of the Internet before he received a reverse mentor, Trotter said, "I knew it was there."

The *Journal* story also shares the perspective of Trotter's mentor, Rachel Dorman: "For her part, Ms. Dorman, who at 27 is exactly half Mr. Trotter's age, says the sessions have made her more comfortable in hobnobbing with her boss. 'I can teach him things,' she says. 'I know things he doesn't know.' At the same time, she says, she is learning through her relationship with Mr. Trotter the skills a manager needs to run a big operation, such as the ability to communicate with different people."

"Classic" mentoring of younger talent by experienced talent has been around for ages, but the rise of the Internet changed the power and information dynamic between older and younger professionals. As Welch realized, modern mentoring needs to flow in all directions.

Mentoring

According to the Association for Talent Development, 75 percent of executives point to mentoring as playing a key role in their careers. And rest assured that tomorrow's executives value mentoring just as much. When PwC surveyed recent university graduates globally about what training and development opportunities they most value from an employer, the number one answer by far was "working with strong coaches and mentors."

Furthermore, mentoring generally has little to no cost associated with it, and reaps valuable rewards. Deloitte's global 2016 Millennial Survey found that Millennials intending to stay with their organization for more than five years were twice as likely to have a mentor than not.

Mentors are especially important if you are a new leader. When Millennial Kevin Grubb was promoted to executive director of the career center at Villanova University, one of his first moves was to set up weekly lunches with Nancy Dudak, his former boss, who had recently retired from the role after twenty-eight years. She is an invaluable mentor and sounding board as he grows in his role.

Business owners and freelancers can find it harder to obtain guidance and support, but many resources exist. When my mother was starting a business back in the 1990s, she had no existing professional network, so she reached out to SCORE—the Service Corps of Retired Executives—a nonprofit that offers free business mentoring to entrepreneurs. SCORE is still active today, along with many new organizations catering to entrepreneurs across industries, regions, and specific demographics.

Mentoring can be particularly important for people of color, first-generation Americans, veterans, people with disabilities, and other marginalized groups. According to James Frick of Management Leadership for Tomorrow, employees from underrepresented populations often want mentors who appear like them or come from similar backgrounds, who can "tell me what it is I don't know."

Mentoring has even proved effective as a strategy to lower the unconscionably high rates of young men, particularly men of color, sent to prison in our country. Darnell Epps, who became a student at Cornell University after serving seventeen years in prison for a murder he committed with his brother in 2000, writes poignantly about how he was mentored at Five Points Correctional Facility in upstate New York by "old-timers" who were decades older and committed to keeping younger inmates out of trouble.

The mentoring and support was so helpful to Darnell and his brother Darryl that they themselves began mentoring younger inmates and became leaders of two organizations designed to mentor young men both already in prison and those on probation or in rehabilitation programs.

The brothers credited their early parole and amazing path from prison to the Ivy League (Darryl is now a student at Columbia) to the mentoring they received in jail. They now advocate for the granting of parole to reformed older prisoners—there are 160,000 prisoners in state and federal prisons over the age of 55—to reenter their communities and work to mentor young people with the mission of reducing crime and violence.

A remix, remember, does not mean that anything is necessarily "wrong" with a classic practice. Mentoring is the perfect example of this. Mentoring is an extraordinarily important practice for people across generations, ethnicities, personality types, functional roles, and regions of the world. It is a fundamental, evergreen experience that reaps extraordinary benefits. The remix, in this case, involves several additions and options to make mentoring even more effective and beneficial.

Reverse Mentoring

In a workplace as multigenerational as ours is today, mentoring can be enhanced by the kind of two-way learning experienced by Lloyd Trotter and Rachel Dorman at GE two decades ago. Reverse mentoring is back and, I would argue, more vital than ever. What better way to thrive in the multigenerational workplace than to encourage as many cross-generational conversations as possible?

SoulCycle CEO Melanie Whelan, a Gen Xer, speaks frequently about her Millennial mentor, whom she refers to publicly as "one of her most important advisers" and meets with regularly. When I asked Melanie about her experience, she told me, "Partnering with my Millennial mentor has been truly impactful and one of my best decisions. She offers a different perspective on everything from how this important consumer segment thinks about purchase decisions, to what new apps I should be using for inspiration, to what matters in culture now. I believe that innovative ideas can come from anywhere, and she's no exception! She keeps me proactively informed and is a great sounding board, so that we can better support our people, riders, and community."

At The Estée Lauder Companies, three hundred senior leaders in twenty countries are currently matched with Presidential Reverse Mentors, who are junior employees at the organization. The program grew out of a small pilot reverse mentoring program about four years ago in which president and CEO Fabrizio Freda asked his team to put together a retail immersion day, at which a small group of the company's Millennial and Gen Z employees would take executives shopping to help them better understand the retail habits of young consumers. "We knew that our future success was in the hands of the young consumer," Freda has said, and he deliberately wanted to tap the young talent in the company rather than engaging outside experts.

The day proved eye-opening for executives, who observed the ways in which their young colleagues completely integrated their mobile phones into their in-store shopping experiences, from reading product reviews, comparing prices, watching online tutorials, taking selfies in-store, and ordering their afternoon lattes in advance so they could skip the lines and fit in more time for shopping. After this one experience, Freda made the reverse mentoring program permanent and rolled it out globally.

While these executives and companies have taken a more formal approach to reverse mentoring, the concept can be applied on a more casual basis as well. One manager in the insurance industry recently told me that he walks up to his junior team members each Monday morning and asks them to put a new app on his phone. "I want to use what they're using," he told me.

Reverse mentoring is particularly valuable if you are in an industry that serves a younger demographic of clients or customers or you want to serve that cohort. Manny Contomanolis, whom you met in the previous chapter, is adamant about staying current in order to best serve the Millennial and Gen Z students at Northeastern University. One of the ways he does this is by spending as much time as possible listening to his youngest employees.

"The newest professionals are closest to the actual clients that we serve," he told me. "The longer you're in the higher ed business or any business working with a certain younger customer or client base, you have to be careful. Young professionals coming into higher ed or career services were fairly recently students themselves. They can often anticipate how students will respond and what they want—sometimes in a way that the rest of us don't always see.

"That has been tremendously invigorating and good for the business. Prior generations of leaders often said, 'New kid? Just be quiet and listen.' Now it's 'New kid? Sit down! Fill me in! What don't I know?' That's a huge shift."

Co-mentoring

While most reverse mentoring duos organically engage in a back-and-forth dialogue, sometimes that is not the case. And some organizations find that reverse mentoring is hard to sell to senior executives, especially if they operate in a highly hierarchical corporate or global culture.

If you are seeking the benefits of reverse mentoring for your organization but that concept is a step too far, there is another, similar concept to consider. It's called co-mentoring, and I first learned about it more than a decade ago when I was writing my first book, *Getting from College to Career*. Co-mentoring is a supportive relationship between generations in which the advice flows in both directions. Co-mentors might even be peers.

MaryLeigh Bliss of Ypulse has found that the concept of co-mentoring can be more appealing and more accurate. "While reverse mentoring is wonderful, we have found people are more receptive on both sides if it's clear the mentoring will go both ways. We don't want to imply the onus is all on the Millennials for the mentoring relationship to succeed. It has to be clear the two people involved will be mentoring one another."

Again, this is not to imply that mentoring or reverse mentoring is wrong in any way, but precision about the shared nature of the relationship can be valuable, especially if you face resistance to the concept of reverse mentoring.

Here are some best practices for remixing your mentoring, reverse mentoring, or co-mentoring efforts, whether you intend to launch a company-wide program or simply ask a colleague of another generation to meet for lunch. Try this:

SECURE SUPPORT FROM THE TOP. The organizations with the best reverse mentoring outcomes have support from their most senior leaders. Every organization I have met or researched with a reverse or co-mentoring program says this is the most important success factor, including Jack Welch at GE in the 1990s and Fabrizio Freda at The Estée Lauder Companies more recently.

According to Ana Tereza Guimaraes, who works on the team that runs The Estée Lauder Companies' Presidential Reverse Mentor program, "It is critical to have an executive sponsor who is at the CEO or senior executive level. Without that, others will not make the time and treat it with the same level of gravity that it needs for a reverse mentoring program to flourish and succeed."

PROVIDE CONTEXT. MaryLeigh Bliss and Ypulse have found, through experience launching co-mentoring programs at such organizations as Intel and Godiva, that it increases success when a program is explained to participants in the context of generational change. "Often it goes a lot better if everyone goes into a co-mentoring program with some knowledge of the generations and not working off of assumptions and stereotypes. For example, you might have a kickoff event where everyone discusses each generation's core characteristics, background, and current trends. This also gives them conversation fodder for their first meetings."

ENCOURAGE DIVERSITY BEYOND GENERATIONAL. Remember that Millennials and Gen Zs are significantly more ethnically diverse than Gen Xers, Boomers, and Traditionalists, so reverse mentoring relationships can help generate more new employee relationships as well. According to Jennifer Brown, CEO of a diversity consulting firm and author of *Inclusion: Diversity, the New Workplace & the Will to Change* and *How to Be an Inclusive Leader: Creating Trust, Cooperation, and Community Across Differences*, "People tend to be more comfortable approaching and supporting those in their same identity group, making cross-gender and cross-race mentoring relationships a new and potentially transformative experience.

"Acknowledging that difference is present early on and discovering shared experiences or common ground across that difference can ease the relationship. It can also build the capacity for leaders to challenge themselves and grow in awareness and skills, in the relative safety of an individual pairing."

Do keep in mind that there is an important and necessary discussion taking place at many organizations today around the need for women and people of color in particular to supplement mentoring (in any form) with the cultivation of more formalized sponsors. Sponsors are senior leaders who actively advocate on behalf of more junior employees, such as recommending them for a promotion. Mentors are a supplement, not a replacement, for sponsors, and mentoring and reverse mentoring relationships can and should turn into sponsorship alliances.

TRAIN THE MENTEES. Ana Tereza Guimaraes also advocates the importance of training reverse mentors, often Millennials or Gen Zs. "A lot of our Presidential Reverse Mentors haven't had senior-level exposure," she points out, "so we need to make sure they are fully prepared and have the resources to succeed." Remember Remixer Rule #5: Common sense is not so common; many companies are now offering "mentee training" for employees engaging in their first mentoring experience. I have facilitated such trainings and find them a helpful way to make sure that participants are clear on the etiquette of such actions as requesting mentoring meetings, asking for an appropriate level of advice, and demonstrating gratitude.

AGREE TO RULES AND RESPONSIBILITIES. At BNY Mellon's Pershing, reverse mentors are advised to eliminate all aspects of hierarchical titles during meetings. Pairs are directed to engage as equals who are both in a learning relationship. Key responsibilities are agreed to by both parties, including:

- Invest time in getting to know one another, building trust, and respecting one another.
- Discuss the desired goals, outcomes, and expectations, while adjusting if necessary.
- Agree how you are going to track progress.
- Plan and commit to meetings, and stick to the commitment.
- Be explicit about maintaining and respecting confidentiality.
- Give and receive constructive feedback and challenge each other.
- Be prepared to share personal experiences and collaborate as equal learning partners.
- Meet at least once a month for one year.

Such clear guidelines can minimize the chance of misunderstandings or disappointment with a mentoring experience.

CONNECT REVERSE MENTORS TO EACH OTHER. At The Estée Lauder Companies, the company's more than three hundred Presidential Reverse Mentors across twenty countries participate in an online platform to build community, share news articles, and discuss product differences around the globe. The company recently brought a portion of the reverse mentors together for an in-person event in Oxford, England, where I had the opportunity to present to them about generational differences.

The reverse mentors joined together in groups to work on real business challenges, which they then presented to the company's general manager for the United Kingdom and several members of his leadership team. I was amazed at how this global group of

Millennial and Gen Z employees came together so quickly to solve problems. Because they had already engaged with one another online, there was a lower barrier to diving right in. I couldn't help but feel like I was looking out at an audience of future corporate leaders who already had a strong group of trusted, global peers. I honestly felt a bit of envy that they are starting their careers in an age when all of this is possible.

HAVE CO-MENTORING TEAMS WORK ON REAL BUSINESS CHALLENGES. MaryLeigh Bliss of Ypulse strongly recommends assigning meaningful business projects to co-mentoring teams. "The idea is that generations working together can actually have an end result that will better the company, not just to train Xers and Boomers to tolerate Millennials." In one program Ypulse advised on, the assignment was for each co-mentoring team to work together to come up with an idea and a business plan, then to pitch their ideas to top executives at an event, *Shark Tank*–style. The younger member of each team was tasked with presenting each idea. At the end, the executives gave each team critiques and chose winners.

It should be noted that reverse and co-mentoring programs are also contributors to retention. At BNY Mellon's Pershing, the retention rate of Millennials who participated in the firm's reverse mentoring program stands at 95 percent.

Micro-mentoring

Thus far we've talked about more formalized cross-generational mentoring programs. Mentoring can also take place in much shorter segments. From the first time I heard the term, I fell in love with the concept of "micro-mentoring." Every mentoring relationship doesn't have to be a long-term marriage; sometimes it's great to have a little mentoring fling.

This concept is similar to "speed networking" events, which I've always liked. The more limited the amount of time available, the more people tend to cut to the chase with their questions and guidance. Now, I am not suggesting that you literally walk up to a member of another generation at a conference or meeting and say, "Hi! Can you give me some micro-mentoring?"—although I'm not totally against that tactic, if that's your style. But think of all the opportunities you have in your personal or professional life to gain intergenerational insights and share some of your own.

Here are some questions to spark a quick insight from a short conversation with a person of another generation. I have personally used these with clients, vendors, my daughter's babysitters, people standing next to me in the kitchen of my coworking space, Uber drivers, people who follow me on Twitter, and more. It's kind of my personal version of the Proust Questionnaire:

- What are you currently reading that you recommend: books, blogs, newsletters, magazines, etc.?
- What are you currently listening to that you recommend: music, podcasts, audiobooks, etc.?
- What are your favorite apps and tech tools and why?
- What are your favorite brands and why?
- What companies do you think are the best employers and why?
- What people do you most admire and why?
- How do you think people view your generation?
- What is the biggest myth or misconception about your generation?
- What do you most wonder about other generations?
- Have you ever had a notable cross-generational experience at work? Tell me about it.

Author Chip Conley, who refers to himself as a "modern elder" and joined the Millennial-led team at Airbnb at age 52 after running his own boutique hotel company for a quarter century, is also a fan of asking a lot of questions across generations. He says that his best tactic for being a Baby Boomer among Millennials was "to reconceive my bewilderment as curiosity, and give free rein to it. . . . In fact, in my experience it can be easier for older people to admit how much we still don't know. Paradoxically, this curiosity keeps us feeling young."

Internal Networking: Employee Resource Groups

Beyond mentor-mentee relationships, leaders in the multigenerational workplace are wise to expand their professional networks to be more diverse. It's one of the oldest sayings in the book and it's as true as ever: Success is not about what you know; it's about who you know. And who knows you. Diversity and inclusion expert Jennifer Brown defines inclusive workplace cultures as those that enable all talent to feel valued and not just "tolerated" for their differences, but sought out and valued for them. We saw some examples of this in chapter 3 related to the recruiting of diverse talent. Let's now explore the role of employee resource groups, as a way to remix employee networking opportunities.

The start of employee resource groups (ERGs), also known as affinity groups, is attributed to Joseph Wilson, then CEO of the Xerox Corporation, who formed a group with Black employees in 1964 following race riots in Rochester, New York, where Xerox was founded and headquartered. The group's goal was to address discrimination and create a fair corporate environment.

Today, 90 percent of *Fortune* 500 companies have ERGs consisting of groups for people with a wide variety of identities, including women, Black, Asian, Latinx, LGBTQ, people with disabilities, veterans, working parents, and Millennial employees. Some companies are also adding a plus sign or the word "ally" to their ERGs to signify that people who support but are not part of the community—for instance, family members, friends, or colleagues—are welcome.

An area where ERGs are due to expand is in providing a network of support for older workers. Patricia Milligan, senior partner and global leader at Mercer, has said, "At the most respected multinational companies, the single class not represented from a diversity and inclusion perspective is older workers. LGBT, racial and ethnic diversity, women, people with physical disabilities, veterans—you can find an affinity group in a corporation for everything, except an older worker."

A note of caution to ERGs comes from Riley Hanson, an engineer who is a nonbinary, transgender femme Millennial who is Black and Indian. Riley describes their experience of attending ERG meetings at their company but not feeling comfortable in any of them. The African-American ERG meetings excluded their experience of being transgender, and the LGBTQ meetings excluded their experience of being Black and Indian. Riley ended up creating an informal lunch support group that felt more inclusive of their experience and concerns.

Knowing that many companies want to recruit and retain diverse young talent, especially engineers, I asked Riley what made them accept a job with their current employer, a large multinational organization. "I chose this company because they were the only one honest enough to say, 'We are terrible at diversity!'" While job hunting, Riley would ask potential employers how many Black femme engineers they had. Instead of providing a number, which Riley was specifically requesting, recruiters would give answers like "We will look into that for you" or "We have someone working on that."

"If the answer is zero, I want to hear zero," Riley says. "I don't want the wool pulled over my eyes. I want to know what I'm getting into." Being an inclusive leader requires transparency, even—or especially—when it can be uncomfortable.

If you or your organization don't know where to begin to address or remix your employee diversity and inclusion efforts, Riley recommends finding a consultant—external if you are in a small organization or possibly internal in a large one—who is multiply marginalized and as different from you as possible.

If employee resource groups are not possible in your organization due to size or other factors, here are some additional recommendations for making your internal employee networking opportunities more diverse and inclusive to all employees:

CREATE—AND CELEBRATE—MIXED-GENERATION TEAMS AND TASK FORCES. In the e-commerce business at Pitney Bowes, managers created mixed-age teams of about fifteen employees from different departments, in which all decisions are made collaboratively. "The old way of working no longer works," said one manager, referring to the previous practice of segregating employees by age and skill level and allowing longest-tenured employees to have the most authority.

This same strategy applies to special projects, planning committees, and task forces. I actually receive the most complaints from Generation Xers who feel left out of such projects; leaders think of the farthest ends of the age spectrum and sometimes forget the middle. Remember to specifically call out and celebrate the successes of multigenerational teams. Consider putting together case studies to document how employees of all ages and tenures contribute to your organization together.

BOND MORE INCLUSIVELY. Another common dilemma is how to plan a team bonding event that is truly inclusive. It is impossible to plan an event that incorporates the preferences of every single person, but no doubt most events could be far more inclusive than they are now.

Here are some issues to consider:

- Are you planning events that are comfortable for non-drinking members of your team? Of course, anyone can choose to order a Diet Coke instead of a cocktail at the bar, but non-drinkers can feel left out of events centered on drinking. Partly as a response to the #MeToo movement and increased awareness of sexual harassment and abuse in work-related situations, several organizations are now choosing to host alcohol-free events to make sure all attendees feel welcome, valued, and safe.

- Are you considering whether events are accessible to people with different abilities, such as securing interpreters for Deaf colleagues or ramps for those who use wheelchairs?

- Are you planning events that take place at different times of day? Depending on family obligations and commuting distances, the scheduling of events can impact different employees' ability to attend or truly enjoy an event. Can you rotate among breakfast events, luncheons, and dinner or evening activities, to incorporate all needs? If you have any remote team members, you will want to consider their ability to potentially attend in person as well. Some teams even have virtual coffee chats where everyone grabs a beverage and logs into Skype together to chat and catch up.

- Are you varying the kinds of activities you offer for different interests? Can you balance a 5K race with a trivia night or a museum visit, or a cooking party with a volunteer outing? (In fact, when I have polled multigenerational audiences about their most desired team-bonding activity, volunteering always comes out number one.)

- Are you incorporating a social media element? As appropriate, where can you engage employees by inviting them to share a work experience with their broader networks of friends and family on social media? This tactic used to be considered a way to engage Millennials, but today I would argue it engages everyone. As I have mentioned, my social media feeds are multigenerational, and work-related events are often shared proudly by all generations. Why not give an event a hashtag, set up a step-and-repeat background, or provide some fun props to inspire people to snap photos and share? No one is compelled to share if they don't want to, and people can choose whichever social networks they prefer.

The Personal Networking Remix:
Lunch Is Dead and CrossFit Is the New Golf

J. Kelly Hoey is a model multigenerational networker—and she should be, given the fact that she wrote a book called *Build Your Dream Network: Forging Powerful Relationships in a Hyper-Connected World.* Kelly, a Gen Xer, recently told me the story of how she met business guru Tom Peters, a Traditionalist by age, thanks to her participation in a Twitter chat for Millennials.

"I was participating in a Twitter chat, and one of the participants quoted 'move fast and break things,' the famous Silicon Valley mentality. I tweeted, 'Time out. Read Tom Peters's latest blog post on the benefits of going slow.' The participants criticized that older generation and I said, 'Hold on here! Don't paint them all with the same brush.'"

Kelly knew about Tom Peters's post because she frequently engages with him, and many other professionals, on Twitter. Overall, she views Twitter as a big cocktail party, as "an opportunity to find new communities of interest, enrich my life, and enable me to do my job better. I find people of mutual interest who are generous in their conversation. On Twitter, we are not limited by geography, or age, or gender, or ability, or education.

"So, like a good guest at a cocktail party," Kelly continues, "I had been listening and engaging in conversations with Tom Peters on Twitter. To me, a 'like' or retweet is like a nod or saying, 'mm-hmm'— the way you would acknowledge someone when you are actively listening to them in a group of people.

"At some point, Tom started to follow me like he did with a lot of people. In the fall of 2016, he indicated he had preordered my book and I fell over!"

Kelly and Tom became friends on Twitter and eventually met up in person in New York, where Kelly is based. "I went and met him and it was the exact same conversation that had started in the digital world. We were just not limited by characters now. There was no stumbling over the threshold from online to off-line. It was exactly the same person. I consider him a friend and most definitely a mentor. Subsequently, when I told him my book was going to paperback, he reached out to me and offered to write the foreword.

"We feel completely like equals and have a mutually beneficial relationship, but I had been brought up to be deferential to people in authority, so I kept wanting to call him Mr. Peters! The most amazing part is that, before Twitter, when would I have formed a relationship or even met him?"

If you have never formed a professional relationship on a social media site, now would be a good time to start. And as you can tell from Kelly's story, this method of networking is not just for Millennials and Gen Zs. (However, it is certainly most common among younger people. A Ypulse survey found that 63 percent of 13- to 35-year-olds say they have friends on social media they've never met in person.)

Here are some additional ways to build a more multigenerational network. Try this:

REMIX YOUR EXISTING ACTIVITIES. Review some of the activities you are already involved in—perhaps nonprofit volunteer work, professional association memberships, or serving on a local government committee. Kelly Hoey recommends that you find ways to participate in the same activities you enjoy, but in a new way. For example, maybe you are involved in a not-for-profit, but you currently spend all your time with fellow members of the board. What if you got in the field with the volunteers for a project or two to expand your work with the organization and meet some new people? Conversely, if you like to volunteer but have not taken on a leadership position, try joining a committee or stepping up to a role with more responsibility. You will expand your skill set while also diversifying your existing professional and personal network.

ASK FOR INTRODUCTIONS. If you are less experienced in your industry and you'd like to "level up" your networking to meet more experienced professionals, Kelly advises that you lean on your mentoring relationships and more senior colleagues. "I had a mentor who did this for me," she explains. "I told her, 'I'd really like to get on this committee of the association of the bar. (Kelly began her career as a lawyer.) Can you help me?'" When you know exactly what communities, committees, or organizations you want to be part of, be focused and ask for a specific referral or introduction. Don't be shy.

In a neat remix of the parent-child networking dynamic in which children tap their parents' connections, I have also heard of Millennial children helping their Boomer parents to connect professionally. Marci Alboher of Encore.org once told me a great story about her poker game, which she has been playing with a regular group of media professionals for the past fifteen years. Older members of this poker network used to ask the group to help find job opportunities for their children. These days, Marci says, it's the reverse: the mostly Gen X and Baby Boomer players talk about scanning the LinkedIn profiles of one another's Millennial kids as they hunt for new professional opportunities.

FIND NICHE COMMUNITIES ONLINE. I mentioned that Kelly first met Tom Peters while they were participating in a Twitter chat. You can also seek out communities of interest on social media. The best way to do this is to find hashtags and chats around the things you are interested in. You can do this by searching on your own or by asking people you know IRL for recommendations. Even if you don't naturally gravitate to connecting with people online, you might find it easier to connect over specific discussion topics and questions during a one-hour chat on a single network. And then, if anyone interests you, you can reach out through a direct message and continue the conversation privately or even off-line.

TRY A NEW SCENE. Few business clichés are as common as the image of executives (usually older white men) doing business while playing golf or enjoying a white tablecloth lunch—with martinis, of course. Well, both those "classic" images are fading fast in the new era of business. Country club membership and the sport of golf are having trouble attracting younger generations. In the 1990s there were more than 5,000 golf and country clubs in the U.S. Today there are fewer than 4,000. According to the National Golf Foundation, golf participation has fallen nationally by 20 percent since 2003.

The numbers of people eating out for a business lunch at a restaurant is following the same trend. In 2018, Americans made 433 million fewer trips to restaurants during lunchtime, representing the lowest level of lunch traffic in at least four decades. ("I put [restaurant] lunch right up there with fax machines and pay phones," said one 55-year-old sales director who used to dine out for lunch every workday but now says he doesn't have the time.) And it's not just fancy restaurants: lunch traffic at fast casual restaurants is down, too.

What is the remix of doing business over golf or lunch? Several different kinds of activities are picking up the slack, proving yet again that one size fits none. One hot new professional networking trend is "sweatworking," or doing business while exercising— usually at trendy fitness spots like CrossFit, SoulCycle, Flywheel, Barry's Bootcamp, or Orangetheory. (To get in on this trend, some country clubs are adding activities like gym classes, yoga, and wellness lectures.)

Physical activities are not appealing or possible for all people, so, as always, you should ask people what their preferences are. A more introverted person might not want to express her preference for a quieter location but will suggest one when asked. Likewise, a colleague inexperienced with formal dining might suggest a less intimidating location than an executive who eats out every day might choose.

Speaking of intimidation and discomfort, what I've always found curious about the topic of networking is how scary and awkward many people find it to be. Have you noticed that people rarely even use the word "networking" anymore? More than a few professionals, across generations, have told me that the word gives them the "ick." What gives? To me, networking is simply the building and maintaining of relationships, which is what humans have been doing for all time.

Yes, networking, along with mentoring, involves some different rules of etiquette, but it's just about people. If you can make friends, you can network and build successful professional relationships. If you are a member of a family, you can network and build successful professional relationships across generations. However, as we will discuss in the next chapter, I will admit that the physical spaces in which we are now being asked to do this relationship building are getting a little bit complicated.

CHAPTER 8: KEY TAKEAWAYS

- The mentoring remix involves mentoring that flows in all directions, from senior to junior person, junior to senior person, and peer to peer.
- Mentoring is as important as ever to all generations. Seventy-five percent of executives point to mentoring as playing a key role in their careers, and university graduates say their most desired training and development opportunity is working with strong coaches and mentors.
- Reverse mentoring involves a less experienced employee providing guidance and insight to a more experienced employee. This is particularly valuable if you are in an industry that serves a younger demographic of clients or customers or you want to serve that cohort.
- Co-mentoring is yet another option and involves employees from two different generations coaching and advising one another.
- When implementing any kind of mentoring program, formal or informal, do provide some training and guidelines to foster success. This might include a list of ground rules, assignment of logistical responsibility to one person, or scheduling shared events to help relationships grow.
- In addition to more long-term mentoring relationships, consider adding micro-mentoring moments to your regular routine. Think of all the opportunities you have in your personal or professional life to gain intergenerational insights and share some of your own simply by asking good questions and engaging in a dialogue with someone who is different from you.
- Beyond mentoring, now is the time to build a more cross-generational professional network. Try engaging in dialogue in niche communities on social media, participating in new activities outside of work, and asking for introductions from people in your network to a wider variety of people.

9 THE WORKSPACE REMIX

"Work" Is No Longer a Place

MY VERY FIRST desk at WorkingWoman.com was in a windowless former conference room where they had removed the large table and replaced it with as many desks as could fit. I sat approximately eighteen inches from my boss.

I remember being terrified when I negotiated a contract on the phone that she would hear me saying something wrong. I remember wondering if she was reading over my shoulder the e-mails I typed all day long. I remember being hyperaware of the smell level of anything I ate for lunch in case it would bother her or the other seven people in the room. I remember hiding in the stairwell to make personal calls, which kind of backfired because when I or anyone else came back from such a call the rest of the group would say, "Ooh, who were you calling out there?"

Since we were employed in the brand-new dot-com division of a legacy magazine company (which published *Working Woman*, *Working Mother*, and other titles), everyone else at the company had an office or a decent-sized cubicle. I have distinct memories of these longer-term employees walking by our crammed conference room, saying, "That must be so much fun in there!"

We employees were told that this office layout was to encourage collaboration and innovation and synergy and other dot-commy late-'90s buzzwords. This being the late '90s, I had of course read all about the headquarters of Google and other Silicon Valley start-ups, who were thriving in open spaces. And I had friends who worked in newsrooms and trading floors who loved the energy of their workplaces. I thought something was wrong with me for struggling to work in an open space.

It's not hard to figure out why employers like mine embraced them: open offices are significantly less expensive because you can fit more people into a smaller amount of space. And because open floor plans have been successful in Silicon Valley start-ups, there is the added benefit of saying that the switch to an open office is a way to appeal to the kinds of young, tech-savvy workers who want to work at such Silicon Valley start-ups. By 2015 approximately 70 percent of offices had converted to open plans.

It is only recently that the downsides of the now-ubiquitous open floor plans have been more widely acknowledged. This is another reminder that one size fits none. Yes, Google, which is often credited with launching the open office trend—and the use of scooters to move around that office—designed a workspace to embody its corporate culture and to cater to the job needs of its employees, many of whom are programmers who sit silently at their desks all day writing code. Their office is right for their work and their culture. That does not mean an open space is right for every organization that wants to be as successful and desired an employer as Google.

According to Nikil Saval, author of *Cubed: A Secret History of the Workplace*, the original design concept of open floor plans and cubicles was created in Germany in the 1950s to enable individualized, autonomous space for workers that was flexible, modular, and easily changed as circumstances in the office changed—which makes total sense.

Unfortunately, as Saval details, most organizations decided that cubicles and open floor plans could also be a way to cram as many people as possible into as little space as possible. In many offices today, employees sit elbow to elbow at long tables.

In my experience and observation, whether or not a person likes to work in an open space has far more to do with the work they are doing and their personal preferences than their age or generation. While Millennials and Gen Zs often have the expectation that they will work in an open-plan space because that has been the dominant model in their lifetimes, it doesn't necessarily mean it is their preference. Personality type—introvert versus extrovert, for example—can often have much more to do with how different individuals prefer to work.

It is also the case that not all offices today are open-plan. Especially in more traditional industries, closed-door offices with mahogany desks and metal filing cabinets are still quite common. I have been in office building elevators where the doors open onto a bright, colorful, loft-like tech company, and then on the next floor they open onto a dark and formal wood-paneled office that seems straight out of 1975.

Let me be clear that I am not necessarily against wide-open lofts or the use of taupe and green banker's lamps in office décor. What I am against is choosing a workspace design by default. The workspace remix involves rethinking professional environments from a one-size-fits-all approach to more flexible, deliberately designed spaces. If you want to lead a multigenerational team to success, you have to put serious thought into the environment in which they will be able to get their jobs done.

"Headphones Are the New Wall"

What concerns me most is the way in which employees are criticized for how they adapt to a work environment over which they have little to no control. Leaders should not be surprised when employees find workarounds and adaptations to make a work environment better fit their individual preferences and work needs.

For example, have you ever noticed how, even in the most staid office spaces, some employees find ways to decorate their cubicles or desks with bright colors, personal photos, and inspirational quotes? Or how extroverted employees stuck in private offices tend to invite people in for unnecessary meetings or wander around hoping for people to talk to?

And then there is the issue of headphones in open offices.

If I had to name the question about generational differences I receive more than any other, it would be this:

"What do I do about my Millennial employees wearing earbuds?"

As we discussed early in this book, many managers, often but not always Baby Boomers or Gen Xers, complain about young employees who always wear headphones or earbuds in the office. "They're not engaging with the world around them," managers will lament.

"Why are your employees wearing headphones?" I will ask in reply.

"Because they say it helps them focus."

"And why can't they focus?"

"I have no idea. The office is silent!"

And therein lies the rub. Sure, sometimes employees in open offices wear headphones to avoid noisy distractions. But a deeper reason is to find a modicum of privacy in a wide-open, boundary-less space in which everyone can hear everything, which is especially important for employees doing work that requires deep thinking or personal creativity. As one open-plan office worker commented, "Headphones are the new wall."

It turns out open floor plans are actually destroying the very innovation and collaboration they were meant to enable. A 2018 Harvard study found that switching to an open-plan office space decreased employees' face-to-face interactions by over 70 percent and increased the use of e-mail and instant messenger by 67 percent and 75 percent, respectively. Rather than increasing face-to-face collaborations, open architecture had the exact opposite effect: it was more likely to make people socially withdraw. Workers became less productive and the quality of their work decreased.

Open offices have always been the norm in certain industries and actually enhance productivity and interaction. The difference is likely the level of overall movement and background noise in, say, a newsroom or a trading floor, where people are talking on the phone and interacting frequently. But when there is no constant buzz in the background, people have less privacy and feel more self-conscious about any sound they make—just as I did in my early job.

Some organizations are putting a Band-Aid on the problem by installing "pink-noise" systems, which pump in an almost imperceptible whooshing sound designed to match the frequency of human voices and therefore be less distracting when people talk in an open floor plan. Not only does Pink Noise sound like the name of a punk band, it seems to me like an unnecessarily expensive and high-tech solution when simplicity would suffice. (Of course, if you are curious to check it out, YouTube has you covered with a video of ten full hours of pink noise.) Other companies are experimenting with music and nature sounds, like those sleep machines that create an atmosphere of rain or waves.

I personally love and crave quiet workspaces, especially when I am writing. I never leave home without my Hearos earplugs; in my college library I favored the private little study cubicles called "weenie bins"; and if you've ever been shushed in the Amtrak Quiet Car, it was probably by me. But when I need to collaborate with clients, meeting them in a quiet office can feel uncomfortable, as if we are bothering other people.

While you as an individual leader may or may not be able to

control the physical environment in which you and your team work, you can pay attention to the ways your employees have been adapting to their physical workspace. Once you empathize with the tensions that might be lurking, you can begin to research and advocate for solutions.

The Remix: "A Diversity of Spaces"

As you walk through Capital One's corporate location in New York's Flatiron district, you might forget you are in the offices of one of America's largest banks. You will certainly see work taking place all around you, but you might feel more like you are in an airport lounge or the lobby of a popular hotel in the middle of a dynamic conference.

When I visited, I walked past a series of sliding walls that the bank's associates had arranged in various ways to accommodate meeting groups of different sizes. I rounded a corner into a wide hallway and found three employees huddled around a laptop in one of the private diner-style booths built into the walls.

In a more open area, a few people worked alone on stools at high tables. Others sat on overstuffed armchairs that reminded me of the ones I had considered for my own living room. I observed still other employees on video calls in small glass-walled "phone booths." And everywhere I turned there were plants and sunshine.

"Six years ago, we looked around our organization and saw a fundamental shift in how people were doing work," says Stefanie Spurlin, vice president of workplace solutions at Capital One and my Slack mentor from chapter 6. "Our focus was on co-location, getting all the teams together who were collaborating on the same work product together. We needed to create an environment to fuel innovation and collaboration that would allow our people to ultimately support our customers, and also to be inclusive of different people's work styles."

Stefanie's team even changed its name to reflect the changing way space is part of our work lives today. Her team, which used to use the more traditional name Corporate Real Estate, rebranded to Workplace Solutions to demonstrate that its role went beyond facilities management. "We were very deliberate in rebranding ourselves with the idea that we are solution providers to our lines of business from a real estate perspective."

So, what is it like to truly collaborate and solve people's space challenges? According to Stefanie, this requires a lot of personal involvement and listening from leaders like her. Not surprisingly, it can be especially challenging for long-tenured employees to change the way they have worked, perhaps for decades.

"In a very early generation of our workplace strategy and my initial involvement, people said, 'This isn't going to work,' 'We can't have a centralized printer,' 'I can't lose my office,' etc. Because at this point it was all theoretical, I took the most concerned people to the construction space—a behind-the-scenes tour with hard hats and everything. Once they saw it, it brought the plans to life. They understood it better and could orient around it. In the end, some of the biggest initial naysayers became the biggest advocates."

In other cases, some compromise was necessary. For example, one of the redesigns involved moving a team of lawyers out of their offices. When Stefanie met with the head of the team, they discussed why the lawyers needed more enclosed spaces. Stefanie talked about the overall desire for more cross-functional collaboration. There was education, and ultimately compromise, on both sides. In the end, the team came out of offices but were provided more huddle and collaborative space for confidential calls to do the work they needed to do.

The workspace remix, as exemplified by Capital One, boils down to this: give people a variety of spaces in which to accomplish a variety of types of work. At a time in which we are asking employees to be more agile, innovative, disruptive, and multidimensional than ever before, we need to provide spaces that allow for agile, innovative, disruptive, and multidimensional work to take place.

Sometimes we need spaces to work alone, and sometimes we need spaces to work with others. According to architecture firm Gensler's 2013 Workplace Survey, this is true no matter what your business: "Across industries, we found that balanced workplaces—those prioritizing both focus and collaboration—score higher on measures of satisfaction, innovation, effectiveness, and performance."

And don't get too caught up in the terminology of whether your space is "open-plan" or not. As Stefanie says, "Don't let labels define your space. We don't want labels as people, and so we don't want labels for our workspace, either." In fact—and I promise this is a total coincidence—Capital One doesn't call their office changes "renovations." They call them remixes.

Your Workspace Remix

Ready to remix your workspace on a large or small scale? Try this:

OFFER OPTIONS. Wherever you are located, remember that your office is firmly in the jurisdiction of Customization Nation. Research out of Great Britain has shown that when workers can choose their working conditions, productivity on cognitive tasks increases by 25 percent or more. Organizational psychologists call these environments "empowered offices," and it's a concept any organization can implement in some way. For example, when Stefanie is traveling, as she does frequently, her team members know that they are welcome to the large meeting table in her office for impromptu group meetings or for an individual to spread out to work on a complicated project.

Choice also means that fun elements can be included in a professional environment. While we would all agree that many dot-com-era start-ups went too far with the playground aesthetic (call me old-fashioned, but I'm just not convinced that ball pits correlate to positive work outcomes), this doesn't mean the pendulum has to swing entirely in the other direction. For example, software company Janeiro Digital removed its large shuffleboard table but opted to keep a small, tabletop foosball game and a video game system that employees can connect to a big office TV if they need a break. But both the foosball and the gaming console can be moved out of the way for client events, staff meetings, and other professional needs. As another tech executive, Amy Spurling, CEO of Compt, has said, "We need to have a work environment that makes more than just one group of people happy."

PROVIDE PRIVACY. While many workplaces now offer private spaces such as lactation rooms for breastfeeding mothers, there are a wide variety of reasons employees in other life stages can require privacy to accomplish their jobs. An entry-level salesperson, for example, might be more successful if he or she can make cold calls without feeling that colleagues are overhearing. If you don't provide such spaces, either these important calls won't get made at all or you'll stumble over junior employees camped out in your stairwells trying to find a little slice of seclusion.

On the other end of the age spectrum, one executive admitted she was embarrassed to place a fan on her desk in an open office setting because she didn't want her colleagues to know she was suffering through hot flashes related to menopause. Having the option to slip into a private phone booth allowed her to continue working without awkwardness. Where in your workspace can you repurpose an unused office or storage area as a private space for employees to use when they need it?

If you can't provide privacy for each individual, team privacy can be effective as well. At JotForm, a company that makes online forms, employees work in cross-functional teams of five or six people. Each team has its own room, with whiteboards, desks, space to move around, and a door that closes. The company has found that these private team offices have increased productivity and eliminated the need for employees to use noise-canceling headphones. JotForm's founder calls this setup a "happy medium" between private offices and wide-open spaces. As for the cost of providing a bit more space? "It's worth every bit of the investment."

ADD "IN-BETWEEN" SPACES. Formal conference rooms can feel too big and stuffy when all you want to do is have a quick private chat with a colleague. Instead, "in-between" areas like alcoves and booths allow for a mix of both the proximity and camaraderie of an open space and the privacy all humans desire. Can you remix an unused corner of your space into an in-between space by placing a few chairs or a bench there?

If you currently have an open floor plan that you want to make more interaction-friendly, you can rearrange bookshelves, rolling whiteboards, flipcharts, or even tall plants to create semiprivate areas away from people's desks where colleagues can casually gather for conversation. Capital One includes a variety of residential furniture, such as couches, armchairs, and side tables, to make it easier for employees to move the furniture around to accommodate groups of all sizes and a variety of meeting needs.

INCREASE TRANSPARENCY. I once consulted with a financial services company where the highest-level executives all had offices on a private floor of the organization's headquarters, set apart from the rank-and-file employees. The offices were all in a row down a long white-marble hallway. Employees referred to it as "the mausoleum." Not a good image.

In contrast, another large organization in the same industry redesigned its space so that executive offices were on the same floors as other employees, and each office featured glass walls. This not only provided more light to employees working in the middle of the floor but also literally gave workers transparency into their leaders' domains. Remember Remixer Rule #7: Be more transparent, whatever that "more" may be in your environment.

ENGINEER OPPORTUNITIES FOR "CASUAL COLLISIONS." When Steve Jobs was designing Pixar's headquarters, he intentionally placed the restrooms in the building's main atrium, a long walk away from where people worked. This encouraged impromptu interactions between people of all departments and levels in the company.

In an example that requires no architectural changes, Capital One removed all individual trash and recycling bins from beside people's desks. Now employees need to stand up and walk to centralized bins to discard anything, which encourages more interaction (and, as a bonus, adds to everyone's daily step count).

If you don't want to do that, consider moving the water cooler or snack dispensers to a farther location from where they are now. This can even be as simple as making an employee break room more inviting by swapping out several smaller tables and replacing them with a larger, family-style farm table where more employees can sit together.

Marketing software company HubSpot takes the concept to the extreme. Almost all employees at the company shift seats every three months. Chief people officer Katie Burke explains, "Our founders realized that in every office there are good seats and bad seats, so they set up a lottery in which everyone, including them, participated. . . . The point is to eliminate perceptions of power imbalances. The reshuffles also emphasize that change is constant, so you need to be adaptable. And we want people to get out of their entrenched social patterns so that they will collaborate and learn."

In my favorite multigenerational component of this reshuffle system, Burke says, "We keep teams together, but we change adjacent groups and mix up the people within each team. We also try to put interns and new hires near people who have been here a while so that they can learn more about how we work."

ENCOURAGE SOME PERSONAL EXPRESSION. I remember touring through a newly designed financial services company office floor a few years ago with a group of employees who were about to move in. The reactions were generally positive, but I'll never forget one woman, a self-identified Baby Boomer, who said with great concern, "But without a dedicated desk, where will I keep my cardigan?"

"We have lockers!" said the executive leading the tour proudly, but anyone could tell that was not going to cut it. This woman, a longtime, loyal employee, wanted more. That cardigan was clearly part of her identity and she wanted a home for it. And that is a cross-generational human desire: to mark a place of our own in the space where we spend a large part of our lives.

So, how do we create collaborative, innovative spaces for today's work while still fulfilling our employees' need for self-expression? If we are asking people to change the physical space in which they work, we need to be creative about providing new ways for them to express themselves and feel comfortable. How can people find ways to create personalization even without a bulletin board for family photos, a shelf to display industry awards, or a hook on which to hang a favorite cardigan?

Since Millennials and Gen Zs have come of age in a world with fewer offices and dedicated workspaces, we can observe how they have adapted. One place to do this is at your local coffee shop. One of my pastimes when I am standing at the counter, waiting for my tall skim latte, is to notice the various stickers on people's laptop covers. You can often predict each person's employer or industry simply from the sticker assortment.

While young people might be leading this trend, I see plenty of stickers on the laptops of people of other generations as well. Plus, we all personalize our various screens with photos of our families, favorite vacation spots, sports team logos, and more. Capital One even designs laptop stickers for various special events at the company to help employees customize their work devices while building company pride at the same time. Maybe the next iteration of workspace personalization is not on our walls or furniture but on the things we carry with us at all times: our devices, our notebooks, and our personal items.

Going back to our Baby Boomer friend, what if her company awarded her a chic company tote bag for her work on an exciting project in which she could carry her favorite cardigan? Perhaps it's not the same as having a regular seat, but it would be a refreshing remix.

(P.S. This might be a stretch, but I wonder if the rise of the acceptability of tattoos in many workplaces is related to the need for self-expression at work. If people can't have an office in which to hang images, then they will display them on their skin.)

BRING THE OUTSIDE IN. I love to share an enlightening statistic. And there are few statistics I like to share more than this one, because it's so simple and actionable and gives you the best result for the least amount of money or effort of perhaps any suggestion in this book. According to Capital One's Work Environment Survey, when asked what feature employees most desire in a workplace, the number one answer by far is . . .

Natural light.

Fifty-seven percent of employees say that they want more sunshine at work. That's right: while I encourage you to think about the various ways you can improve the lives of your employees across generations, you'll get the most bang for your buck if you simply raise the blinds. This goes for adding live plants to your work environment, too. We love sunlight and greenery in our homes, so of course we want these reminders of nature and health in our offices, where we spend the majority of our time.

INVITE IDEAS AND FEEDBACK. As with so many suggestions in this book, many of the best workspace remix ideas will come from your own multigenerational employees, who know your business best. Whether you send out an online survey or stick a suggestion box in your reception area, employees are usually more than willing to share their ideas for workspace improvements.

This is particularly important to make sure you reach employees who work in all different types of environments, from call centers to operations centers to factory floors. Just be sure to manage expectations by explaining that not all suggestions will necessarily be implemented.

At Capital One, the Workplace Solutions team, as part of its change management process, goes back to those teams whose workspaces have changed after 90 to 120 days to check in about what is and isn't working. While they are clear that large changes are permanent, these check-ins often lead to important findings. For example, at the first focus group after a remix to one of the bank's Plano, Texas, buildings, the focus groups determined one major oversight. Employee after employee said, "I know it's rarely cold in Plano, but sometimes it is, and we don't have anywhere to put our coats!" A few coatracks were purchased and people were happy.

To provide another example, a few years ago I was facilitating a workshop for executives at a construction company. Given the long hours, hard physical work, and remote locations of many of the company's job sites, they were struggling to attract and retain Millennials and Gen Z workers. One site manager shared that he had asked his existing young employees to offer suggestions for customizing a particular job site's trailer to better appeal to their generational peers.

The suggestions, he said, were notable for their simplicity—and applicability not just to young people but also to all employees. The suggestions included a stronger Wi-Fi signal so people could more easily communicate with their families when they were far from home. They asked for healthier food options in the fridge. And they requested some room to place weights and other light exercise equipment for the team members who spent most of the day sitting in the trailer. Yet again, Millennials and Gen Zs often want what all generations want. They are often just more willing to speak up about their desires.

These workspace enhancements were relatively easy and inexpensive to implement, and the site manager appreciated that his employees were respectful of reality. Out of curiosity, he asked them what they would want in a "trailer of the future" if a new design were being created from scratch. Perhaps not surprisingly, the most common answer was timeless: more windows.

REMIX YOURSELF. Finally, when was the last time you changed your own physical workspace? Have you tried standing up to do work, even if it's just answering e-mails with your laptop perched on top of a bookcase? How about adding a plant, or installing a softer lightbulb in your desk lamp? Make a small change and see what happens.

Telecommunication Nation: Rise of the Remote Worker

After I left that crowded conference room at WorkingWoman.com and started my own business in 2002, I worked from a desk in the corner of my studio apartment and sat in what was possibly the least comfortable wooden chair ever created. (I bought it for $10, which may have had something to do with it.)

This setup was a perfectly fine place for me to make calls, send e-mails, write blog posts, and plan my campus workshops. Besides the neighbor's yapping dogs next door, it was a pleasant work environment. What I struggled with was the fact that none of my friends at the time, who all had full-time jobs in more traditional work environments, believed I was actually working.

Everyone seemed to assume I was bingeing *Law & Order* episodes and perfecting my yoga poses just because I wasn't in an office. The reality, as many work-from-home professionals know, is that I often worked *more* than when I had been in a traditional office because I no longer had a commute or any physical way to "leave work." But people who worked in offices had a stigma against those of us who worked from home.

This is not surprising. I was on the early fringe of one of the biggest changes to today's labor market: the rise of remote work by both entrepreneurs and employed professionals, made possible by the spread of broadband Internet and mobile devices. In 1996 only 20 percent of employers offered telecommuting as a benefit. By 2016 that number had reached 60 percent.

And yet, I continue to observe a stigma against working from home. Some organizations and individual managers shun the practice or outright ban it. (IBM and Yahoo are notable examples of companies that have called all employees back to the office.) And I am not proud to say that, even as someone who worked from home myself for over a decade, I understand the arguments people have against remote work.

It's important to remember that for the generations who came up the ranks in the twentieth century, working from home was not possible for most employees. This is why my friends were so confused by my working from home. I've had many Gen Xers, Boomers, and Traditionalists confess to me that while they want to be supportive of their employees working from home, they can't help but feel it's better to have everyone in the office or that people aren't really working if the boss can't see them.

"I know it's ridiculous," one attorney admitted to me. "We all travel all the time and do conference calls from the airport and our firm's offices around the world. It shouldn't feel different talking to an associate who is at home versus at a desk at another office, but for some reason it does."

I have empathy for this point of view, and if you have a manager with this perspective, I'd encourage you to have empathy, too. It's a pretty radical shift to go from everyone being in the office for ten, twenty, or thirty years or more to now never knowing where anyone is. And as with other changes technology has enabled, it's okay to mourn what has been lost.

Some people miss the camaraderie of seeing their colleagues every day or occasionally working late together and bonding over midnight pizza. Some senior executives have shared with me how they think younger workers today are missing out on the incidental learning opportunities that took place when more people worked on-site. And more than a few long-tenured professionals have shared with me that they miss having a distinct separation between work and home.

I truly get it.

And I advise anyone who is resistant to embrace remote work anyway.

My first argument in favor of flexibility in work location is pretty basic: the ship has sailed. As workplace strategist Cali Williams Yost has said, "We'll never return to the time when 'work' meant going to the same physical space with the same people every day."

When I speak about telecommuting and remote work to corporations, law firms, professional associations, and universities, I often ask audience members to raise their hands if they have ever worked from home. I can't remember the last time every hand in the room wasn't raised. Sara Sutton, founder and CEO of FlexJobs, has a similar story of speaking at a technology conference on a panel about remote work, with thousands of professionals in the audience. "It was a very savvy, multigenerational audience," Sara described to me.

"I asked the audience," Sara said, "'How many of you work remotely or consider yourself remote workers?' and maybe 30 percent of the hands went up, which is in line with what I get at any conference. Then I said, 'How many of you work from home on weekends, work during your commute, or work on vacation?' and every single hand went up. Every one.

"There's a really big misconception about what is happening with remote work. In order to be a competitive, forward-thinking, evolving company, you have to understand this trend is already happening."

My second argument is that offering flexibility will better help you achieve your goals with a multigenerational workforce. If there were any benefit for which one size really does fit all generations of employees, remote work options would be it. Yes, younger workers expect flexibility because of their connection to technology, but half of telecommuters are 45 years of age or older. Yes, working mothers appreciate flexibility to care for children, but the percentage of women and men who telecommute is about equal and has been for the past decade.

The ability to work remotely helps employees economically by lessening the expense of commuting; it benefits the environment by lowering the carbon emissions associated with commuting; it serves employees with caretaking responsibilities for not just children but also elderly or sick relatives and those with pets; and it keeps people safe and productive during our increasingly extreme weather events.

While many organizations and leaders still consider flexibility to be a benefit or perk, I prefer to think of it as a multigenerational management and retention strategy. Isn't it time to drop the remaining stigma?

Remote Control: How Do You Manage a Multigenerational, Multi-located Team?

No matter your personal feelings around remote work, thanks to business travel, geographically distributed companies, and remote work policies that you yourself may not have implemented, it is almost a guarantee that as a leader today you will have to manage multigenerational workers who are not in the office. Here are some strategies to guide you:

BE DELIBERATE WITH YOUR TERMINOLOGY. Cali Williams Yost is an advocate for shifting the language from "working from home" to "working remotely," and I agree. For too many of us, particularly those with longer workplace tenures, fairly or not, "working from home" has those soap-opera-watching, bonbon-eating connotations that plagued me. Get in the habit of referring to people as "working remotely" even when they are in another office or on-site with a client. This removes the perceived hierarchy of one location being more "appropriate" than any other.

BE CREATIVE AND INCLUSIVE. Some leaders resist remote work because they have employees who need to be on-site. They fear that allowing flexibility for some employees will make others feel excluded. If this is the case for you, I'd encourage you to think creatively about whether it is possible to offer some degree of flexibility—even 5 percent of a person's job—to keep up with the times and allow people some wiggle room. Even a call center employee, distribution center worker, or driver might spend a few hours a month writing up reports, which could be done from home.

SET GUIDELINES FOR REMOTE WORK. It is totally appropriate to set guardrails and expectations around remote work, whether at the organizational level or among members of an individual team. Here are a variety of guidelines I have observed organizations implement.

Pick and choose the strategies that are appropriate for your culture and needs:

- Have a shared calendar on which workers indicate when they will be working remotely so people know where to find one another.
- Whenever anyone on a team is working remotely, have all meetings by phone or teleconference to ensure a level playing field and no "sidebar" conversations that remote workers miss out on.
- Determine core days or core hours during which all members of the team agree to be on-site for in-person meetings.
- Set clear expectations for professionalism and work hours. For example, no pet sounds in the background on conference calls, no taking calls at the grocery store or other non-quiet environment, and have a professional background for teleconference calls taken remotely.

Of course, a sense of humor is always important, just as it is in the office. We all remember the BBC interview with the very serious and professional professor whose children burst into his home office during a live TV interview. It was pretty adorable and an experience shared by many of us across generations who have ever worked from home. Sometimes the little snafus become the most memorable and bonding workplace experiences we have.

TRACK RESULTS. In the indelible words of Peter Drucker, "That which is measured, improves." Measurement is particularly important if you have leaders or colleagues who are skeptical about remote work—or if you yourself are resistant. Sara Sutton of FlexJobs advises teams to "have an open conversation about what flexibility and remote work means, what are the fears, what are the potential benefits? Clear the air on it," she says. "Find out from your workers what kind of flexibility is wanted. Some teams might lean toward remote work and some might lean toward a flexible schedule. The most common fear is that people aren't going to do their job, so decide how you will measure if somebody is doing their job. It doesn't have to be this scary process. It can be pretty logical, with some guidelines that you will follow through and check in."

To set up remote workers—and yourself as a leader—for success, decide if and when you will require remote workers to check in each remote day with you or their teams. Will you require an end-of-day write-up of accomplishments? Will you track any specific results and compare remote workdays with in-office days?

Also ask remote workers what they perceived as the successes and challenges of working from home. Did they have all the tools they needed? Every person is different, so results and needs will surely vary. Some remote workers may want or need a lot of oversight; some may not. Some bosses may like to instant message throughout the day with remote workers; others may have no problem with a daily check-in. What is most important is to clearly state your expectations as a leader and listen to your remote workers about what support they may or may not need.

KEEP UP WITH TECHNOLOGY ADVANCEMENTS. Remember that remote work really became possible because of the ubiquity of mobile devices and broadband Internet. There are many emerging technologies today that will make it even easier for more people to work remotely on more types of projects, such as drones, virtual reality, and, of course, robots.

If you've been in the workplace awhile, you'll remember that large companies once fiercely resisted the iPhone and subsequently Android devices, citing security concerns. (Maybe they just seemed too cool and fun to be considered professional.) I have memories of people sitting in my workshops with two phones stacked on top of the other—a personal iPhone on the bottom and a professional

BlackBerry on top. It was an equal sign of change how brazenly people were willing to show their need to stay connected both professionally and personally in a work setting.)

What this says to me is that the devices that currently frighten us will become commonplace, too. This likely includes drones, artificial intelligence devices, and Internet-enabled glasses like those tested by Google and Snap. Employees will continue to expect that the devices they use at home will be available to them in the workplace and that their use will be accepted.

To give an example that will likely apply to Gen Z, last summer my family went on vacation to Maine. My daughter, age 6 at the time, walked into the hotel room and said, "Alexa! What's the weather?" She assumed that anywhere she goes there will be an AI device at her service. You can blame my husband's and my tech-permissive parenting, or you can observe what technologies young people consider to be essential as you plan for the next several years of your tech budget.

Work Is Everywhere

As we come to the end of this discussion about workspace, I can't help but wonder: Where did you work today?

Were you in an open office space wishing for more privacy? Or were you alone in an office nursing a desire for more companionship and collaboration? Perhaps you worked from home: If so, did you feel lonely or empowered? Or maybe you shared a communal table with three other freelancers at a restaurant that offers its space for independent workers during the day. Did you plug in on a flight with unconscionably expensive Wi-Fi?

As for me, I wrote this chapter at a coworking space in New York City, where I rent a private office. But as soon as my Apple Watch buzzes that it's time to stand up, I might go read through this draft on a couch in the open seating area where there are often wandering puppies and an occasional tray of leftover conference room treats to snack on. And after that I might take my laptop to a coffee shop for a change of scenery. Even as an entrepreneur working alone, I like a variety of work location options.

Are any of us right or wrong in where we work or how we feel about it? To me it seems fitting that, given the extraordinary diversity of our workforce, we have an array of places from which we can work every day. Limiting workplace options feels counterproductive and unnecessary. As leaders, we will only benefit from increasing the options people have of where to complete their daily goals. Everybody really can win. In the next chapter, we'll take our experience of physical space and add in the emotional and psychological spaces we inhabit at work, otherwise known as culture.

CHAPTER 9: KEY TAKEAWAYS

- The workspace remix involves rethinking professional environments from a one-size-fits-all approach to more flexible, modular spaces and remote work options.
- While you as an individual leader may or may not be able to control the physical environment in which you and your team work, you can begin to pay attention to the ways your employees have been adapting to their physical workspace. Once you empathize with the tensions that may be lurking, you can begin to explore potential solutions.
- Keep in mind that people's workspace preferences are often unrelated to their generation and can have more to do with personality type, physical abilities, and the kinds of work they need to accomplish.
- Open floor plans are actually working against the innovation and collaboration they were meant to enable. This is why younger workers often wear headphones or earbuds to find a modicum of privacy in a wide-open, boundary-less space.
- Ideally, give people a variety of spaces in which to accomplish a variety of types of work. When we ask employees to be more agile, innovative, disruptive, and multidimensional, we need to provide spaces that allow for agile, innovative, disruptive, and multidimensional work to take place.
- When asked what feature employees most desire in a workplace, the number one answer by far is natural light. You'll get the most bang for your employee satisfaction buck if you simply raise the blinds in your office space.
- We'll never return to the time when "work" meant going to the same physical space with the same people every day. The ship has sailed and the desire for remote work options is perhaps

the only example of one benefit appealing to all generations. Think creatively about whether it is possible to offer some degree of flexibility—even 5 percent of a person's job—to keep up with the times and allow your people some wiggle room in their schedule.

10 THE CULTURE REMIX

A Widening of the Mind and of the Spirit

WE HAVE ESTABLISHED that people do not accept a job offer or stay in a position because of money, Ping-Pong tables, free lunches, or other "things." These can be important and appreciated, but the personal experience someone has every day and the emotions they have about their work—including whether they feel welcome, acknowledged, and included—matter significantly more. I'm talking about culture.

People love to quote the famous Peter Drucker line, "Culture eats strategy for breakfast," and I agree it's a great line and has some truth to it. But it doesn't define what culture is. I've always been fond of this definition from Jawaharlal Nehru, the first prime minister of India: "Culture is the widening of the mind and of the spirit."

As a leader, while you don't always have the power to raise someone's salary, change your office's location, or alter the benefit offerings, you can absolutely support the widening of people's minds and spirits.

Every person in every organization contributes to its culture. Which means that when we talk about culture, we are also talking about diversity and inclusion—about how to create work environments that are truly welcoming to all people, across generations and every other aspect of identity.

The remix involves rethinking organizational culture from being dictated top-down by leaders to growing bottom-up through the day-to-day experience of each and every employee.

In this final chapter, we will explore a variety of ways that leaders can be more inclusive in listening to and serving the needs of the diverse individuals who make our organizations thrive, including the ways we approach purpose, work/life integration, employee benefits, and more.

Leadership from Every Chair

Earlier in the book I mentioned the concept of intrapreneurship, which refers to acting like an entrepreneur within an organization. At LinkedIn, for example, one of the company's core values is "Act like an owner." That includes the existence of "InDays" one Friday a month when employees can work on personal projects and an internal platform on which any employee can pitch an idea to the executive team.

The concept of intrapreneurship has expanded in recent years to be more inclusive of individual contributors who see themselves as independent leaders but perhaps don't necessarily identify as entrepreneurs. The Estée Lauder Companies president and CEO Fabrizio Freda, for example, encourages all the company's employees to embrace "leadership from every chair."

I find this to be such a generous and empowering concept for employees of all generations, and one that is particularly suited to our times. As we have discussed, in a world in which everyone has a voice on social media, it feels natural to want to have a voice in one's workplace as well.

I also love this concept because leadership from every chair can be applied on a smaller scale within a team or in a small business. Everyone can generate ideas and help to solve challenges. As Laszlo Bock, former head of People Operations at Google, says, "Pick an area where people are frustrated and let them fix it. If there are constraints, limited time or money, tell them what they are. Be transparent with your people and give them a voice in shaping your team or company. You'll be stunned by what they accomplish."

As an example, one leader at a consumer packaged goods brand engaged her team across all generations, lengths of tenure, and functional roles to identify and suggest solutions to any little irritations they were experiencing at work. She called the project "100 Paper Cuts"—a term borrowed from computer programming—and it became a fun group effort. One "paper cut" the team identified was that they had nowhere in their small and crowded office to eat lunch together and socialize a bit. Their proposed solution was to designate the company conference room as a lunchroom each day from noon to 1 p.m. The boss loved the idea and implemented it immediately. That simple solution boosted morale and gave employees a sense of pride and ownership in their office culture. And the financial cost? Zero.

The Power of Purpose

One area in which many employees want to engage more deeply with their employers is corporate social responsibility and volunteering. According to one study, 84 percent of Millennials want

employers to give them ways to get involved in their communities—
and 65 percent of older generations want the same opportunity.

But I sometimes find a disconnect between the support that organizations provide to their communities or to charitable causes
and the way they treat their own employees. Doesn't community
include what is happening inside the walls of our organizations? As
you think about the culture of your organization or team, I would
encourage you to think about ways that your employees can find
meaning and purpose and do good within their everyday work, in
addition to thinking about opportunities to do so outside their
jobs.

KPMG is one of the "big four" accounting and professional services firms. Like others in its elite ranks, the firm boasts admirable
charitable work, and employee surveys showed strong engagement
and retention. But we are not living in times of maintaining the
status quo, so KPMG wanted to further improve its standing as a
best-in-class employer for current and future employees.

A review of internal survey results showed that one factor most
strongly drove employee engagement and retention at the firm. It
was agreement with the statement "I feel like my job has special
meaning and is not just a job."

As a result, in 2014 the company launched what it called the
Higher Purpose Initiative and asked employees all across the organization to submit posters that shared their own stories about how
their work is making a difference. The program kicked off with a
video of how the firm has contributed to many historic events, like
certifying the election of Nelson Mandela in South Africa.

The project's goal was to collect 10,000 posters. The idea proved
so popular that employees submitted 42,000 posters (note that the
firm has 27,000 employees). Some examples include, "I keep jobs
in the U.S.A.," submitted by an employee who helped clients obtain federal tax credits for keeping research and development jobs in

America. Another said, "I combat terrorism," from an employee who helped financial institutions prevent money laundering. Yet another declared, "We restore neighborhoods," from a team that audits development programs for low-income communities. The faces on the various posters are notable for their diversity of age, ethnicity, and gender.

The result of this increased attention to purpose? When workers were surveyed, 90 percent said the initiative had increased their pride in working for the firm. When asked if KPMG is a great place to work, 89 percent of employees agreed, up from 82 percent a year earlier. Importantly, KPMG noted a drop in morale on teams where employees felt their manager was *not* embracing the commitment to purpose. These managers were offered additional training and support.

Overall, the initiative contributed to KPMG rising seventeen positions on the prestigious *Fortune* 100 Best Companies to Work For list, making KPMG the number one–ranked big four accounting firm for the first time in the company's history.

And all they did was ask employees to make posters about how their work was making a difference. To me, that shows how desperately people of all generations want to find meaning in their work.

While purpose resonates across all generations, it is a particularly important factor for Millennials. One 20-something computer programmer for a global retail chain told me, with great pride, how his boss told him that every line of code he writes will impact millions of customers around the world. That is purpose. And culture. And a pretty effective retention strategy.

I often laugh when leaders complain about how their "entitled"—there's that word again—Millennials come into their jobs on day one and want to make a difference. "How dare they!" I like to reply in mock horror. Why on earth would we as leaders not consider it a good thing that Millennials want to contribute as much and as early as possible? Maybe because it puts more pressure on us to make sure *we* are clear on the purpose of the work we are doing and assigning?

Work/Life Integration

When we talk about meaning, we inevitably talk about how people see the role of work in their lives. And emphasizing a sense of purpose with employees does *not*, of course, replace the need to compensate everyone appropriately. One of the main reasons we all work is to make money to pay for our needs and wants. That said, I've always been intrigued by the term "make a living," because it shows how aligned our personal and professional selves truly are. Even those who say they "work to live" still spend a lot of life doing their jobs. So many Millennials have told me how they don't really understand the term "work/life balance." "Isn't it all my life?" they say.

My preference is for the term "work/life integration," which is not perfect, but to me it feels more reflective of our times. "Balance" implies a desire to place equal time and emphasis on two separate "sides" of life. The word "integration" feels more holistic and real in a world in which our devices keep us connected to all aspects of our lives at all times. Cali Williams Yost coined the term "work/life fit" as another option to describe how work and home obligations are involved in an ongoing recalibration that ebbs and flows over the course of one's career.

The idea of work/life "balance" implies that you can somehow leave your life behind when you go to work—or "leave your drama at the door," as one of my editors told me one of her bosses used to say. Workers in past decades could more easily separate from the factory or office after work hours. Today we can no longer do that, which means a leader's policies and expectations must be adjusted accordingly, as we addressed related to remote work in the last chapter.

Several young people have pointed out how unfair it is for a boss to expect an employee to answer e-mail messages after work hours but criticize that same employee for texting a friend or doing a little online shopping during the day. I am not saying that you should encourage your team to shop on their phones all day, but more leeway for managing one's life during work hours is appropriate. Rather than bemoan that or try to turn back the clock, the best leaders today accept the reality that work and "life" are more interrelated than ever.

This is why so many companies now offer employee benefits to make it easier to manage working while being human, with such offerings as on-site car oil changes and flu shots and even selling stamps to save employees from long post office lines. If you are not in a position to change your company's benefit offerings, sometimes just acknowledging the work/life issue is appreciated. One nonprofit employee who works long hours caring for children with disabilities told me that it meant the world to her when her manager asked about her weekend or made sure she left on time on days when she had after-work plans.

Generationally, work/life balance was not really a consideration for the first several decades of Traditionalists' and Baby Boomers' careers. To put it bluntly, the workplace—and especially leadership roles—were dominated by middle- to upper-middle-class married white men whose wives managed their homes and children. This was not by any means all Traditionalists and Boomers, but it was a very common scenario. Many working women of these eras chose either not to have children or not to discuss their children during the workday for fear they would be discriminated against or viewed as not committed and on the "mommy track."

As the workplace began to be populated by more women, dual-income families, and single parents, "work/life balance" gained more traction as Gen Xers like me were rising in the ranks. But often, as I remember it, "work/life" concerns were still usually reserved for people with children who might need to leave early to care for a sick child or attend a sporting event or play. Everyone else was expected to work standard hours. And remember, it was not until well into our careers that most Gen Xers had the technology that would enable us to work from anywhere other than on-site.

And then Millennials, the generation who *were* those sick children and childhood athletes and actors, began to enter the workplace. Perhaps because so many members of this generation saw their parents struggle with work/life issues, they came in with their eyes wide open. And the Internet, high-speed Wi-Fi, and mobile devices enabled them to work from anywhere. When I started speaking on college campuses in the early 2000s, it would have been unthinkable for a student to ask a question about finding a job with work/life flexibility. Today, I would say it is the most common question I receive on campuses, from any gender, as early as their first year.

As a sign of how much the world has remixed its thinking on this issue, a report by Accenture found that 52 percent of employees globally, across all generations, turned down a job offer because of concerns about work/life integration. In fact, Capital One's 2018 Work Environment Survey found that 65 percent of employees expect the next company they work for to have flexible hours. Note that this is not a preference; it is an expectation. Across the board, studies show that workers with some degree of flexibility in when, where, and how they work report feeling more productive, more engaged, and more creative. PwC says that 90 percent of its employees incorporate some kind of flexibility into their schedules and report "zero shift in our productivity as a firm" as a result.

Flexible schedules are also a way to attract and retain older workers, who may have worked long hours earlier in their careers. Many workers over 50 even say they would be willing to exchange high salaries—often a concern among employers about hiring older workers—for flexible schedules. Some companies are offering specific flexibility programs for this population. CVS's "Snowbird" program allows older employees to travel and work seasonally in different CVS pharmacy locations around the country; Steelcase offers workers a phased retirement program with reduced hours; and Brooks Brothers has restructured assignments to offer enhanced flexibility for its aging workforce.

Law firms have traditionally been notorious for long hours and lack of balance—think billable hours, up-or-out career paths, and high expectations for 24/7/365 client service—but some firms are rejecting that stereotype and remixing for a new generation of attorneys. Reed Smith remixed their billable hour policy to offer more flexibility to firm associates by crediting different activities as billable. "For example," Casey Ryan of Reed Smith explained to me, "we've added fifty 'development hours,' which gives an associate the opportunity to attend depositions or an opening argument in trial, which are really valuable experiences."

At Vetter Health Services, leadership had to think creatively about how to provide flexibility in an industry, nursing home operations, in which employees traditionally work lengthy shifts. In a great example of asking, "What do we do because we've always done it?" president Glenn Van Ekeren and his team took a fresh approach to the issue of scheduling. "Just because we have always had eight- or twelve-hour schedules, why can we not have someone work two hours?" And so now they do.

The productivity start-up Doist, creator of the Todoist app, faced a dilemma in figuring out a company-wide vacation policy for its sixty employees across twenty-six countries. I've already mentioned my hesitation about unlimited vacation policies, and Doist had the same perspective. No existing system of vacation days seemed appealing. As Amir Salihefendić, Doist's founder, said, "Some of the companies building the most innovative technologies in the world are still using principles of work that are hundreds of years old."

What the company came up with to be most fair to its diverse workforce is to eliminate company holidays altogether and give everyone forty days off a year to use as they see fit—for national holidays in their countries, religious holidays, personal time off, vacation, or whatever else they choose. And as an additional boundary to promote fairness, the time off is mandatory.

The Employee Benefits Remix

Given the diversity of people in today's workplace, it is imperative to address the wider range of employee benefits they will want and expect. The benefits offered by an organization send a strong message to employees about how much they are valued. Whereas benefits used to be a once-a-year consideration when employees had to check a few boxes on a form for what insurance and pension or 401(k) investment plan they wanted, now employee benefits are infused in our everyday experience and are often considered part of an organization's culture.

Laura Marzi, chief marketing officer for the benefits division of The Hartford, puts it this way: "What we are hearing from employees today is a very different perspective on the value of work and their desire for benefits that address their 'whole self.' The message we are hearing is 'If I give you my talent and time, you will reciprocate by understanding that I am a human being with many interests and desires.'"

If you haven't been paying close attention to the benefits industry, you might be surprised by how many more options are now available for employers to consider. In just the past twenty years, the Society for Human Resource Management (SHRM) has gone from tracking 60 employee benefits in 1996 to 330 benefits today. And yet, as we have discussed, some major benefits like employee pensions have virtually disappeared in this same time period.

Here are a few notable changes over time:

- In 1996, 54 percent of employers offered wellness resources and information. Today, 72 percent do. (Wellness benefits include bonuses for completing certain health and wellness programs, standing desks, and on-site fitness centers.)
- The share of *Fortune* 1000 companies offering "summer Fridays"—days on which employees can leave early for a long summer weekend—doubled from 21 percent in 2015 to 42 percent in 2018.
- The share of corporations offering paid maternity leave increased from 26 percent in 2016 to 35 percent in 2018.
- While only about 15 percent of U.S. employers offer any paid paternity leave, the average amount of that time offered by top companies has grown from four weeks in 2015 to eleven weeks in 2017.

As a working parent myself, I must note that too many employers do not offer adequate parental leave and child care support, and our country overall is woefully behind in supporting working parents. One of the reasons I advocate so strongly for child care benefits is the impact parents' working lives have on their children's perceptions of work. As we have discussed, when you are a child and witness a parent lose a job because of family needs or struggle to manage work and family obligations, it has an enormous impact on your own views about work.

Studies show that child care support is especially helpful for lower-income families, because it can help move generations of children forward toward higher earnings, better jobs, improved health, and more education as adults.

Another reason is that it just makes good business sense. Particularly as more Millennials need two adult incomes to support a family and top talent is harder to retain, many employers have found a competitive advantage in recruiting and retaining talent by providing benefits like paid parental leave and child care assistance, which have also proven to increase productivity, employee engagement, and financial performance.

Here are some more examples of how employers have adapted to the changing benefit needs of diverse multigenerational workers. If you as a leader cannot necessarily change the benefits offered to your employees, you can build your awareness of what kinds of benefits are being offered in the marketplace and how your suite of offerings compares. With this awareness, you can advocate for your organization to provide benefits that will serve your company's particular mix of employees in a more inclusive way.

STUDENT LOAN REPAYMENT. Like Abbott, which we discussed in chapter 2, many employers are now offering their Millennial and Gen Z employees some relief for their student loan debt. About 4 percent of employers today offer some sort of student loan repayment benefit, up from 3 percent in 2015, according to the SHRM. The way it usually works is employers make a lump-sum after-tax payment, monthly or annually, toward the employee's student loans. Right now such programs are mostly offered by large corporations such as Fidelity, Hewlett Packard Enterprise, and Aetna. The U.S. Congress has begun to offer staffers up to $10,000 for student loan debt repayment, and it is my hope that more people, especially those entering public service, will have access to such programs in the future.

MENTAL HEALTH SUPPORT. Gen Z are reporting higher levels of anxiety and depression than any previous generation. Some attribute this increase to the pressures of online life and constant connectivity, while others note that it is more accepted societally today to report mental health concerns. About one in eight college first-years reported feeling depressed frequently in 2016, the highest level in the three decades such statistics have been collected.

I suspect higher rates of mental health concerns also have to do with the fact that there are fewer boundaries around work today. This has proven problematic for entrepreneurs in particular, especially those who make a living documenting their lives on YouTube. Famous YouTubers like Lilly Singh, Elle Mills, and Rubén "El Rubius" Gundersen have very publicly admitted to burning out.

This doesn't surprise experts like Katrina Gay, national director for strategic partnerships at the National Alliance on Mental Illness, who has said how dangerous it can be when no one tells you when to stop working. What Gay says is positive is the ways in which the very public acknowledgment of mental health concerns by YouTube stars has modeled healthy behavior for their millions of followers.

As someone who struggles with anxiety and workaholism myself, I have been gratified to find an increase in the number of companies that offer and promote mental health benefits through their health insurance plans and provide counseling through short-term employee assistance programs (EAPs).

Mental health concerns are certainly not limited to younger generations. They are also prominent in employees who frequently work remotely. Although many employees desire and appreciate flexible work schedules, these come with some risks, including the feeling of isolation. No one is immune to mental health concerns. This is why a few years ago Ernst & Young launched "We Care," a company-wide mental health program that includes a hotline for struggling workers. Other organizations are turning to technology-based programs to help support employees with mental health as well as other personal development issues. BetterUp, a benefit offered by such employers as Facebook, Logitech, and Buffalo Wild Wings, provides virtual counseling and executive coaching with licensed therapists and executive coaches.

LIFE PLANNING ACCOUNTS. Another growing trend in Customization Nation is employers' fully or partially funding a taxable account with cash that workers can use to spend on a variety of approved expenses, such as student loan payments, a child's or grandchild's college education, a gym membership, professional memberships, home closing costs, or more. Currently, such accounts range from about $500 to $2,500 per year and are known as life planning accounts.

Most employers can't afford to provide all the benefits that employees might want—or that their deeper-pocketed competitors might—so this strategy allows employees to pick and choose their perks. This also ensures that no one cohort feels ignored or less important. When LinkedIn employees without children felt left out of the company's generous paid parental leave policy, the company decided to offer all employees a benefit that provides up to $500 a quarter to spend on lifestyle perks such as massages, a personal trainer, or even a professional dog walker.

The life planning account model also provides leaders with flexibility to remix the scope of your benefit offerings depending on the changing needs of your workers. For example, as the age of parenthood has been rising, more Millennials have expressed interest in pet insurance for their animals. Given the many recent technology breaches of people's personal information and the security-minded nature of Generation Z, we will find an increased interest in personal identity theft insurance as well.

All this said, benefits experts are quick to point out that employers cannot ignore the fundamental benefits that employees need. Remember Remixer Rule #6: Don't change what works. Laura

Marzi cautions employers not to get so caught up in "on-trend" benefits that their employees disregard the importance of "bedrock" protections, such as health, life, and disability insurance that previous generations took for granted, since their employers often provided them for free.

"It is quite easy for people to be attracted to spend money on benefits they understand the most, like pet insurance," she says. "But if you have no protection for your health through health insurance or your income through disability insurance, it is extremely difficult to live the life you want if something happens to you."

Laura's best advice to leaders is to make benefits information and selection help available, and then honor how much engagement employees want to have with their leaders about choosing benefits.

She says, "I have encountered 23-year-olds who will research on Google if their dental or health insurance is worth spending extra money on for a value-added service. And I have encountered 64-year-olds who have signed up the same way for the same benefits their entire career. It's really important to meet people where they are."

In the past it was enough for an employer to provide a brochure on benefits to each employee. Now many companies are using segmentation analysis to offer the right mix of benefits to employees at various life stages. For individual leaders, my best advice is to be clear on the resources your company offers to help employees make smart decisions.

What We Wear

We've talked a lot about what we say at work, think at work, expect at work, the people we work with, and the spaces in which we work. Let's spend a moment on the clothes we wear while doing all of this. Clothing is a part of culture and it is another area in which the workplace is shifting under our feet.

When I landed my job at WorkingWoman.com, my mom took me to the mall to buy my first-ever suit. How did I know I had to wear a suit to this brand-new job? Because the job was in an office and everyone I had ever met or watched on TV who worked in an office of any sort wore a suit. For anyone starting a new job today, this assumption is no longer correct.

Some of the most common questions I receive from young professionals, particularly women, relate to appropriate and inappropriate dress. Although a lot of people didn't like wearing suits every day, the old rules of "looking professional" were a lot easier. But now, as society has become more casual overall and different industries and organizations have vastly different cultures, getting dressed for work is daunting. The longer you've been getting dressed for work, the more drastic the change has felt. As one history professor put it, "Americans began the twentieth century in bustles and bowler hats and ended it in velour sweat suits and flannel shirts—the most radical shift in dress standards in human history."

While many Boomers dressed casually on the weekends, they still wore suits to work in offices. It was the dot-com era and the rise of the Silicon Valley ethos that changed everything. According to the SHRM, just 24 percent of companies had some sort of casual dress policy in 1992. By 1999, 95 percent of U.S. companies had one. Some employers reinstated more formal dress codes after the 2008 recession, but it is a rare organization today that requires suits every day. Many companies have no dress code at all, allowing jeans, shorts, yoga pants, flip-flops, and basically anything short of a swimsuit (unless you're, you know, an 80-year-old lifeguard).

Cindi Leive, former editor in chief of *Glamour*, explains the situation like this: "There's the overall demolition of every old rule you can think of about how people should dress. The concept of work dressing versus casual dressing is gone in a lot of fields. So is the idea of dressing for day versus night, or of what makes a January outfit versus a July outfit, or of what's appropriate for a 20-year-old versus for a 50-year-old."

It's no wonder young people first entering the workplace have no idea how to dress for work. Men have the benefit of just wearing the default khaki pants and collared shirt, but it's more challenging for women, who have many different options. I am reminded of the confusion I felt when I was invited to a networking event on a boat for which the requested dress was "festive nautical." Huh?

If you are not providing clear guidance on what you expect employees to wear (and not wear), you can't blame them for showing up in what members of a different generation (and, possibly, the same generation!) deem inappropriate.

Anecdotally, most employees tell me they think it is ridiculous to dress formally for work if you will be sitting at a desk all day and it's just for protocol's sake. And as far as I have found, there is no definitive research on whether casual dress makes us more or less productive, more or less engaged, more or less loyal to an employer. What seems to make the most sense is—as with so many issues—a flexible policy with some guardrails that aligns with your overall culture and the work that people do. As discussed earlier, if dressing in a suit and tie is core to your culture but members of your team are complaining, it is critical to explain the "why" behind that dress code.

If you're not sure what kind of policy to implement, my favorite dress code remix is the increasingly popular "dress-for-your-day" policy, which puts trust in employees to know if they need to wear a suit because they have a client meeting or can wear jeans because they'll be heads-down at a desk all day working on code. However, this type of flexible policy works best when it is accompanied by some very clear guidelines and boundaries, usually a website featuring a few visual examples of diverse employees dressed for different situations.

And in case you are wondering, for the festive nautical event I went with head-to-toe navy and a ribbon in my hair.

Perks That Walk the Walk

Coming full circle to our discussion of creating a culture of purpose at work, some organizations are tying their employee benefits more closely to their mission and values. Retail stores have long offered employee discounts on products for employees, and schools and universities offer discounted tuition to employees and their families; now other kinds of businesses are becoming more creative in this area, and it's a win-win across generations.

Airbnb gives employees an annual allowance of $2,000 to travel and stay in an Airbnb listing anywhere in the world. Reebok provides free CrossFit classes. Qualtrics is a company that provides experience management software for such activities as market research, employee surveys, and customer loyalty programs. Because it is in the "experience" business, one of Qualtrics' benefits is to give each employee $1,500 per year to spend on an experience, like swimming with sharks, volunteering abroad, or visiting one of the Seven Wonders of the Ancient World.

These companies believe, as I do, that employees of all generations want to feel aligned to the missions of their employers.

As an individual leader, you can apply this same principle without flying your staff to Greece or Egypt. You can offer small, personal benefits that improve your team's culture, acknowledge individuality, and improve people's work/life integration. All it takes is a simple question: What makes you feel appreciated?

When you take the time to acknowledge an employee, try to do it in a way that will truly resonate with that person. Some employees might blossom from a company-wide e-mail that would make others blush or cringe. Some people would love for their boss to be cc'ed on your praise; others would prefer a private note.

And if you're offering something more than just a note or verbal thanks, find out what small gestures might mean the most to each of your employees. Group dinners may sound fun, but not to the employees who have to shell out for a babysitter when they've just been away from their kids all day. Leaving early on Fridays may seem blissful to you, but someone with a tough commute may prefer to come in later in the morning instead. You might not care at all about social media, but being featured in a company Instagram post might mean the world to one of your employees.

I was so impressed when one of my vendor partners asked me for a short list of my gift preferences so they could get me the ideal personal recognition for my birthday or holidays. Knowing what makes your employees (or clients) feel valued will make them value you. And, wow, do I enjoy it when they send me my favorite white wine and gift certificates for a mani-pedi.

Author and workplace expert Keith Ferrazzi says, "Little choices make big impressions," and when I talk about workplace culture, I find myself quoting that line more than any other. When people think about their careers, they usually remember moments that made them feel special and acknowledged as individuals: the time the CEO praised your work in a meeting; how your boss gave you extra time off when your grandmother died; the note from the long-tenured employee saying the new all-gender restroom policy you advocated for changed their life; the moment a junior employee said she joined the company because your success inspired her.

Every moment matters, and every moment is an opportunity to improve yourself and your organization's shared culture a little bit more.

CHAPTER 10: KEY TAKEAWAYS

- The culture remix involves rethinking organizational culture from being dictated top-down by leaders to growing bottom-up by the day-to-day experience of each and every employee.
- In a world in which our devices keep us connected to all aspects of our lives at all times, "work" and "life" have become more integrated and inseparable. Think about ways that your employees can find and express meaning and purpose within their everyday work.
- Have as open a conversation as possible with multigenerational employees at all levels about what flexibility means to them. Once you know what people want, you can prioritize what flexible options you decide to offer. The data can show priority, and then you can experiment and regroup.
- Employee benefits are part of your organization's culture. Consider widening the benefits you offer to appeal to more employees and their needs, and provide support for making benefits decisions.
- When thinking about the impact you personally can have on your organization's culture, especially in a large organization, it's okay to start small. Remember that little choices make big impressions.

CONCLUSION: Your Personal Career Remix

I ONCE ATTENDED a conference celebrating the top thirty companies for executive women. At the end of the event, there was a panel featuring the highest-ranking woman at each of these companies. Near the conclusion of this panel, the moderator asked each executive, "If you could go back to the very beginning of your career and give yourself one piece of advice, what would you tell your younger self? What do you most wish you had done then, knowing what you know now?"

One piece of advice stood out among all the others. It was from a chief marketing officer, who said, "If I could go back to the beginning of my career and give myself one piece of advice, I would tell myself not to be so afraid. When I think back on my career—and I have been very successful and achieved a lot—but to this day I still think about and regret the jobs I didn't apply for, the raises and promotions I didn't ask for, the ideas I had and didn't share. I don't regret my mistakes or embarrassments or failures; what I regret are the times I held myself back."

I have tried to keep this wise and candid advice in mind in my own career, and I share it with my youngest audiences, especially college students. But as I have been writing this book and thinking more and more about multigenerational success, it strikes me that this advice is relevant to all generations at every stage of our careers and leadership journeys. How often have you held yourself back from applying for a position, or starting a new venture, or connecting with a new person because you felt too old, too young, or any other "too" to take the action?

We have talked about all the different ways to remix the workplace. Let's take a final moment to focus solely on how you as an individual can remix your own career now and in the years to come.

Applying Remixer Rule #2: Empathize, I have an enormous amount of empathy for how hard change can be at every stage of one's career. I originally started my business to help college graduates with the difficult transition into the "real world." Then I began to advise Gen X and Baby Boomer managers on the challenges of managing multiple generations. I have been mixing and remixing and adapting and reinventing myself and my own career for years. While people have finally stopped asking me why I don't have a "real" job, it is still really hard to constantly adapt and change.

It is especially painful when circumstances or other people's biases push us away from things we love—when your beloved employer goes out of business, when the product you worked so hard to build is discontinued, when someone opines that you are "too old" or "too expensive" for your current role, or when your entire industry becomes obsolete. Sometimes we can't even see where an alternate path might lead, even though we have little choice but to follow it.

I would also suggest that each person's personal career path today represents a microcosm of the macro changes we have been exploring throughout this book: from one-size-fits-all/need-to-know-basis/up-or-out-career-ladders to a collective desire for more personal development, customization, variety, flexibility, work/life integration, meaning, and purpose. It is a rare person I meet today who isn't concerned about the future of their industry, that of their organization, or their own career longevity.

The challenge is that we are still in the early days of this new model and so many critical issues are still unclear. How much gig work does it take to support oneself? Will benefits be fully portable from one part-time or short-term job to the next? How will fair wages be determined as work becomes more transient and fragmented and lasts later in life? How many jobs will automation and augmentation really eliminate or add?

With so much uncertainty, your only choice as an individual is to continually stay alert and adapt. This does not mean changing everything—remember Remixer Rule #6—but taking the existing, recognizable tunes and rhythm of your career and adding to and subtracting from them as necessary. Fortunately, we already have many examples of how to do this. Tiffany, Natalia, Bill, Jon, and Diana are a few of them. Here are their stories.

The Career Path Remixer: Tiffany Dufu

Tiffany Dufu is a women's leadership advocate, bestselling author, speaker, and fellow Gen Xer. Tiffany has had a job since she was sixteen and, to her, a regular paycheck represented stability and financial security. "Direct deposits were the pathway to financial freedom," she says.

But a conversation with a Millennial changed her perspective.

Tiffany had recently begun to grow what she calls a portfolio career, combining a day job as an executive at a technology company with being an in-demand public speaker and author. She was itching to write another book and was exploring launching her own company, but, as she lamented one day to her Millennial assistant, she didn't have the time to do either.

"Why are you still working at the tech company if you want to start a company and write another book?" her assistant asked.

Tiffany explained that of course there was no way she could leave her job. It was her "anchor" and—most important of all—it provided health insurance for her family of four.

"How much does your health insurance cost annually?" the assistant asked.

When Tiffany told her the amount, she replied, "That is a lot of money. But didn't a client just pay you that exact amount to give one keynote speech?"

That was an aha moment.

"I literally sat back in my chair when she said that," Tiffany tells me about this exchange. "I realized how I had been making decisions based on this old dinosaur model of what a career was and what success was. If I had considered the actual economics of my situation, it made perfect sense to leave my job. Her insight awakened me to how our old paradigms can hinder us from executing on new models in the new economy."

Less than a year after this conversation, Tiffany quit her tech company job and launched her new venture, The Cru, a peer coaching service for women wanting to accelerate their professional and personal growth. And she is writing that second book.

Are any "old dinosaur" beliefs holding you back from your next move?

The Diversity and Inclusion Remixer: Natalia Oberti Noguera

Natalia Oberti Noguera is CEO of Pipeline Angels, which she founded in 2011 when she was 27 years old. Pipeline Angels is changing the face of angel investing and creating capital for women and nonbinary femme social entrepreneurs. Natalia is a cis gender queer Latina and prefers the term Gen Y to Millennial.

When I requested an interview with Natalia and told her that the theme of this book was "the remix," she immediately brought up the musical concept of sampling as an important addition to discuss. While remixing involves adding, changing, or modifying an original piece of music, sampling is taking a portion of one recording and reusing it directly in a new recording. The distinction, as Natalia put it to me, is that sampling gives credit to and amplifies the original.

Amplifying and sampling are exactly what Natalia excels at. She has said, "When the most marginalized are leading the conversation, that's when inclusion happens." You've already met Pipeline Angels' Gen Z chief of staff, Anisa Flowers, who is Deaf. Natalia found a Deaf employee by sharing across social media a part-time paid opportunity that encouraged Deaf and hard of hearing people of color to apply. According to Natalia, "If you want to be inclusive, be explicit." (While I was writing this book, I noticed Natalia's tweet, "Searching for Black and/or Latinx and/or Indigenous women/femme photographers and videographers for a paid project next week in NYC.")

To teach a portion of the orientation program for the members of her angel investing boot camp (most members of Pipeline Angels are new to angel investing and making an investment for the first time), Natalia hired Riley Hanson, the half-Black, half-Indian, nonbinary femme engineer you met in chapter 8. By having Riley lead this conversation, Natalia says, "The academic and theoretical become real."

Natalia describes herself as a "huge believer" in the value of intergenerational relationships and says she doesn't mind being invited to certain events or discussions due to her young age, gender, orientation, or ethnicity. "I just think about how many rooms I *haven't* been invited into because of that identity, so I just say yes and then leverage that."

She is also transparent about the mistakes she has made regarding inclusion. She quips, "Best practices often come from best mistakes." Pipeline Angels is a remote team from around the country, and last summer Natalia brought everyone together for a dinner in San Francisco. "I was so excited and proud," she says. "I found a sustainable, organic, woman-led restaurant and hired what felt like the one Black woman/femme American Sign Language interpreter in SF—this is how I realized that most ASL interpreters are white women.

"After dinner, I was so excited and asked Anisa how the dinner had gone and Anisa told me that the restaurant hadn't been Deaf-friendly. It had dim lighting, which made it harder to lip-read and follow the interpreter, and the table wasn't round, which helps in terms of keeping up with the conversation.

"I was so crestfallen," Natalia admits.

A month later she shared this experience when she was interviewing Ellen Pao, the venture capitalist who sued Kleiner Perkins for gender discrimination in 2012, about Pao's book *Reset*. Ellen Pao replied positively. "Anisa told you," she said. "You have created a culture at Pipeline Angels where Anisa felt comfortable telling you that it hadn't been a Deaf-friendly restaurant."

When Natalia shared this story with me, she quoted Maya Angelou's wise words, "Now that I know better, I do better." Being an inclusive leader does not mean being a perfect leader, but it does mean learning from your missteps and creating a culture of "brave space," as activist and writer Micky ScottBey Jones says, where people can have brave conversations.

How can you better amplify and "sample"—properly crediting them, of course—the people on your team? Where do you know better but are not doing better yet? How could you be creating a "brave space" for your team?

The Corporate Remixer: Bill Fisse

When I think of the stereotype of the Baby Boomer "company man," I can't help but think of the résumé of Bill Fisse, whom you met in chapter 3. He has worked for the banking giant Citi for thirty-eight years in roles of increasing responsibility and is currently a managing director of human resources and global head of talent and diversity for Citi's Institutional Businesses.

When I think of the actual IRL person Bill Fisse, I can't help but think of the definition of an enthusiastic remixer. He has spearheaded Citi's approach to attracting and engaging young talent and, true to form, he insisted on bringing his Gen Z colleague to our interview. (And, yes, Bill is the "banking industry veteran" from the introduction who now loves to sit at a different desk every day. "I just swivel my chair and there are my colleagues!" he says with genuine delight.)

Bill is a master of mixing the old and the new in a scalable way. "In my nearly four decades at Citi," Bill says, "the core of our culture has never changed. We have always been known as a place that promotes career mobility across business lines, products, functions, and geographies. What has changed tremendously is the nature of the mobility Millennials and Gen Zs want.

"On the old Wall Street, it was all about the vertical nature of careers," Bill says, citing his own career path to the top as an example. But he understands that today's young people want something different. "Now it is much more about experiences. Millennials and Zs do not want a straight line to managing director. They want to work for a company whose values are aligned with things that are important to them."

To this end, Bill and his team knew they had to get creative. Over the past several years, they have piloted new offerings for entry-level employees, including being the only firm in the country that invites incoming banking analysts to defer for one year to take a service year—paid for by Citi—to give back and build their leadership skills. They also offer a program to help employees obtain positions on junior nonprofit boards, to amplify their connection to meaning and purpose and to enhance and expand their leadership skills.

Bill has also supported the company's move to a two-pronged

performance rating system to improve the people management skills of the company's leaders. The new system assesses the firm's managers, many of whom oversee Millennials and Gen Zs, on both *what* they achieve (work accomplishments) and *how* they go about achieving that (leadership and interpersonal effectiveness with the people they manage). "We are moving away from rewarding people for technical expertise alone," Bill explains, "because we know that to attract and keep early-career people at the firm, we need high-quality managers to lead them."

According to Bill, the most significant change he and the firm have had to embrace is the breaking down of the hierarchical barriers of a large, global financial services organization. This is Wall Street, after all. "When I first started," Bill recalls, "you would think long and hard before talking to someone a 'skip level' ahead of you in the vertical structure of the banking environment. And now a very junior person can walk up and share an idea with a managing director—and, in fact, is encouraged to do so."

Bill's enthusiasm for the changes on Wall Street is infectious and a model for treating generational change not as a burden to bemoan but as an opportunity to genuinely relish. I can only imagine how many of those junior people are not only sharing great ideas with him but also viewing him as a role model of multigenerational success.

What gets you excited about the future of work? Where can you pilot an idea to see what changes it might lead to? If you sit in an office, would you consider moving around more often to be more available and interactive with your team?

The Entrepreneurial Remixer: Jon Steinberg

Jon Steinberg is the former president of BuzzFeed and currently founder and CEO of Cheddar Inc., a Millennial- and Gen Z–focused news network. A true remixer, Jon analyzed the data that the median age of the MSNBC and Fox News viewer was 65, and CNN's was 60, and realized it might be time for a fresh news option. Besides leading a network for Millennials and Gen Zs, the majority of Jon's employees come from this demographic as well.

The future, he believes, will be a compromise between the past and the present: a remix. He exemplifies this in the business model for Cheddar and the way he leads his company. And he is one of the most transparent and authentic leaders I have come across.

"You can't change everything. It's too hard and takes too much time and is too jarring," he tells me about launching Cheddar. "We decided to change the content, the casting, and the delivery of news. And we decided to keep the structure, the desks, and the concept of talking heads on-screen largely the same. We largely changed the content, distribution, and technology and kept the rest traditional."

Jon, a Gen Xer, is sympathetic to the environment in which Millennials have started their careers: growing up in the aftermath of 9/11, enduring the Great Recession, being saddled with enormous college debt. "I do understand their situation," he says.

But, he says, most business leaders deal with Millennials in that situation by changing how they talk to them, managing Millennials in a way Jon considers to be patronizing. "My attitude," he says, "has always been to speak to them—and everyone—very directly, tell them how opportunity in the organization works. The functions and practices of the organization are the same for everybody."

As you can imagine, this directness is not always easy for people to hear, but it certainly represents a change from the time when leaders spent their days behind closed doors, inaccessible to the rank and file.

"When you speak to a 19-year-old intern like they are an adult, they are often shocked by it. They will come to me with a random idea and I will tell them when their idea is not very useful. 'Vague ideas I can't use. If you put together a document with financials, I can react to it,' I will tell them. Honestly, they kind of love it. They've been so patronized by other people. Half of them come back with an amazing document."

Jon is equally direct and transparent with informing employees about business issues related to the company overall, and hosts a weekly all-hands meeting that shares the company's financials and coming deals. "There are very few things that are secrets," he says. "Most information about the company can be shared. There is actually a very small list of things that cannot be said and need to be kept in a lockbox, like an HR issue with confidentiality, for example."

As a young media executive—most of his CEO peers are decades older—Jon is a voracious reader of business books and frequently turns to his board of directors for advice. But the "classic" advice he often reads and receives does not feel relevant to running a business in today's environment.

For example, when he was leading BuzzFeed, Jon employed an intern named Melissa to work with him on creative sales proposals. Melissa, who had not yet graduated from college, was paid $15 an hour. After a while, she was promoted from intern to employee and continued to do the creative sales work. As the company grew, Melissa kept taking on more responsibility, eventually running Buzz-Feed's creative services unit.

This is when Jon applied the "classic" management step of hiring a "real executive" over Melissa to handle her growing team. It was a total failure.

"It was at that moment that I decided the people that are involved in building an organization will be better at it. If they want to learn management, we can teach them that. But the creativity and ideas and grit—that is much harder to build."

Melissa is now the head of the entire business team at Cheddar.

"Longtime media executives tell me that they hate how Millennials have changed their industry with Netflix and Google and Facebook. They had this great, lucrative business of cable channels, but then a new generation came along that doesn't want to pay for these channels. I love the idea of young people driving culture and bringing new trends and ideas. I'm genuinely curious about what they are curious about. I want them to help us get the content and culture right."

In a multigenerational, constantly shifting workplace, and particularly in an entrepreneurial venture, a deep and genuine curiosity might be just as valuable as an MBA. Where can you expand your curiosity to be a more successful and innovative leader?

The Community Remixer: Diana Fersko

When Diana Fersko, a Xennial in her mid-30s, first arrived as associate rabbi at Stephen Wise Free Synagogue in New York in 2012, one of her mandates was to attract more young people into Friday night Shabbat services. Like many religious organizations, the synagogue had a strong population of children and older adults but was missing the Millennial demographic. Diana set out to help Stephen Wise better reflect one of its key values, "community across generations."

What she knew was that the traditional model of bringing young people into synagogues was to have a "young people's service" during which 20- and 30-somethings could interact on their own. "That pressed all my buttons!" Diana told me. "Because being a youngish person myself, I didn't want to condescend to this group or separate them from everybody else. That sends the wrong message to everybody."

And so, instead of creating a separate experience for Millennials, Diana dreamed up an add-on to the existing experience. While all generations would still attend the traditional Friday night service together, she launched an additional reception option following the service, exclusively for young congregants, which she named Shabbat After Dark.

I am delighted to report that Shabbat After Dark is named after the Peach Pit After Dark, from the 1990s TV phenomenon *Beverly Hills 90210*. (Diana says she watched a lot of TV with her older Gen X siblings.)

The first Shabbat After Dark, featuring wine and treats from Insomnia Cookies, drew forty people. The second one, as with so many sequels, was not as strong, drawing only twenty or so ("and two were my own siblings," reports Diana). But then the idea spread through word of mouth and a fair amount of Facebook sharing, drawing two hundred, then three hundred young people who attend the events held every other month.

Diana attributes the success of Shabbat After Dark to the fact that it gives young people the same communal worship experience as all other generations *and* an event to meet their peers.

Relating this to a business context, it is a powerful reminder that, when recruiting any group of people to your organization, it is important to promote both the aspects of your organization that appeal to their specific generation and the shared, communal aspects that bring all your employees together.

Oh, and when I asked Diana how many of the Millennial attendees of Shabbat After Dark understand the very Gen X–y reference to *90210*, she replied, "Zero."

Diana is in a position of not only being a voice for younger congregants but also of presiding over important life events for congregation members of all ages. One of these roles is leading funeral services for elderly congregants.

"Many times, I meet a family I've never met before to bury a loved one. They often say, 'Wow, you look like my granddaughter.'

And I accept that and I honor it. I probably do look like their grand-daughter!

"I know that I have to show them through my skills what I have to offer them. I have to be good at my job, do research, and be prepared. I often find I have to earn respect before I'm given it, and I'm fine with that."

Diana has also experienced the unique gifts of empathy in the multigenerational mix. "Sometimes," she says, "people say, 'My deceased loved one would be so happy to know a young woman was officiating their ceremony.' I get a lot of affirmation. People appreciate when you take a role seriously and pursue an opportunity that wasn't there for them."

Diana is also keenly aware of the impression she is making on the next generations of congregants as well. Whereas many American Jews grew up with only male rabbis—it was not until the early 1970s that the first female rabbi was ordained in the United States—"Nothing is better than knowing young boys and girls will *not* grow up saying, 'I didn't know young women could be rabbis,'" she says.

How can you connect across all generations, from the very oldest to the very youngest, to make more of a difference in your community?

The Future of Work

We have talked a lot about the past and the future, the new and the old, the young and the not-so-restless. All of this leads to the inevitable question: Where to from here? Some of my predictions and those of the experts I have cited will prove true. Others will prove false. But as Abraham Lincoln said, the best way to create the future is to invent it.

I can only imagine that one day, perhaps ten or twenty years from now, we will remember the early part of the twenty-first century as a time of tremendous transition—in how we work, where we work, when we work, and with whom we work. Like Tiffany, Natalia, Bill, Jon, Diana, and the many people and organizations I have profiled in this book, as a leader, you hold enormous power to contribute to the future work experiences of yourself and the people you lead. The actions you take today will ripple through your organization and the careers of everyone you oversee, and the people they oversee, and on and beyond.

We will ask ourselves in that distant future: Did I do everything I could back then to create the world I wanted to live in now?

Did I lead with integrity and purpose?

Did I adapt my own skill set to change with the times?

Did I create a work environment where every individual felt included?

If you answer those questions right now, would you be happy with your progress? If not, then right now is the time to take action to lead and succeed in the multigenerational workplace. At no time in history has there been more opportunity to make a personal impact. Mix and remix and experiment and adapt and grow and speak up and go viral! When you think back on this time of extraordinary, unprecedented transition, what will you wish you had done?

Now go do it. Generations of the future will thank you.

ACKNOWLEDGMENTS

IT HAS BEEN a privilege and pleasure to work with the first-rate team at Harper Business once again. Thank you to Stephanie Hitchcock for your wise and supportive guidance, and to Hollis Heimbouch for your longtime support and for mixing (and remixing!) the idea for this book. To each member of the team who made this book possible, including Rebecca Raskin, Brian Perrin, Laura Cole, Leslie Cohen, Emily VanDerwerken, Cindy Achar, and John Jusino, I am deeply grateful.

Thank you to my literary agent, Michelle Wolfson, for many years of encouragement, advice, support, and calming influence.

For assistance with key elements of the writing and editing, thank you to Natalia Oberti Noguera and Cathie Ericson. And huge gratitude to Eileen Coombes for helping to keep my business running through it all.

Many thanks to all the subject matter experts and remixers who made introductions and shared your insights and experiences for this book: Michael Abrams, Ziad Ahmed, Marci Alboher, Ashton Applewhite, MaryLeigh Bliss and the Ypulse team, Jennifer Brown, Dan Coates, Laine Joelson Cohen, Manny Contomanolis, Briana Craig, Farouk Dey, Daryl Dickson, Tiffany Dufu, Diana Fersko, Bill Fisse, Anisa Flowers, James Frick, Kevin Grubb, Ana Tereza Guimaraes, Riley Hanson, Emma Lee Hartle, Kelly Hoey, Stephen Kennedy, Jaime Klein, Tiffany Kuck, Donna Kalajian Lagani, Sally Leyes, Alexandra Levit, Tricia Linderman, Laura Marzi, Phebe Farrow Port, Casey Ryan, Stefanie Spurlin, Jon Steinberg, Sara Sutton, Sharine Taylor, Glenn Van Ekeren, Jeff Wald, Caroline Waxler, Melanie Whelan, Cali Williams Yost, Shaina Zafar, and Erica Cordova Zinkie.

I am extremely fortunate to have an amazing network of friends, family, mentors, clients, and colleagues who support me personally and professionally. I am grateful for every encouraging word, generous referral, coffee date, forwarded article, social media like, and shared laugh. Thank you in particular to Meredith Bernstein, Derek Billings, Lisa Brill, Fred Burke, Kerry Coke, Cher Duffield, Wanda Echavarria, Ilana Eck, Carol Frohlinger, the Goodman/ Ramsay family, the Gotlib family, John Hill, Natasha Hoehn, Colleen Hoy, Mignon Lawless, Etel Lima, Danielle Martin, Solana Nolfo, the Raho family, Amanda Schumacher, Melea Seward, Cari Sommer, Trudy Steinfeld, Manisha Thakor, and Amy Vanderwal. Special thanks to the communities of which I feel so incredibly fortunate to be a part: our beloved PS9 crew and the extraordinary women of the Li.st.

Thank you to Mom, Dad, Rob, Laura, Anne, Betty, Jon, Owen, and Will for your support and love.

And to Evan and Chloe, thank you for every day. I love you.

NOTES

1: FROG STEW

5   Americans over the age of 65 today: Ben Steverman, "Working Past 70: Americans Can't Seem to Retire," Bloomberg, July 10, 2017, https://www.bloomberg.com/news/articles/2017-07-10/working-past-70-americans-can-t-seem-to-retire.

5   In the words of Peter Cappelli: Carol Hymowitz, "The Tricky Task of Managing the New, Multigenerational Workplace," *Wall Street Journal*, August 12, 2018, https://www.wsj.com/articles/the-tricky-task-of-managing-the-new-multigenerational-workplace-1534126021.

6   Another outcome of the extraordinary multigenerational mixing: Debra Auerbach, "Generational Differences in the Workplace," CareerBuilder, August 27, 2014, https://www.careerbuilder.com/advice/generational-differences-in-the-workplace.

6   According to a 2018 Randstad Workmonitor study: "Age-Diverse Teams Are Innovative, Resourceful, and Preferred to Work In," Randstad Workmonitor Q2 2018, June 18, 2018, https://www.ir.randstad.com/news-and-events/newsroom/2018/2018-06-18.

7   I appreciate Nilofer Merchant's concept: Nilofer Merchant, "Onlyness (The Topic and the Talk at TEDxHouston)," NiloferMerchant.com, January 17, 2013, http://nilofermerchant.com/2013/01/17/onlyness-the-topic-and-the-talk-at-tedxhouston.

8   48 percent of Gen Z Americans identify as racial or ethnic minorities: Richard Fry and Kim Parker, "Early Benchmarks Show 'Post-Millennials' on Track to Be Most Diverse, Best-Educated Generation Yet," Pew Research Center, November 15, 2018, http://www.pewsocialtrends.org/2018/11/15/early-benchmarks-show-post-millennials-on-track-to-be-most-diverse-best-educated-generation-yet.

8   65 percent of Traditionalists were married by age 32: Richard Fry, Ruth Igielnika, and Eileen Patten, "How Millennials today compare with their grandparents 50 years ago," Pew Research Center, March 16, 2018, http://www.pewresearch.org/fact-tank/2018/03/16/how-millennials-compare-with-their-grandparents.

9   Between 1988 and 2018: "Trends in College Pricing 2017," College Board, October 2017.

9   For the first time in more than 130 Years: Richard Fry, "For First Time in Modern Era, Living with Parents Edges Out Other Living Arrangements for 18- to 34-Year-Olds," Pew Research Center, May 24, 2016, http://www.pewsocialtrends.org/2016/05/24/for-first-time-in-modern-era-living-with-parents-edges-out-other-living-arrangements-for-18-to-34-year-olds.

9   In 1978, 58 percent of American teenagers had paid summer jobs: Drew DeSilver, "The Share of Teens with Summer Jobs Has Plunged Since 2000, and the Type of Work They Do Has Shifted," Pew Research Center, July 2, 2018, http://www.pewresearch.org/fact-tank/2018/07/02/the-share-of-teens-with-summer-jobs-has-plunged-since-2000-and-the-type-of-work-they-do-has-shifted.

9   Generational experts Neil Howe and William Strauss explain it like this: William Strauss and Neil Howe, *Generations: The History of America's Future, 1584 to 2069* (New York: Harper Perennial, 1991), 8–9.

13   As writer Theresa Danna describes her Joneser peers: Theresa Danna, "Meet Generation Jones, Born 1955–1965: Who They Are, What They Want, and How They Buy," LinkedIn, October 11, 2015, https://www.linkedin.com/pulse/meet-generation-jones-born-19551965-who-what-want-how-theresa-danna.

14   From 1973 to 1982, the U.S. endured three recessions: Richard Pérez-Peña, "I May Be 50, but Don't Call Me a Boomer," *New York Times*, January 6, 2014, https://www.nytimes.com/2014/01/06/booming/i-may-be-50-but-dont-call-me-a-boomer.html.

15   From 1960 to 1980, the divorce rate in the U.S. more than doubled: W. Bradford Wilcox, "The Evolution of Divorce," *National Affairs*, fall 2009, https://www.nationalaffairs.com/publications/detail/the-evolution-of-divorce.

16   The term, invented by journalist Sarah Stankorb: Sarah Stankorb and Jed Oelbaum, "Reasonable People Disagree About the Post-Gen X, Pre-Millennial Generation," *Good*, September 25, 2014, https://www.good.is/articles/generation-xennials.

16   "We use social media": Ibid.

17   As one generational analyst described: Monica Hunter-Hart, "What Is a Xennial?" Inverse, June 26, 2017, https://www.inverse.com/article/33453-what-is-a-xennial-what-people-born-between-77-83-need-to-know.

17   In fact, while I was writing this book, a lovely story appeared: Audra D. S. Burch, "A New Class of Voting Rights Activists Picks Up the Mantle in Mississippi," *New York Times*, September 25, 2018, https://www.nytimes.com/2018/09/25/us/freedom-summer-mississippi-votes.html.

18   Many Boomer parents positioned themselves more as buddies: Lind-

sey J. Oates, "Parental Pals: Over 50 Percent of Millennials Find Built-in BFFs," *USA Today*, February 14, 2015, https://www.usatoday.com/story /college/2015/02/14/parental-pals-over-50-percent-of-millennials-find-built -in-bffs/37400681.

19 Millennials are more than three times as likely as Traditionalists to identify as LGBTQ: *Accelerating Acceptance 2017*, GLAAD, 2017, https:// www.glaad.org/files/aa/2017_GLAAD_Accelerating_Acceptance.pdf.

19 The average debt burden of Millennials is around $37,000: Jen Williamson, "3 Reasons Millennials Got Shortchanged with Student Loans," Comet, June 5, 2018, https://www.cometfi.com/blog/four-reasons-millennials -get-screwed-with-student-loans.

19 *New York Times* columnist David Leonhardt has written: David Leonhardt, "The Fleecing of Millennials," *New York Times*, January 27, 2019.

20 I was particularly struck by findings of the Pew Research Center: "Millennials in Adulthood," Pew Research Center, March 7, 2014, http:// www.pewsocialtrends.org/2014/03/07/millennials-in-adulthood.

21 This unscientific result gels with the findings of a study by Pew of generational name preferences: "Most Millennials Resist the 'Millennial' Label," Pew Research Center, September 3, 2015, http://www.people-press .org/2015/09/03/most-millennials-resist-the-millennial-label.

21 BuzzFeed, among the most youth-focused media companies of recent times: Benjamin Mullin, "BuzzFeed Admits 'Millennial' into Its Styleguide," Poynter, April 14, 2017, https://www.poynter.org/news/buzzfeed-admits -millennial-its-styleguide.

22 In fact, 2017 marked the lowest number of babies: Brady E. Hamilton, Joyce A. Martin, Michelle J. K. Osterman, Anne K. Driscoll, and Lauren M. Rossen, "Births: Provisional Data for 2017," National Center for Health Statistics, May 2018, https://www.cdc.gov/nchs/data/vsrr/report004.pdf.

22 Consider that the youngest Gen Zs: Fry and Parker, "Early Benchmarks Show 'Post-Millennials' on Track to Be Most Diverse, Best-Educated Generation Yet."

22 Gen Zs are shaping up to be our most educated generation as well: Ibid.

23 Perhaps not surprisingly, statistics show that Gen Z teenagers are more risk-averse: Jean M. Twenge, "The Decline in Adult Activities Among U.S. Adolescents, 1976–2016," *Child Development*, September 18, 2017, https://onlinelibrary.wiley.com/doi/full/10.1111/cdev.12930.

24 I am not the first one to posit this theory: "Gen Z 2025: The Final Generation," sparks & honey, October 21, 2015, https://reports.sparksand honey.com/campaign/generation-z-2025-the-final-generation.

24   Internet entrepreneur Gina Pell coined the term "Perennials": Gina Pell, "Meet the Perennials," *The What*, October 19, 2016, http://thewhatlist .com/meet-the-perennials.

25   "Fathers and sons comparing fantasy football rankings on matching iPhones": Gregg Lipman, "What Generation Gap?" *AdAge*, June 3, 2010, https://adage.com/print/144249.

25   The national Age Discrimination in Employment Act: "Age Discrimination," U.S. Equal Employment Opportunity Commission, https://www .eeoc.gov/laws/types/age.cfm.

2: RULES FOR REMIXERS

30   Even in the youth-dominated technology sector: Isaac Lyman, "If You Don't Hire Juniors, You Don't Deserve Seniors," IssacLyman.com, September 12, 2018, http://isaaclyman.com/blog/posts/junior-developers.

32   Patty McCord, former chief talent officer at Netflix, says that nostalgia: "Learning from Netflix: How to Build a Culture of Freedom and Responsibility," *Wharton@Work* podcast, May 29, 2018, http://knowledge.wharton .upenn.edu/article/how-netflix-built-its-company-culture.

33   According to Cornell University gerontologist Karl Pillemer: Ashton Applewhite, "You're How Old? We'll Be in Touch," *New York Times*, September 3, 2016, https://www.nytimes.com/2016/09/04/opinion/sunday/youre -how-old-well-be-in-touch.html.

33   Consider as well: Christopher Ingraham, "Three Quarters of Whites Don't Have Any Non-White Friends," *Washington Post*, August 25, 2014.

33   In one of my all-time favorite studies, Cisco found: "Air, Food, Water, Internet—Cisco Study Reveals Just How Important Internet and Networks Have Become as Fundamental Resources in Daily Life," Cisco Connected World Technology Report, September 21, 2011, https://newsroom.cisco.com /press-release-content?articleId=474852.

35   For people of color, the challenges can be even greater: Danielle Kurtzleben, "A Black Man with a College Degree Is as Likely to Be Working as a White College Dropout," *Vox*, June 26, 2014, https://www.vox.com/2014/6/26 /5845468/a-black-man-with-a-college-degree-is-as-likely-to-be-working-as-a.

35   Some trade school and reskilling programs: Julie Margetta Morgan and Marshall Steinbaum, "The Student Debt Crisis, Labor Market Credentialization, and Racial Inequality," Roosevelt Institute, October 2018, http:// rooseveltinstitute.org/student-debt-crisis-labor-market-credentialization -racial-inequality.

38   about 4 percent of employers: Alexia Elejalde-Ruiz, "Abbott 401(k)

Program to Help Employees Who Have Student Debt Could Become National Model," *Chicago Tribune*, August 31, 2018, https://www.chicagotribune.com/business/ct-biz-irs-student-loan-perk-0902-story.html.

39 Similarly, in 2015 Netflix announced that it would offer employees up to one year: Shalini Ramachandran and Joe Flint, "At Netflix, Radical Transparency and Blunt Firings Unsettle the Ranks," *Wall Street Journal*, October 25, 2018, https://www.wsj.com/articles/at-netflix-radical-transparency-and-blunt-firings-unsettle-the-ranks-1540497174.

42 Fabrizio Freda, president and CEO of The Estée Lauder Companies, describes this beautifully: Karen Christensen, "Estée Lauder's CEO on Staying Relevant," *Rotman Management Magazine*, January 2018, https://www.pressreader.com/canada/rotman-management-magazine/20180101/281500751594328.

3: THE TALENT REMIX

50 As Rick Wartzman, author of *The End of Loyalty*: Bryan Burrough, "In Good Company," *Wall Street Journal*, July 12, 2017.

51 An astonishing 94 percent of the job growth since the Great Recession: Lawrence F. Katz and Alan B. Krueger, "The Rise and Nature of Alternative Work Arrangements in the United States, 1995–2015," Working Paper #603, Princeton University Industrial Relations Section, September 2016, https://dataspace.princeton.edu/jspui/bitstream/88435/dsp01zs25xb933/3/603.pdf.

51 Thirty-six percent of U.S. workers participate in the gig economy: Shane McFeely and Ryan Pendell, "What Workplace Leaders Can Learn from the Real Gig Economy," Gallup, August 16, 2018.

51 According to one study, only 1 percent of HR professionals believe Millennials to be loyal to an employer: "Beyond.com Survey Uncovers How Veteran HR Professionals Really Feel About Job Seekers from Millennial Generation," PR Newswire, May 28, 2013, https://www.prnewswire.com/news-releases/beyondcom-survey-uncovers-how-veteran-hr-professionals-really-feel-about-job-seekers-from-millennial-generation-209155161.html.

52 According to the U.S. Department of Labor, the median length of time young people work for one employer: "Workers Are Not Switching Jobs More Often," *Economist*, October 21, 2017, https://www.economist.com/finance-and-economics/2017/10/21/workers-are-not-switching-jobs-more-often.

52 Overall as of 2018, the median number of years that wage and salary workers: "Employee Tenure in 2018," Bureau of Labor Statistics, September 20, 2018, https://www.bls.gov/news.release/pdf/tenure.pdf.

53   As Hoffman, Casnocha, and Yeh describe the benefits of the tour-of-duty model: Reid Hoffman, Ben Casnocha, and Chris Yeh, "Tours of Duty: The New Employer-Employee Compact," *Harvard Business Review*, June 2013, https://hbr.org/2013/06/tours-of-duty-the-new-employer-employee-compact.

53   One study found that one-third of freelancers: Upwork and Freelancers Union, "Freelancing in America: 2017," Edelman Intelligence, September 2017, https://www.slideshare.net/upwork/freelancing-in-america-2017/1.

55   The legislature in Vermont, currently the fastest-aging state in the U.S., passed a bill: Corinne Purtill, "Vermont Will Pay You $10,000 to Move There and Work Remotely," Quartz, May 31, 2018, https://qz.com/work/1289727/vermont-will-pay-you-10000-to-move-there-and-work-remotely.

55   Other areas offering cash and other incentives for young transplants: Brit Morse, "5 Cities That Will Pay You to Live There," *Inc.*, May 1, 2018, https://www.inc.com/brit-morse/5-cities-that-will-pay-you-to-live-there.html.

55   If you move to the state of Maine: Christina Maxouris and Saeed Ahmed, "Maine Will Help You Pay Off Your Student Loans If You Move There," CNN, October 25, 2018, https://www.cnn.com/2018/10/25/health/maine-student-loan-relief-trnd/index.html.

56   Pfizer offers a good example of this strategy: Joan Snyder Kuhl and Jennifer Zephirin, *Misunderstood Millennial Talent* (Los Angeles: Center for Talent Innovation, 2016), 137–39.

57   "Back when *Baywatch* was on the air": Abha Bhattarai, "Why Your Pool's Lifeguard Is More Likely to Be a Senior Citizen," *Washington Post*, July 3, 2018, https://www.washingtonpost.com/business/economy/why-your-pools-lifeguard-is-more-likely-to-be-a-senior-citizen/2018/07/03/2bed1a9a-74bf-11e8-805c-4b67019fcfe4_story.html?utm_term=.3ef4904de0b1.

59   Two major health care organizations recently changed their dress code policies: Rheana Murray, "Nurses with Pink Hair and Tattoos? Why This Hospital System Is Changing the Rules," *Today*, August 31, 2018, https://www.today.com/health/indiana-university-health-changes-tattoo-policy-nurses-t136365.

59   An estimated 47 percent of Millennials in the United States have at least one tattoo: Larry Shannon-Missal, "Tattoo Takeover: Three in Ten Americans Have Tattoos, and Most Don't Stop at Just One," Harris Poll, February 10, 2016, https://theharrispoll.com/tattoos-can-take-any-number-of-forms-from-animals-to-quotes-to-cryptic-symbols-and-appear-in-all-sorts-of-spots-on-our-bodies-some-visible-in-everyday-life-others-not-so-much-but-one-thi.

60   Finally, some of the country's most prestigious employers: Courtney Connley, "Google, Apple, and 12 Other Companies That No Longer Require

Employees to Have a College Degree," CNBC, October 8, 2018, https://www
.cnbc.com/2018/08/16/15-companies-that-no-longer-require-employees
-to-have-a-college-degree.html.

62   One study found that 80 percent of American workers across generations would rather have a boss who cared: Shawn Achor, Andrew Reece,
Gabriella Rosen Kellerman, and Alexi Robichaux, "9 Out of 10 People Are
Willing to Earn Less Money to Do More Meaningful Work," *Harvard Business Review*, November 6, 2018, https://hbr.org/2018/11/9-out-of-10-people
-are-willing-to-earn-less-money-to-do-more-meaningful-work.

62   Back in 1974: Ibid.

63   The average age of an insurance agent in the United States is 59: Caitlin
Bronson, "One in Four Insurance Agents Will Be Gone by 2018," *Insurance
Business America*, February 23, 2015, https://www.insurancebusinessmag.com
/us/news/marine/one-in-four-insurance-agents-will-be-gone-by-2018-17943
.aspx.

64   Toyota Motor Corp.'s manufacturing plant in Indiana, for example,
holds "Parents' Night Out" events: Jennifer Levitz, "To Recruit Workers,
Manufacturers Go to Parents' Nights," *Wall Street Journal*, December 17,
2017, https://www.wsj.com/articles/to-recruit-workers-manufacturers-go-to
-parents-nights-1513425600.

65   Currently about 1 percent of companies invite employees' parents:
Te-Ping Chen, "Cornering Your Boss, Snapping Pictures at Your Desk: It's
Take Your Parents to Work Day," *Wall Street Journal*, November 12, 2018,
https://www.wsj.com/articles/mom-please-stop-talking-to-my-boss-parents
-invade-the-office-1542042333.

66   The company reports that 3,700 parents have signed up for LinkedIn
profiles: Ibid.

68   Construction materials maker USG Corporation now accepts applications by mobile phone: Aili McConnon, "How Manufacturers Are Recruiting
Millennials," *Wall Street Journal*, June 7, 2016, https://www.wsj.com/articles
/how-manufacturers-are-recruiting-millennials-1465351261.

69   Research has shown that Black and Hispanic: Derek R. Avery, Mo-
rela Hernandez, and Michelle R. Hebl, "Who's Watching the Race? Racial
Salience in Recruitment Advertising," *Journal of Applied Social Psychology* 34,
no. 1 (2004): 146–61. Cited in Dolly Chugh, *The Person You Mean to Be* (New
York: Harper Business, 2018), 27–28.

69   Location Labs, a technology company: "This Company Retains 95%
of Its Employees—Here's Its Secret," *First Round Review*, no date, https://first
round.com/review/this-company-retains-95-percent-of-its-employees-heres
-its-secret.

69   Similarly, Intel implemented: Jay Moye, "Hire Power: How Social Media Is Changing the Way People Search for Jobs," *Coca-Cola Journey*, January 3, 2013, https://www.coca-colacompany.com/stories/hire-power-how -social-media-is-changing-the-way-people-search-for-jobs.

4: THE LEADERSHIP REMIX

73   A few years ago, there was a college football head coach who led his team all the way to the NCAA Championship game: Jonathan Clegg, "Why the Oregon Ducks Don't Believe in Yelling," *Wall Street Journal*, January 7, 2015, https://www.wsj.com/articles/oregon-college-footballs-kinder-gentler -team-1420663969.

74   This coach is not the first to take a positive approach to leadership in sports: Austin Murphy, "A Message to Coaches: Stop Screaming and Start Teaching," *Sports Illustrated*, April 24, 2013, https://www.si.com/college -basketball/2013/04/24/college-coaches.

77   One study found that an A is the most common grade: Scott Jaschik, "Grade Inflation, Higher and Higher," *Inside Higher Ed*, March 29, 2016, https://www.insidehighered.com/news/2016/03/29/survey-finds-grade -inflation-continues-rise-four-year-colleges-not-community-college.

78   As recently as 1995, 40 percent of young adults had a direct connection to a service member: Jim Garamone, "DoD Launches Initiative to Inform Americans About Military Life," U.S. Department of Defense, January 29, 2018, https://dod.defense.gov/News/Article/Article/1426748/dod -launches-initiative-to-inform-americans-of-military-life.

79   teen summer employment dropped precipitously after the 2001 recession: Drew DeSilver, "The Share of Teens with Summer Jobs Has Plunged Since 2000, and the Type of Work They Do Has Shifted," Pew Research Center, July 2, 2018, http://www.pewresearch.org/fact-tank/2018/07/02 /the-share-of-teens-with-summer-jobs-has-plunged-since-2000-and-the -type-of-work-they-do-has-shifted.

79   This is not because today's teenagers don't want to work: Roy Maurer, "Why Are Fewer Teens Working Summer Jobs?" Society for Human Resource Management, June 6, 2018, https://www.shrm.org/resourcesandtools/hr -topics/talent-acquisition/pages/why-fewer-teens-working-summer-jobs.aspx.

80   Martha Ross of the Brookings Institution has noted: Ben Steverman, "Why Aren't American Teenagers Working Anymore?" Bloomberg, June 5, 2017, https://www.bloomberg.com/news/articles/2017-06-05/why-aren-t -american-teenagers-working-anymore.

82   According to a recent study out of the UK, the most common theme: Leigh Buchanan, "Why All the Bosses in Disney Movies Are Terrible," *Inc.*,

March 12, 2018, https://www.inc.com/leigh-buchanan/how-bad-cartoon
-bosses-are-shaping-kids-ideas-about-work.html.

84   Leadership expert Daniel Goleman recommends the coaching style:
Robyn Benincasa, "6 Leadership Styles and When You Should Use Them,"
Fast Company, May 29, 2012, https://www.fastcompany.com/1838481/6
-leadship-styles-and-when-you-should-use-them.

5: THE PEOPLE MANAGEMENT REMIX

89   The data definitively revealed: David A. Garvin, "How Google Sold
Its Engineers on Management," *Harvard Business Review*, December 2013,
https://hbr.org/2013/12/how-google-sold-its-engineers-on-management.

89   Google defined being a good coach: Michael Schneider, "Google Managers Use This Simple Framework to Coach Employees," *Inc.*, July 30, 2018,
https://www.inc.com/michael-schneider/google-discovered-top-trait-of-its
-most-effective-managers-you-can-develop-it-too.html.

94   One study found the traditional performance-review process: Kim
Runyen, "Millennials Think Your Performance Reviews Suck and Here's
Why," TriNet, October 29, 2015, https://www.trinet.com/hr-insights
/blog/2015/millennials-think-your-performance-reviews-suck-and-heres
-why.

95   According to a PwC study: Maren Hogan, "5 Employee Feedback
Stats That You Need to See," *LinkedIn Talent Blog*, February 8, 2016, https://
business.linkedin.com/talent-solutions/blog/trends-and-research/2016/5
-Employee-Feedback-Stats-That-You-Need-to-See.

96   For example, Paul Irving: Paul Irving, "When No One Retires," *Harvard Business Review*, November 2018, https://hbr.org/cover-story/2018/11
/when-no-one-retires.

99   Some organizations, such as IBM and Warby Parker, have replaced
their annual performance reviews: Pavithra Mohan, "Ready to Scrap Your Annual Performance Reviews? Try These Alternatives," *Fast Company*, April 13,
2017, https://www.fastcompany.com/40405106/ready-to-scrap-your-annual
-performance-reviews-try-these-alternatives.

100 One Harvard Business School study found that managers with the
lowest levels of respect: Francesca Gino, "'Rebels' Approach Work in a Completely Different Way Than Their Peers. Here Are 3 Things They Do Better,"
Money, May 1, 2018, https://amp.timeinc.net/time/money/5259919/rebels
-at-work-research-francesca-gino?__twitter_impression=true.

103 A study by the nonprofit Common Sense Media found that 33 percent
of teens: "Social Media, Social Life: Teens Reveal Their Experiences," Common Sense Media, September 10, 2018, https://www.commonsensemedia

.org/about-us/news/press-releases/common-sense-research-reveals-everything
-you-need-to-know-about-teens.

103 Seattle-based law firm Perkins Coie, one of the few "biglaw" firms: Kevin
Mckeough, "Perkins Coie," *Crain's Chicago Business*, March 1, 2008, https://
www.chicagobusiness.com/article/20080301/ISSUE02/100029390/16
-perkins-coie.

105 Gallup research has found that 80 percent of employees across generations said recognition is a strong motivator: Kellie Wong, "Why Employee
Recognition Matters," *Engage: The Employee Engagement Blog*, December 6, 2016, https://www.achievers.com/blog/2016/12/employee-recognition
-matters.

108 When Volvo wanted to turn around its brand and business: Ram
Charan, Dominic Barton, and Dennis Carey, "How Volvo Reinvented Itself
Through Hiring," *Harvard Business Review*, March 12, 2018, https://hbr.org
/2018/03/how-volvo-reinvented-itself-through-hiring.

6: THE COMMUNICATION REMIX

111 According to research, generational differences: "Impact of a Multigenerational Workforce," Randstad Workmonitor Q2 2018 Report, June 2018,
https://workforceinsights.randstad.com/hr-research-reports-workmonitor
-q22018.

112 When he was mayor of New York City from 2002 to 2013, Bloomberg:
Chris Smith, "Open City," *New York*, September 26, 2010, https://nymag
.com/news/features/establishments/68511.

114 This was a key practice of former Land O'Lakes Inc. CEO Chris Policinski: Rachel Feintzeig, "CEOs Spend More Time on Campus," *Wall Street
Journal*, February 1, 2017, https://www.wsj.com/articles/ceos-spend-more
-time-on-campus-1485962223.

115 The firm's CEO at the time: Susan Dominus, "Rethinking the Work-
Life Equation," *New York Times*, February 25, 2016, https://www.nytimes
.com/2016/02/28/magazine/rethinking-the-work-life-equation.html.

115 Another leader who comes to mind when I think about visibility and
transparency is Massimo Bottura: Callan Boys, "Chef Massimo Bottura
Shares the Secrets of Italian Cooking," *Good Food*, October 21, 2014, https://
www.goodfood.com.au/archived/chef-massimo-bottura-shares-the-secrets
-of-italian-cooking-20141016-115nos.

116 a recent survey by the Institute for Women's Policy Research: Andrew
Chamberlain, "Is Salary Transparency More Than a Trend?" Glassdoor, April
2015, https://research-content.glassdoor.com/app/uploads/sites/2/2015/04
/GD_Report_2.pdf.

117 A 2010 experimental study by economists found that sharing information about workers' pay relative to others: Ibid.

117 Angela Cornell, director of the Labor Law Clinic at Cornell Law School, has said that open discussion of salaries: Tim Herrera, "Why You Should Tell Your Co-Workers How Much Money You Make," *New York Times*, August 31, 2018, https://www.nytimes.com/2018/08/31/smarter-living/pay-secrecy -national-labor-rights-act.html.

118 A recent survey reported that 75 percent of workers aged 18 to 24 are connected with colleagues on social media: "Impact of a Multigenerational Workforce," Randstad Workmonitor Q2 2018 Report.

118 As Joan Snyder Kuhl and Jennifer Zephirin: Joan Snyder Kuhl and Jennifer Zephirin, *Misunderstood Millennial Talent* (Los Angeles: Center for Talent Innovation, 2016), 56.

121 Fortunately, there is a solution: Daniel Jacobson, "COPE: Create Once, Publish Everywhere," ProgrammableWeb, October 13, 2009, https://www.pro grammableweb.com/news/cope-create-once-publish-everywhere/2009/10/13.

122 Warby Parker has always conducted all-hands meetings with its employees: "How Warby Parker Makes Every Point in Its Employee Lifecycle Extraordinary," *First Round Review*, no date, https://firstround.com/review /how-warby-parker-makes-every-point-in-its-employee-lifecycle-extraordinary.

127 Author and psychologist Adam Grant: Scott Judd, Eric O'Rourke, and Adam Grant, "Employee Surveys Are Still One of the Best Ways to Measure Engagement," *Harvard Business Review*, March 14, 2018, https://hbr .org/2018/03/employee-surveys-are-still-one-of-the-best-ways-to-measure -engagement.

7: THE TRAINING AND DEVELOPMENT REMIX

138 According to one study, a whopping 65 percent of Millennials: "Millennials at Work: Reshaping the Workplace," PwC, 2011, https://www.pwc .com/co/es/publicaciones/assets/millennials-at-work.pdf.

138 Writing in the *Atlantic* about why Millennials aren't buying homes at the same rate as previous American generations: Derek Thompson and Jordan Weissmann, "The Cheapest Generation," *Atlantic*, September 2012, https://www.theatlantic.com/magazine/archive/2012/09/the-cheapest-gen eration/309060.

139 Liz Wiseman, author of *Rookie Smarts: Why Learning Beats Knowing in the New Game of Work*, advises employers: Liz Wiseman, "Why Your Team Needs Rookies," *Harvard Business Review*, October 2, 2014, https://hbr .org/2014/10/why-your-team-needs-rookies.

144 CEO Thomas Crosby has said: Leigh Buchanan, "Training the Best

Damn Fry Cooks (and Future Leaders) in the U.S.," *Inc.*, April 23, 2014, https://www.inc.com/audacious-companies/leigh-buchanan/pals-sudden -service.html.

145 World Economic Forum predicts that machines will do 42 per-cent of our labor: Oliver Cann, "Machines Will Do More Tasks Than Hu-mans by 2025 but Robot Revolution Will Still Create 58 Million Net New Jobs in Next Five Years," World Economic Forum, September 17, 2018, https://www.weforum.org/press/2018/09/machines-will-do-more-tasks -than-humans-by-2025-but-robot-revolution-will-still-create-58-million -net-new-jobs-in-next-five-years.

145 According to futurist Tom Cheesewright: Tom Cheesewright, "Don't Confuse Automation and Augmentation," TomCheesewright.com, no date, https://tomcheesewright.com/dont-confuse-automation-and-augmentation.

146 Researchers from Deloitte: Jeff Schwartz, Heather Stockton, Laurence Collins, Darryl Wagner, and Brett Walsh, "The Future of Work: The Aug-mented Workforce," Deloitte Insights, February 28, 2017, https://www2 .deloitte.com/insights/us/en/focus/human-capital-trends/2017/future-work force-changing-nature-of-work.html.

146 An example of augmentation: Amit Kothari, "AI Is More Than Machine Automation: It's About Human Augmentation," CMS Wire, December 7, 2016, https://www.cmswire.com/digital-workplace/ai-is-more-than-machine -automation-its-about-human-augmentation.

146 BMW and Nissan: Paul Irving, "When No One Retires," *Harvard Busi-ness Review*, November 2018, https://hbr.org/cover-story/2018/11/when-no -one-retires.

146 Freelancers, it appears, are leading the way: "Freelancing in America 2017," Upwork, 2017, https://www.upwork.com/i/freelancing-in-america /2017.

147 AT&T, which employs 250,000 people, determined nearly half of its workers lacked the skills: Susan Caminiti, "AT&T's $1 Billion Gambit: Re-training Nearly Half Its Workforce for Jobs of the Future," CNBC, March 13, 2018, https://www.cnbc.com/2018/03/13/atts-1-billion-gambit-retraining -nearly-half-its-workforce.html.

147 Salesforce is not only reskilling its own workforce: Sophia Kunthara, "Salesforce's Answer for Jobs: An Online Training Site with 1 Million Users," *San Francisco Chronicle*, September 16, 2018, https://www.sfchronicle.com /business/article/Salesforce-s-answer-for-jobs-an-online-13231337.php.

148 In 2018, MIT took the ambitious step: Steve Lohr, "M.I.T. Plans College for Artificial Intelligence, Backed by $1 Billion," *New York Times*,

October 15, 2018, https://www.nytimes.com/2018/10/15/technology/mit
-college-artificial-intelligence.html.

149 Recently, Laszlo Bock, formerly of Google: Laszlo Bock, "Employee
'Poaching' Is Good Business—Here's Why," *Fast Company*, August 22, 2018,
https://www.fastcompany.com/90222242/companies-should-get-rid-of
-their-non-solicitation-clause.

153 According to Charlie Schilling, a general manager at General Assembly:
Jeffrey Selingo, "The Future of College Looks Like the Future of Retail," *Atlantic*, April 16, 2018, https://www.theatlantic.com/education/archive/2018/04
/college-online-degree-blended-learning/557642.

154 According to the National Association of Colleges and Employers
(NACE), about 43 percent of large employers: NACE Staff, "Rotational Programs Yield Higher Retention Rates," NACE, March 22, 2017, http://www
.naceweb.org/talent-acquisition/onboarding/rotational-programs-yield
-higher-retention-rates.

155 A worrisome study by CareerBuilder found that 58 percent of managers:
David Sturt and Todd Nordstrom, "10 Shocking Workplace Stats You Need
to Know," *Forbes*, March 8, 2018, https://www.forbes.com/sites/davidsturt
/2018/03/08/10-shocking-workplace-stats-you-need-to-know/#2642e10cf3af.

156 According to Gallup, while 96 percent of chief academic officers:
Preety Sidhu and Valerie J. Calderon, "Many Business Leaders Doubt U.S.
Colleges Prepare Students," Gallup, February 26, 2014, https://news.gallup
.com/poll/167630/business-leaders-doubt-colleges-prepare-students.aspx.

159 One of the pioneers of this practice is Dr. Philip Pizzo, founding
director of the Stanford Distinguished Careers Institute: Douglas Belkin,
"Baby Boomers Looking for Reinvention Try College—Again," *Wall Street
Journal*, December 28, 2017, https://www.wsj.com/articles/baby_boomers
_looking_for_reinvention_try_collegeagain_1514466001.

8: THE MENTORING AND NETWORKING REMIX

164 In 1999, Jack Welch, CEO of General Electric at the time, required
five hundred(!) of his top executives: Matt Murray, "General Electric Mentoring Program Turns Underlings into Web Teachers," *Wall Street Journal*,
February 15, 2000, https://www.wsj.com/articles/SB950573678484860919.

165 When PwC surveyed recent university graduates globally: "Millennials at Work: Reshaping the Workplace," PwC, 2011, https://www.pwc.com
/co/es/publicaciones/assets/millennials-at-work.pdf.

165 Deloitte's global 2016 Millennial Survey found that Millennials intending to stay: "The 2016 Deloitte Millennial Survey: Winning Over the

Next Generation of Leaders," Deloitte, 2016, https://www2.deloitte.com /content/dam/Deloitte/global/Documents/About-Deloitte/gx-millenial -survey-2016-exec-summary.pdf.

166 Darnell Epps, who became a student at Cornell University after serving seventeen years in prison: Darnell Epps, "The Prison 'Old-Timers' Who Gave Me Life," *New York Times*, October 6, 2018, https://www.nytimes.com /2018/10/06/opinion/sunday/aging-inmates-prisons-mandatory-sentencing .html.

172 At BNY Mellon's Pershing: "Reversing the Generation Equation: Mentoring in the New Age of Work," 2018, https://information.pershing.com /rs/651-GHF-471/images/per-reversing-the-generation-equation.pdf.

174 Author Chip Conley, who refers to himself as a "modern elder": Chip Conley, "I Joined Airbnb at 52, and Here's What I Learned About Age, Wisdom, and the Tech Industry," *Harvard Business Review*, April 18, 2017, https://hbr.org/2017/04/i-joined-airbnb-at-52-and-heres-what-i-learned- about-age-wisdom-and-the-tech-industry.

177 In the e-commerce business at Pitney Bowes: Carol Hymowitz, "The Tricky Task of Managing the New, Multigenerational Workplace," *Wall Street Journal*, August 12, 2018, https://www.wsj.com/articles/the-tricky-task-of-man aging-the-new-multigenerational-workplace-1534126021.

180 A Ypulse survey found that 63 percent of 13- to 35-year-olds say: "Who Are Gen Z and Millennials Really Following on Social Media?" Ypulse, July 5, 2018, https://www.ypulse.com/post/view/who-are-gen-z-millennials-really -following-on-social-media.

182 In the 1990s there were more than 5,000 golf and country clubs in the U.S.: Kelsey Lawrence, "Why Won't Millennials Join Country Clubs?" *CityLab*, July 2, 2018, https://www.citylab.com/life/2018/07/will-millennials -kill-the-country-club/563186.

182 In 2018, Americans made 433 million fewer trips to restaurants during lunchtime: Julie Jargon, "Going Out for Lunch Is a Dying Tradition," *Wall Street Journal*, May 30, 2017, https://www.wsj.com/articles/going-out-for -lunch-is-a-dying-tradition-1496155377.

9: THE WORKSPACE REMIX

186 By 2015 approximately 70 percent of offices: Evan Rawn, "When One Size Does Not Fit All: Rethinking the Open Office," *ArchDaily*, February 5, 2015, https://www.archdaily.com/595033/when-one-size-does-not -fit-all-rethinking-the-open-office.

186 According to Nikil Saval, author of *Cubed*: Joseph Stromberg, "How the Universally Hated Cubicle Came to Be," *Vox*, December 19, 2014, https://

www.vox.com/2014/5/20/5731692/the-surprising-history-of-the-cubicle
-and-the-rest-of-the-modern.

188 As one open-plan office worker commented: John Tierney, "From Cubicles, Cry for Quiet Pierces Office Buzz," *New York Times*, May 19, 2012,
https://www.nytimes.com/2012/05/20/science/when-buzz-at-your-cubicle
-is-too-loud-for-work.html.

188 A 2018 Harvard study found that switching to an open-plan office
space: Christian Jarrett, "Open-Plan Offices Drive Down Face-to-Face Interactions and Increase Use of E-mail," *British Psychological Society Research
Digest*, July 5, 2018, https://digest.bps.org.uk/2018/07/05/open-plan-offices
-drive-down-face-to-face-interactions-and-increase-use-of-e-mail.

192 Research out of Great Britain has shown that when workers can choose:
Steve Lohr, "Don't Get Too Comfortable at That Desk," *New York Times*, October 6, 2017, https://www.nytimes.com/2017/10/06/business/the-office-gets
-remade-again.html.

193 For example, software company Janeiro Digital: Andy Rosen, "Not
Your Parents' Office? Now It Is: Tech Workspaces Start to Grow Up," *Boston
Globe*, April 5, 2018, https://www.bostonglobe.com/business/2018/04/05
/this-really-your-parents-office-tech-workspaces-start-grow/ZYsLyd6ya83
qwHQykz1x3O/story.html.

194 At JotForm, a company that makes online forms: Aytekin Tank, "Why
Open Office Design Makes You Less Productive," *JotForm Blog*, October 12,
2018, https://www.jotform.com/blog/kill-your-open-office.

195 Chief people officer Katie Burke explains: "Why You Should Rotate
Office Seating Assignments," *Harvard Business Review*, March/April 2018,
https://hbr.org/2018/03/why-you-should-rotate-office-seating-assignments.

202 half of telecommuters: Kate Lister, "When Will We Stop Calling Remote Work Something Different? It's Just the Way People Work," *Global
Workplace Analytics*, October 6, 2017, http://globalworkplaceanalytics.com
/tag/flexjobs.

10: THE CULTURE REMIX

213 According to one study, 84 percent of Millennials: "2016 Millennial
Employee Engagement Study," Cone Communications, April 2016, http://
millennialemployeeengagement.com/#purpose-culture2.

214 KPMG is one of the "big four" accounting and professional services
firms: Bruce N. Pfau, "How an Accounting Firm Convinced Its Employees
They Could Change the World," *Harvard Business Review*, October 6, 2015,
https://hbr.org/2015/10/how-an-accounting-firm-convinced-its-employees
-they-could-change-the-world.

218 As a sign of how much the world has remixed its thinking on work/life integration: Cathy Leibow, "Work/Life Balance for the Generations," Huffington Post, December 16, 2014, https://www.huffingtonpost.com/cathy-leibow /worklife-balance-for-the-_1_b_5992766.html.

218 PwC says that 90 percent of its employees: Corinne Purtill, "PwC's Millennial Employees Led a Rebellion—and Their Demands Are Being Met," Quartz at Work, March 20, 2018, https://qz.com/work/1217854/pwcs -millennial-employees-led-a-rebellion-and-their-demands-are-being-met.

219 Some companies are offering specific flexibility programs for this population: "Flexible Work Arrangements Attract Older Workers," AARP, June 2013, https://www.aarp.org/work/employers/info-06-2013/flexible -work-attracts-older-workers.html.

219 The productivity start-up Doist, creator of the Todoist app: Simone Stolzoff, "A Vacation Policy Built for a New Age: 40 Days Off to Use as You Choose," Quartz at Work, September 27, 2018, https://qz.com/work/1402886 /the-startup-behind-todoist-has-a-novel-new-vacation-policy.

221 In 1996, 54 percent of employers offered wellness resources and information: Stephen Miller, "Past Two Decades Saw Big Shifts in Employee Benefits," Society for Human Resource Management, June 20, 2016, https://www .shrm.org/hr-today/news/hr-news/pages/past-two-decades-saw-big-shifts -in-employee-benefits.aspx.

221 The share of Fortune 1000 companies offering "summer Fridays": Jena McGregor, "More Than 40 Percent of Companies Now Offer 'Summer Friday' Perk," Washington Post, June 9, 2017, https://www.washingtonpost.com/news /on-leadership/wp/2017/06/09/more-than-40-percent-of-companies-now -offer-a-summer-friday-perk/?utm_term=.fb24a628a738.

221 The share of corporations offering paid maternity leave increased: Kathryn Mayer, "The 15 Most Popular Employee Perks," Employee Benefit News, October 16, 2018, https://www.benefitnews.com/list/the-15-most-popular -employee-benefits.

221 While only about 15 percent of U.S. employers offer any paid paternity leave: Kenneth Matos, Ellen Galinsky, and James T. Bond, National Study of Employers (2016), http://whenworkworks.org/downloads/2016-National -Study-of-Employers.pdf.

222 Studies show that child care support is especially helpful for lower-income families: Claire Cain Miller, "How Child Care Enriches Mothers, and Especially the Sons They Raise," New York Times, April 20, 2017, https:// www.nytimes.com/2017/04/20/upshot/how-child-care-enriches-mothers -and-especially-the-sons-they-raise.html.

222 Particularly as more Millennials: Patrick Ball, "How We'd All Benefit from an Investment in Child Care," *Care@Work*, November 14, 2017, http:// workplace.care.com/investments-in-child-care-pay-off.

222 Right now such programs: Erica Pandey, "The Future of Student Debt: How Employers Might Help," Axios, October 11, 2018, https://www .axios.com/student-loans-debt-assistance-401k-28f36662-fa66-42f5-9650 -110f0fcd02d1.html.

223 This doesn't surprise experts: Julia Alexander, "YouTube's Top Creators Are Burning Out and Breaking Down En Masse," Polygon, June 6, 2018, https://www.polygon.com/2018/6/1/17413542/burnout-mental-health -awareness-youtube-elle-mills-el-rubius-bobby-burns-pewdiepie.

226 As one history professor put it, "Americans began the 20th century in bustles and bowler hats": Deirdre Clemente, "Why American Workers Now Dress So Casually," *Atlantic*, May 22, 2017, https://www.theatlantic.com /business/archive/2017/05/history-of-business-casual/526014.

226 Cindi Leive, former editor in chief of *Glamour*: Alexandra Schwartz, "Rent the Runway Wants to Lend You Your Look," *New Yorker*, October 22, 2018, https://www.newyorker.com/magazine/2018/10/22/rent-the-runway -wants-to-lend-you-your-look.

228 Qualtrics is a company that provides experience management software: Melia Robinson, "A Tech Company Is Giving Each Employee $1,500 to Spend on Experiences—and It's a Millennial's Dream Perk," *Business Insider*, April 29, 2018, https://markets.businessinsider.com/news/stocks/qualtrics-gives -employees-money-to-spend-on-experiences-2018-4-1022780983.

RECOMMENDED READING

INTRODUCTION

Pollak, Lindsey. *Getting from College to Career: Your Essential Guide to Succeeding in the Real World*. Rev. ed. New York: Harper Business, 2012.

Strauss, William, and Neil Howe. *Generations: The History of America's Future, 1584 to 2069*. New York: Harper Perennial, 1991.

CHAPTER 1

Merchant, Nilofer. *The Power of Onlyness: Make Your Wild Ideas Mighty Enough to Dent the World*. New York: Viking, 2017.

Stillman, David, and Jonah Stillman. *Gen Z @ Work: How the Next Generation Is Transforming the Workplace*. New York: Harper Business, 2017.

Taylor, Paul, and the Pew Research Center. *The Next America: Boomers, Millennials, and the Looming Generational Showdown*. New York: PublicAffairs, 2015.

Twenge, Jean M. *iGen: Why Today's Super-Connected Kids Are Growing Up Less Rebellious, More Tolerant, Less Happy—and Completely Unprepared for Adulthood—and What That Means for the Rest of Us*. New York: Atria Books, 2017.

CHAPTER 2

McCord, Patty. *Powerful: Building a Culture of Freedom and Responsibility*. Silicon Guild, 2017.

CHAPTER 3

Freedman, Marc. *How to Live Forever: The Enduring Power of Connecting the Generations*. New York: PublicAffairs, 2018.

Hoffman, Reid, Ben Casnocha, and Chris Yeh. *The Alliance: Managing Talent in the Networked Age*. Boston: Harvard Business Review Press, 2014.

Hyman, Louis. *Temp: How American Work, American Business, and the American Dream Became Temporary*. New York: Viking, 2018.

Terkel, Studs. *Working: People Talk About What They Do All Day and How They Feel About What They Do.* New York: The New Press, 1974.

Wartzman, Rick. *The End of Loyalty: The Rise and Fall of Good Jobs in America.* New York: PublicAffairs, 2017.

CHAPTER 4

Dweck, Carol S. *Mindset: The New Psychology of Success.* New York: Random House, 2006.

Pollak, Lindsey. *Becoming the Boss: New Rules for the Next Generation of Leaders.* New York: Harper Business, 2014.

CHAPTER 5

Applewhite, Ashton. *The Chair Rocks: A Manifesto Against Ageism.* New York: Celadon Books, 2019.

Blanchard, Ken, and Spencer Johnson. *The New One Minute Manager.* New York: William Morrow, 2015.

Bock, Laszlo. *Work Rules!: Insights from Inside Google That Will Transform How You Live and Lead.* New York: Twelve, 2015.

CHAPTER 6

Kuhl, Joan Snyder, and Jennifer Zephirin. *Misunderstood Millennial Talent.* Los Angeles: Center for Talent Innovation, 2016.

Watkins, Michael D. *The First 90 Days: Proven Strategies for Getting Up to Speed Faster and Smarter (Updated and Expanded).* Boston: Harvard Business Review Press, 2013.

CHAPTER 7

Gratton, Lynda, and Andrew Scott. *The 100-Year Life: Living and Working in an Age of Longevity.* London: Bloomsbury, 2017.

Levit, Alexandra. *Humanity Works: Merging Technologies and People for the Workforce of the Future.* New York: Korgan Page, 2018.

Wiseman, Liz. *Rookie Smarts: Why Learning Beats Knowing in the Game of Work.* New York: Harper Business, 2014.

CHAPTER 8

Brown, Jennifer. *Inclusion: Diversity, the New Workplace, and the Will to Change.* Hartford: Publish Your Purpose Press, 2016.

Chugh, Dolly. *The Person You Mean to Be: How Good People Fight Bias.* New York: Harper Business, 2018.

Conley, Chip. *Wisdom at Work: The Making of a Modern Elder.* New York: Currency, 2018.

Hoey, J. Kelly. *Build Your Dream Network: Forging Powerful Relationships in a Hyper-Connected World.* New York: TarcherPerigee, 2017.

CHAPTER 9

Saval, Nikil. *Cubed: A Secret History of the Workplace.* New York: Doubleday, 2014.

Yost, Cali Williams. *Work + Life: Finding the Fit That's Right for You.* New York: Riverhead Books: 2004.

CONCLUSION

Dufu, Tiffany. *Drop the Ball: Achieving More by Doing Less.* New York: Flatiron Books, 2017.

INDEX

ABOUT THE AUTHOR

LINDSEY POLLAK is a *New York Times* bestselling author, a keynote speaker, and one of the world's leading experts on Millennials and the multigenerational workplace. She is the author of *Getting from College to Career: Your Essential Guide to Succeeding in the Real World* and *Becoming the Boss: New Rules for the Next Generation of Leaders*. She has served as an official ambassador for LinkedIn, a Millennial workplace expert for *The Hartford*, and the chair of *Cosmopolitan*'s Millennial Advisory Board. A graduate of Yale University, she is based in New York City.